The LIVING PRESIDENCY

The LIVING PRESIDENCY

An Originalist Argument against Its Ever-Expanding Powers

✴ SAIKRISHNA BANGALORE PRAKASH

THE BELKNAP PRESS OF HARVARD UNIVERSITY PRESS
Cambridge, Massachusetts
London, England
2020

First printing

Library of Congress Cataloging-in-Publication Data

Names: Prakash, Saikrishna Bangalore, author.
Title: The living presidency : an originalist argument against
  its ever-expanding powers / Saikrishna Bangalore Prakash.
Description: Cambridge, Massachusetts : The Belknap Press of
  Harvard University Press, 2020. | Includes bibliographical
  references and index.
Identifiers: LCCN 2019033132 | ISBN 9780674987982 (cloth)
Subjects: LCSH: Executive power—United States. |
  Presidents—Legal status, laws, etc.—United States.
Classification: LCC KF5050 .P73 2020 | DDC 342.73/062—dc23
LC record available at https://lccn.loc.gov/2019033132

To N. Surya Rashmi Rao,
*whose patience and love always expand
Rashmi, nee samanamevaru?*

CONTENTS

The LIVING PRESIDENCY

INTRODUCTION

The important thing is the presidency. If need be, save
the presidency from the President.

—Richard Nixon to Elliot Richardson, 1973

Modern American presidents wield a vast array of constitutional powers, making their office one of the most powerful
on earth. They take the nation to war, dispatching our men and
women to battle in far-off lands. They make laws with the stroke
of a pen, sometimes adding needful provisions and occasionally
ignoring inconvenient or unwelcome rules. In foreign affairs, they
evade core constitutional clauses, like those related to treaties and
spending, in the way that an impatient motorist might bypass both-
ersome traffic.

It wasn't meant to be this way. Our Founding Fathers certainly
did not fashion a Constitution that authorized presidents to amend
and expand their constitutional office. Likewise, "We the People"
never chose to transform our presidency, making it more royal and
powerful and less executive and duty-bound. As we behold the
modern presidency, mull the modifications of the office, and dwell
on the Constitution's text, most of us can sense that our presidency
is a distortion of the original McCoy. Essentially, our familiar presidency is a funhouse-mirror version of the Founders' presidency,

except in our reality the carnival version is the lived experience, and not just a silly or grotesque reflection.

We are right to feel uneasy about the future. Congress, charged with making our nation's laws, seems obsolete, a place where useless speeches are occasionally punctuated by pointless votes. The courts offer sporadic resistance, but not nearly enough to redirect the trend. They are reactive and slow and, acting alone, are no match for the energetic executive. Attempting to advance policy and personal agendas, our next president likely will continue to push the boundaries of the office outward and grasp at new powers. After all, every modern president supposes that his agenda is wholly just and absolutely necessary, that he alone enjoys a popular mandate, and that the "loyal opposition" is in fact obstinately obstructionist. Presidents may enter office imagining that they can heal the partisan divide and work across the aisle, but reality eventually sets in. In the context of what seems an unreasonable, even rabid, opposition and an urgent need to fulfill campaign promises and do what is best for the nation, presidents seize authority to do what they believe is necessary and right.

What of the Constitution and its limits? Well, today's presidents recognize that the 2020 Constitution is not the 1789 Constitution, and that as the times change, so does our living Constitution. In this context, why does what George Washington thought about the reach of presidential power matter at all? When it comes to their powers, presidents realize that what matters are the rock-solid needs and demands of today, not the hazy limits and outdated conceptions of an obscure, distant, and rather different past. Sure, Alexander Hamilton, James Wilson, and James Madison were smart, but what could they have known about nuclear bombs or our multi-trillion-dollar high-tech economy? The theories and concerns of the Founders are a poor match for the realities and problems of today. While modern presidents may say a few kind words about the Founders here and there, they see no need to live under the outmoded Constitution of the past. Our living Constitution, with its many informal amendments and its potential for more, better suits their needs.

Be alarmed, but not fearful. No aspiring president, no matter his or her party, will stage an actual coup any time soon. America's institutions of representative government are too sturdy for that, and besides, the American people would not stand for it. Yet candor requires admitting that for decades we've witnessed something of a creeping constitutional coup. And creeping coups are more likely to succeed because the change is gradual, sometimes imperceptible. Like the proverbial frog in the pot, we often fail to discern some of these changes in the presidency and mostly haven't noticed these dangers to our Constitution.

Over more than two centuries, the American presidency has been transformed into what Arthur Schlesinger Jr. called an "imperial presidency."[1] In coining the term, Schlesinger largely focused on wars. Yet he certainly understood that the expansion of presidential power was not limited to the martial arena. Modern presidents have advanced on all fronts, pushing the boundaries of their constitutional office outward. They now wield far greater authority over lawmaking, law enforcement, and foreign affairs. What James Madison said in 1788 about legislatures—"[t]he legislative department is everywhere extending the sphere of its activity, and drawing all power into its impetuous vortex"—now applies more aptly to the executive.[2] We have, in short, a living presidency. It is an office with no fixed limits and with the potential to expand by leaps and bounds.

I do not claim that modern presidents rule without constraints. That is manifestly untrue. There remain legal restraints on the executive, such as the universal expectation that presidents will enforce judicial judgments, including ones that they loathe. Likewise, presidents do not punish the accused outside the justice system. Rather the point is that the modern office grows more powerful over time and that *any* existing constraints can be overcome in due course.

The modern presidency has no enduring limits, no permanent frontiers.

We sometimes fail to notice the absence of any permanent constraints on the presidency because we are too often beguiled by a set of comforting constitutional platitudes. "The president cannot make law," we assure ourselves. "Presidents cannot make treaties without the Senate's consent" because it says so in the Constitution. "The Constitution cannot be changed via mere practice." Presidents, because they take an oath to "preserve, protect and defend the Constitution," cannot violate it, much less amend it.[3]

But in the twenty-first century, these feel-good bromides are false. Our living presidency subverts the idea of an executive subject to the Constitution and to the laws. If presidents can unilaterally alter the Constitution, they can circumvent the document that spells out and limits their authority. The president's express obligation to "preserve, protect and defend the Constitution" becomes irrelevant in the face of a practical power to alter, undermine, and subvert the Constitution. Likewise, if presidents can supplement, amend, or ignore federal statutes, they are also lawmakers and they need not take care to faithfully execute Congress's laws.

As this book goes to press in 2020, the incumbent has many on edge. The sense of disquiet surrounding the presidency seems especially acute. Yet despite the pronounced differences in style and rhetoric, Donald Trump's immediate predecessors were little different in their efforts to pursue their agendas and, as a byproduct, expand the office of the chief executive. To be sure, the Republican faithful are quick to blame Democratic presidents; for their part Democrats are apt to indict Republican ones. But if we are honest with ourselves and escape the partisan perspective for a moment, we know in our heart of hearts that the problem has deep roots. Presidents of both parties have aggrandized themselves and the office of the presidency. There are no angels among our recent presidents, at least on questions of presidential power. Whatever noble qualities they may have had—patriotism, compassion, earnestness—each has contributed to inflating the powers of the living presidency.

Consider Barack Obama. Though Senator Obama earnestly promised that he would restore the rule of law to the office, President Obama saw things differently. Obama took America to war in Libya and evaded Congress's laws via dubious interpretations. What transformed a cutting critic of presidential power into one of its most energetic exercisers? There is an iron law of American politics: one's view on the scope of presidential power often depends on where one sits. From the Senate chamber or the gubernatorial chair, the presidency may seem to have gone off the rails. But once in the Oval Office, behind the Resolute Desk, every president quickly comes to see the benefits of a powerful executive. Even ardent admirers were astonished by Obama's U-turn. If Obama, the constitutional law professor who conspicuously and repeatedly vowed to curb the presidency, succumbed to the temptation to grasp and seize authority, constitutional and otherwise, can any occupant of the Oval Office ever resist it?

George W. Bush inaugurated this century's unease with presidential power. His administration's muscular advance of presidential prerogatives provoked fierce responses from the academy and the bar. While signing bills into law, Bush announced that these new statutes contained hundreds of unconstitutional features because they attempted to limit his constitutional authority. Bush also claimed the right to ignore existing laws that constrained his authority as chief executive and commander in chief. When Bush famously said "I'm the decider," some observers could be forgiven for supposing that he was proclaiming a belief that he could and should decide *all* matters of government.[4]

Has the living presidency become a juggernaut? The word *juggernaut* comes from Puri, India, where a celebrated Hindu temple contains three *murthis* (idols). One depicts Jagannath, "lord of the universe." Every year, votaries place the Jagannath *murthi* atop a gigantic, forty-five-foot high chariot and conduct a ceremonial procession. Once this massive carriage gains momentum, it is said to be unstoppable—indeed it has crushed those in its path. Many people fear that our presidency has become a juggernaut, an unstoppable force. Our presidents regularly play offense—grasp for new legal authority—whereas their institutional competitors seem always to be on the defense. Similarly, presidents seem unwilling to cede an inch to their rival, Congress, insisting that the Constitution forbids legislative encroachment on the executive branch. Given the way the game is played, even if presidents prevail only part of the time, the net effect is presidential expansion. Essentially each president says to Congress, "What is mine will remain mine. What is yours now may, in time, be mine."

This book argues that the living presidency is not a juggernaut. It is very much stoppable, and we need not be crushed under its wheels. Just as the modern presidency was formed over the course of many decades, so too must the movement to curb it stretch across many years. There will be no single moment marking the retreat or collapse of the living presidency.

Precisely because the anxieties triggered by the presidency transcend any particular occupant of the office, it is worth considering the contours of the presidency, as it exists today, without obsessing about the particular excesses of any single president, current or past. Our politics and media understandably fixate on the incumbent's personality and controversial acts, offering rapid reactions from partisans, a focus on polling numbers, and predictions about how some act will influence the next election. Can the president be impeached? Will the courts stand up to him? Is this president (Bush, Obama, or Trump) the most lawless? But we need to move beyond the ephemera of whether a particular president was or is the most imperial or whether the incumbent's legal innovations are popular or even desirable. If you are troubled about ever-expanding presidential powers, as I am, you cannot afford to be distracted by tweets, foibles, polling, or for that matter, sound policy.

The time is ripe for a dispassionate appraisal of the modern office, one free of partisanship and a focus on the crisis du jour. This can be hard to do, but if the overarching aim is to diagnose the causes and consequences of a grasping presidency, and curb the condition, some detachment is essential.

When we escape the partisan perspective and today's headlines, we can better see that our presidents take actions not traceable to any plausible reading of the original Constitution. They can and do:

* Veto transborder pipelines, cables, and wires
* Dodge the Treaty Clause and make treaties with foreign nations without securing the consent of two-thirds of the Senate
* Declare war
* Spend money that has not been appropriated by Congress
* Make federal law courtesy of congressional delegations of lawmaking authority and by advancing spurious interpretations of existing law
* Ignore federal laws that restrict the president's use of the military
* Alter congressional laws by repeatedly violating them
* Amend the Constitution via repeated transgressions of it

Some of these claimed powers may be familiar while others are undoubtedly obscure. A few changes arose during the past several decades; others date back more than a century. Finally, a few have the potential to determine the fate of the United States, while some seem trifling.

In reality, each is quite significant. Trivial presidential usurpations pave the way for future encroachments and informal constitutional amendments. If presidents can acquire the power to approve private cross-border pipelines, why won't they seize other authorities? If they can circumvent the Constitution's Treaty Clause, why not the Constitution's intricate rules about lawmaking, in particular the cumbersome process of bicameral passage? Because success breeds success, a successful alteration of the Constitution and federal laws creates a roadmap for further innovation and expansion.

What is the principal engine of this constitutional and statutory change? To borrow from Joseph Schumpeter, it is the alchemy of creative destruction.[5] As strange as this may sound to most Americans, modern presidents can change the law by violating it. More precisely, they change the Constitution and federal law by stretching, bending, and breaking elements of both. Every other American faces consequences, often severe, for breaking the law. But under contemporary practices and approaches, presidents often face little or no real adverse repercussions. To the contrary, presidential lawbreaking benefits the incumbent and expands the office of the presidency. Unlike the rest of us, presidents can liberate themselves through the transformative, emancipating process of law-breaking.

The most famous judicial expression of this theory comes from Supreme Court Justice Felix Frankfurter. In a celebrated case involving the extent of presidential power—whether Harry Truman could seize and operate steel mills during the Korean War—Frankfurter adopted an approach to executive power that has since resonated with presidents and their legal advisers:

> Deeply embedded traditional ways of conducting government cannot supplant the Constitution or legislation, but they give meaning to the words of a text or supply them. It is an inadmissibly narrow conception of American constitutional law to confine it to the words of the Constitution and to disregard the gloss which life has written upon them. In short, a systematic,

unbroken, executive practice . . . may be treated as a gloss on "executive Power" vested in the President by § 1 of Art. II.[6]

Though Frankfurter insisted that traditions cannot "supplant" the law, he basically admitted that repeated practice may trump the original meaning of the "words of the Constitution." Even if the gloss does not exactly supplant the previous meaning, it certainly overwhelms it. This is what I will call the "practice-makes-perfect" school of executive authority. By transgressing a law repeatedly over time, the president actually can change the law's meaning. While Frankfurter was speaking primarily of constitutional change, this way of thinking has also influenced how people understand statutory change, for presidents likewise claim to have the authority to change federal law via repeated violations. Practice can put a gloss on any existing rule, constitutional or statutory, and thereby render its original meaning immaterial.

Writing decades later, Justice Antonin Scalia decried this claim as misplaced "adverse possession."[7] Adverse possession, a property law concept, states that if A squats on B's land long enough—typically decades—squatter A eventually becomes the land's owner and B loses her interest. Scalia fully intended to invoke what he saw as the absurdity of the analogy: presidential trespasses should not serve as a means of amending the Constitution.

A district judge, responding to the claim that presidents had acquired a power to seize private property in the absence of congressional authorization, put it this way: "The fact that a man reaches in your pocket and steals your wallet is not a precedent for making that a valid act."[8] In other words, a pickpocket cannot acquire the legal right to lift wallets through dogged repetition.

Yet this is a principal defense of the living presidency. Essentially, modern presidents are pickpockets. After pilfering particular authority enough times—say, the power to declare war—that originally rested elsewhere, presidents (and their lawyers) eventually claim that the particular authority is now equally theirs. Furthermore, having pilfered many sorts of specific authority over time, they assert a general power to acquire the constitutional authority of others. The living Constitution, they say, authorizes and sanctifies their acquisitiveness.

The practice-makes-perfect approach is perverse and spurs executive lawlessness. Presidents (and their allies) regularly argue that some innovation, recent or otherwise, is legitimate because practice has legitimated it. They also invariably point out the innovation's usefulness, leading the beneficiaries of the innovation to support the executive's assertion in the moment. As the number of presidential amendments swells beyond count, the very idea of legal change through creative destruction becomes more accepted. Whenever presidents cannot change the law via conventional and clearly legitimate means, they will be tempted to say that prior practice authorizes them to take some desired act, whatever the law or Constitution might appear to say.

Consider a president who wishes, for policy or political reasons, to delay implementing a new recycling statute that regulates corporations. If he or she unilaterally grants "transition relief" to these firms, that is, delays enforcing the new law, the president simultaneously advances policy or political interests and makes it more likely that future presidents eventually will acquire a generic authority to delay the enforcement of new statutes, many of which will contain unwelcome provisions.

By a similar process, presidents can also transcend limits on their own authority. Imagine that a congressional law declares that "no federal funds" shall go to foreign rebels, but a president nevertheless supplies money to a popular rebel band. Had an ordinary citizen marched into the Treasury, seized federal funds, and handed them over to the revolutionaries, no one would doubt that she was a lawbreaker. Yet someone who favors executive lawmaking might say that the violation is but an opening pirouette in a complicated dance of legal reform. The president seeks to change the law, to better it. There should be some common-sense exceptions to the absolute rule, the president supposes. Why should we condemn that reformist impulse? After all, few would censure a president merely because he sought a formal change to the law. In any event, what may initially seem illegal may eventually become wholly legal, as the transgressive practices accumulate. With persistence, then, presidents may liberate themselves from any congressional or constitutional constraints.

If many of us welcome particular instances of informal (meaning transgressive) constitutional and legal change, presidents will be eager to gratify our desires and in ways that invariably enhance presidential power. The idea that the Constitution can change via practice systematically favors presidents because they have the best means of influencing and effecting legal change. They have the motive, the opportunity, and the energy to be the most prolific change agents. They can paint a new constitutional picture, sell it to their electoral coalition, implement it, and then influence the Supreme Court through jawboning and appointments to encourage the Court to endorse it.

To be clear, I reject the notion of legal change via the alchemy of repeated violations. More precisely, I deny that presidents, or anyone else, can change the Constitution and laws via practice. This is in keeping with my general approach to legal interpretation, which is "originalist" in bent. Although originalists differ among themselves, they generally seek to discern the meaning of a legal text at the time it was adopted. They further assert that this original meaning ought to be applied to future questions and disputes. As one might imagine, originalists generally oppose living constitutionalism and thus would be expected to resist a living presidency. They certainly would oppose the idea of legal change through repeated encroachments, for the Constitution contains absolutely no hint that constitutional transgressions are a proper means of generating constitutional amendments.

I am no less concerned with how Congress and the courts have seized new authorities. No one can deny that we have a living Congress, because it exercises far broader powers over the nation than it did at the Founding. Long ago, Congress breezed past its enumerated powers, seizing authorities never granted to it. In particular, a power to regulate interstate commerce now encompasses a power to regulate all aspects of American life. If the modern reading of the Commerce Clause is correct, Congress can ban flower gardens, woodworking, and home cooking. That fantastical reading cannot be squared with the Constitution's long list of limited and relatively precise grants of legislative authority to Congress.

Similarly, because the federal courts have seized a power to craft and impose new constitutional rights, we have a living judiciary. The federal courts have long been in the business of recognizing novel rights that strike them as especially worthy of protection. Although the courts typically justify their creation of new liberties as mere interpretations of the existing Constitution, many of their readings are so implausible that it is hard to escape the conclusion that the courts are amending the Constitution—adding to the Bill of Rights—under the thin guise of interpretation. If some law, federal or state, strikes the Supreme Court as sufficiently outrageous, some justices, occasionally a majority, will be disposed to strike it down. In a sense, the Supreme Court resembles a perpetual constitutional convention, continually fine-tuning the Constitution and occasionally churning out major amendments.

If the living presidency troubles us, so should the rise of a living Congress and living judiciary. We cannot deplore presidents who expand their authority while simultaneously supporting a Congress that transgresses its constitutional boundaries and celebrating judicial amendments to our Constitution. Put another way, we should not censure executive pickpockets while lauding congressional thieves and judicial shoplifters.

Yet many progressives adopt this awkward stance. They extol a living Constitution but excoriate a living presidency. Progressives lionize courts that impose rights found nowhere in the Constitution. They endorse congressional exercises of legislative power not traceable to any reasonable reading of the Constitution's grants of lawmaking authority. Yet many living constitutionalists strongly disfavor the living presidency, quite often on originalist grounds. Why living constitutionalism is extoled as the engine of progress except when it comes to presidential powers is never made clear. Why we should revert to the Founders' more limited presidency but not their more limited Congress or constrained courts is likewise a mystery.

In the interest of clarity, some caveats are in order. I do not believe that the Founders were infallible, that their Constitution always generates optimal rules, or that the original presidency was perfect. Many of the Founders were great men; none were flawless. Much the same could be said of the original Constitution and its presidency; both are good, not perfect. Nor do I suppose that originalism always yields clear or readily discernible answers to modern questions. Interpretation of old documents is often laborious and time-consuming, and the painstaking effort sometimes generates uncertain meanings.

Although I criticize recent presidents, I do not mean to suggest that any of them have been constitutional villains. In fact, I rather doubt that there are any true villains in the tale of the living presidency. Presidents have personal and policy agendas and they do their best to implement them. They see themselves as playing a game with extremely flexible rules and they see nothing wrong with further bending those rules to favor their agenda. But they are hardly alone in creating this flexible system, for almost everyone, including Congress, the courts, and the public, has a hand in constructing the presidency we have today. Though each of us is responsible for our predicament, we are not villains either. We too are playing the same game, responding to the same incentives and responding in the same way. That is the problem.

As noted earlier, I do not believe that the presidency is in an inexorable state of expansion. The office can contract, as it has in the past. Indeed, contraction is one aim of this book. And I do not imagine that presidents are uniquely hungry for power and fame. All politicians share this proclivity, to varying degrees. The acquisitiveness of Congress and the courts bears this out. My point is that under the auspices of a living Constitution, the presidency is uniquely positioned to acquire the powers of other branches and the states and to infringe on private rights. In a regime with a living Constitution, presidents will be the most powerful agents of constitutional change.

For more than a quarter century, I've written about the American presidency. In keeping with the originalist tradition, I've consistently sought to unearth and explain the original presidency and, from the vantage point of the Founding, criticize modern innovations and deviations, whether in war powers, the execution of laws, or foreign affairs. Sometimes I have argued that contemporary conceptions of presidential powers are too capacious; other times I have criticized encroachments on the presidency. For instance, I have argued that Congress has unconstitutionally constrained the president's power to direct the execution of federal laws.

This book focuses on the ever-expanding living presidency. But I also briefly touch on congressional encroachments because they reveal how to curb the living presidency. If, in the past, Congress has had the fortitude to occasionally encroach on the presidency here and there, it surely can do something less controversial, namely, reclaim its lost constitutional authority. While we don't want Congress to act as Madison's "impetuous vortex," usurping executive and judicial powers, we do require a more insistent, ornery, and jealous Congress, one keen to hold on to its remaining prerogatives and willing to claw back lost powers.

This book takes as its lodestar a bit of sage advice from Abraham Lincoln. In his 1858 "House Divided" speech, Lincoln began with this powerful observation: "If we could first know where we are, and whither we are tending, we could better judge what to do, and how to do it."[9] I adopt his wise counsel, considering where we were at the Founding, where we find ourselves today, what might come next, and what to do about our predicament.

Although some modern critics suppose that the original executive was designed to be weak, this fundamentally misreads the Founders and their Constitution. Chapter 1 demonstrates that the president was originally a king in all but name. Presidents would occupy a powerful office, one more potent than any previous American executive. A single person had authority (albeit limited) over law execution, foreign affairs, and the military; broad power to forgive offenses; a share of legislative authority (via the veto); and the ability to appoint, direct, and supervise the bureaucracy. Why did many people of that era see the presidency as a monarchy when many of us cannot even make out its outlines? We fail to see the resemblance because when we visualize monarchs, pageantry comes to mind— carriages, thrones, and crowns. We also tend to envision one species of monarchy, the absolute, hereditary sort. Yet in the eighteenth century, limited, elective monarchies were familiar. In crafting a single, powerful, elective executive, the Founders made the semblance to an elective monarchy inescapable.

Though this presidential monarchy was meant to be formidable, the office was far from omnipotent. Among other things, presidents would have no right to make laws or suspend them. They would have no right to take the nation to war. And they would have no right to amend the Constitution or refashion the presidency, via practice or otherwise.

The outcry that the proposed Constitution created a monarchy on the sly quickly gave way to protests claiming that early presidents, including George Washington, ruled like monarchs. Such reproaches were all but guaranteed, because the office's many powers and its unitary structure lent credence to any such charge. Railing against a president's monarchical pretensions is a tried and true part of American politics. It is a polemical trope so tempting that only the most timid of chief executives can hope to avoid its sting.

To be sure, the semblance to monarchy seems even more palpable now. Some of this is superficial—the president has a palace (the White House), a royal guard (the Secret Service), and carriages in the guise of a limousine (the "Beast"), helicopter (Marine One), and airplane (Air Force One). But the vast majority of the criticisms have less to do with pomp and more to do with our modern circumstances, namely the presidency's continual acquisition of authority. Why has this powerful executive become even more mighty?

In Chapter 2, I discuss *why* presidents seek greater constitutional authority. Some reasons relate to the age-old proclivities of pols, namely a thirst for power and a hunger for fame. Greater authority allows politicians to advance their agendas and try to add luster to their names. Every modern president wants to be known as one of the true greats, standing shoulder to shoulder with Washington and Lincoln. Presidents have sensibly concluded that a successful tenure requires boldness, energy, and results. If constitutional or statutory limitations stand in the way, they can—and, indeed, should—be massaged, reconceptualized, or evaded.

Moreover, contemporary presidents feel compelled to keep campaign promises and meet the public's heroic expectations. For first-term presidents, these pressures often stem from a desire to secure reelection. In an era when incumbents invariably run again, a one-term president is a failed president. But the desire to keep promises and meet public expectations continues to be an influence even during a second term, when reelection is impossible. Even lame ducks don't wish to disappoint their base or be seen by the public as unequal to the high office.

A final reason for craving greater power is that many presidents have strong and sincere convictions about what constitutes good policy for the nation. They want health care for all, tax reform, and an America secure from external threats. Presidents recognize that greater constitutional and legal power translates into a greater ability to implement their policy agendas.

How have presidents expanded their authority? Chapter 3 explains that they have exploited their many institutional advantages: an energetic, unified executive branch; perceived textual ambiguity in Article II (the president's part of the Constitution); and hamstrung rivals in the other two branches of government, Congress and the judiciary. Moreover, they have seized upon radical changes in popular perceptions and politics. Modern presidents routinely claim a mandate from the people to implement their policy agendas. Since no other official can claim to represent the entire nation, this argument carries significant weight. Presidents also exploit their status as the undisputed leader of their party to draw congressional and public support for their policies, further fragmenting an already bicameral Congress. Finally, presidents have at their disposal a phalanx of executive personnel predisposed to advance the executive's policy agendas, and in the process, expand executive authority. Fully aware of the weakness of interbranch checks and institutionally committed to the executive, executive branch lawyers are apt to adopt interpretations of laws and the Constitution that advance the president's policies and the presidency more generally.

I address the puzzling relationship between our living Constitution and our living presidency in Chapter 4. Whether we like it or not, we live under a regime of informal constitutional and legal change—though the text of our federal Constitution and our national laws may not change that often, their meanings do change. Congress has far broader legislative power than at the Founding; the courts have acquired authority to construct and impose their preferred constitutional rights; and the states have been the losers, forced to share many powers that were formerly theirs alone. Liberals love this living Constitution. Absent a living Constitution, progressives tell us, school segregation might be constitutional, there would be no right to contraception, and we would be saddled with inadequate criminal procedures. Moreover, Congress would be unable to clean our foul air and water, command a living wage from tightfisted corporations, or fund our retirement via Social Security. From a progressive perspective, an organic, living Constitution makes perfect sense. After all, the stale Constitution of the eighteenth century was a product of a naive political science coupled with prejudiced understandings of race and sex.

Somewhat incongruously, a good many liberals also loathe a living presidency. Many progressives have been quick to denounce the transformation of the presidency, particularly the acquisition of war powers, and wistfully look backward to the Founding's more modest presidency. This inconsistency has largely gone unnoticed and remains unexplained. If the original Constitution is woefully backward because it was a product of a less sophisticated understanding of government and because it reflected a retrograde morality, why are eighteenth-century conceptions of executive authority somehow desirable? There is no reason to imagine that the Founders were singularly sophisticated about the presidency or particularly prescient about the executive's ability to meet the needs of twenty-first-century Americans. Liberals are essentially picking and choosing among constitutional theories to suit their current policy or constitutional preferences. Either the Founders' Constitution, including its more constrained presidency, is of historical interest only, or it is the proper foundation of constitutional law. It cannot be one or the other, as convenience suits.

In Chapter 5, I reassess the presidential oath to preserve, protect, and defend the Constitution and what that oath means in a world of constitutional change and in a regime where the bounds of presidential power regularly shift. I argue that the meaning of the presidential oath has arguably changed, so that presidents do no violence to their sacred pledge when they seek to change the Constitution or Article II in particular. If living constitutionalism can enlarge the powers of the presidency, there is no reason to think that the oath's meaning is uniquely immune from informal transformation. Per the modern meaning of the presidential oath, presidents must preserve the Constitution except when they wish to change it via transgressive practices. They must defend it unless they agree with those outside their branch who wish to alter its meaning. Or, put another way, presidents can preserve, protect, and defend those portions of the Constitution they favor, and they can damage, despoil, and informally amend the rest.

Chapter 6 explores the living commander in chief's burgeoning authority over all military matters. The Founders conceived of the commander in chief as an instrument of Congress. Presidents could not wage (declare) war and had to obey Congress's military commands. Modern presidents, however, have invaded and partially captured Congress's powers over the military. Presidents now declare war, in the constitutional sense, and seek congressional approval at the outset of wars only when they are certain that Congress will oblige. Presidents also insist on great autonomy in how they conduct wars, treating Congress as if it were some meddlesome bystander when it comes to objectives, resources, and methods. For its part, Congress has been complicit in the incursion on its prerogatives, not only by allowing executive encroachment on congressional power, but also by supplying a splendid and supremely capable military establishment always ready to launch a president's overseas adventures.

In other areas of foreign affairs, the subject of Chapter 7, executive creep is less noticeable but still present. The Founders split authority over foreign affairs between the president and Congress.

Presidents were to superintend our relations in foreign affairs, subject to Congress's broad authority over war and foreign commerce. Moreover, the president's ability to conduct diplomacy was originally constrained by the Senate's checks on diplomatic appointments and treaties and by Congress's control of the purse. Today, each of these congressional checks has atrophied. The Treaty Clause, with its requirement of supermajority Senate consent, has become a dusty relic because presidents now make treaties by either bypassing Congress altogether or seeking bare majorities in both chambers. With respect to funds, presidents ignore congressional restrictions on the use of funds in foreign affairs, asserting a constitutional right to conduct diplomacy as they see fit. Finally, presidents have a remarkable degree of control over foreign commerce, usually via congressional delegations of legislative authority. Presidents, not Congress, effectively regulate much of foreign commerce.

Law execution was the president's principal bailiwick—it is what makes the president an executive. Justice Hugo Black once said that the president's duty to faithfully execute the law refutes the idea that he is a lawmaker. But Black's claim is not logically true, and practice no longer bears him out. Modern presidents are lawmakers, as Chapter 8 makes clear. Their lawmaking authority typically comes courtesy of Congress, via delegated authority to make rules and regulations, which are effectively laws by another name. Indeed, Congress has delegated vast swaths of legislative authority to the executive, content to have the executive make the hard choices in lawmaking.

As a means of advancing their policy agendas, modern presidents sometimes adopt rather strained readings of congressional law. For example, they may shun the best reading of a statute when doing so furthers their preferred policies. In the face of perceived necessity, executives sometimes manufacture statutory discretion as a means of doing what is supposedly required. They are especially apt to adopt more extreme and less plausible constructions of federal law when it seems that no court will peer over their shoulder and rap them for their interpretational gymnastics. In other words, as judicial review becomes weaker or nonexistent, executive lawyers find more legal wiggle room and adopt increasingly implausible readings of the law.

The creeping, encroaching, and living presidency is very much a fixture of our modern age, leading some to despair that nothing can be done to stop its expansion. But the other branches have stood up to the executive before. Congress has, in the past, curbed the executive's authority. The constraints on the president's power to remove executive officers, enacted across centuries, and the slew of reforms after Watergate, are obvious examples. Today, Congress can push back again, via an aggressive attitude and clever responses. Chapter 9 lays out some possible steps, including:

- The chambers can censure presidents and their aides as a way of signaling—to the executive, the courts, and the public—the depth of congressional disagreement.
- Congress can create its own team of lawyers to advance Congress-friendly interpretations of its constitutional authority over the executive. These lawyers can craft written opinions and cite them in court briefs.
- Congress can include "poison pills" in its bills to prevent signing statements. Such poison pills would provide that if the president negates any part of a law on constitutional grounds (that is, declares it invalid), the entire law has no force. This strategy would compel presidents to take the bitter with the sweet.

Likewise, just as they have done in the past, our courts can do a better job of checking an aggrandizing, transgressive executive. Courts can abandon doctrines that counsel deference to the executive, because none of these are constitutionally required. They can eschew policies that bar judges from deciding legal questions about the president's war powers. And courts can forsake the idea that practice can put a gloss on (amend) the Constitution and laws.

The people have a preeminent role to play. In any republican system, the people are the ultimate safeguards. We the People will have to reacquaint ourselves with our Constitution and decide whether we truly wish to curb the executive's appetites and its ability to amend our Constitution and laws. If we do wish to curb the living presidency, we will have to stop judging executive actions exclusively through the lenses of partisanship and policy. We will have to condemn presidential acts that rest on power grabs, even when those acts advance policies we fervently admire. Most importantly, we must struggle to make sense of our sometimes incoherent stances and contradictory impulses. Should we favor a living, mutating constitution, one in which the presidency will exert the greatest influence on constitutional change, including on the expansion of presidential power itself? Or should we be faithful originalists, favoring the Founders' Constitution and condemning not only executive pickpockets, but also congressional thieves and judicial shoplifters?

CHAPTER ONE

KINGLY BEGINNINGS

In June 2018, a *Time* magazine cover depicted Donald Trump peering into a mirror, his reflection sporting a glittering crown and royal robes. Captioned "King Me," the message was hardly subtle. Trump was behaving like a monarch.[1]

The president-as-monarch is a tried and true bogeyman of American politics. In condemning an incumbent president, professional politicians, bookish professors, and ordinary citizens alike often argue that the president, by taking some controversial act or exercising some claimed authority, is acting like a monarch; and because the Founding Founders did not want a king and did not create one, the president has acted illegally. He has trampled on our republican Constitution.

This familiar argument is as American as apple pie. It dates back to the first presidency and has been with us ever since.[2] But it is mistaken in several respects. In vesting significant authority in one person, the Constitution did create a monarch, albeit a limited, republican one.[3] By eschewing the regal trappings of monarchy and certain evocative words, the Founders veiled their monarch behind a facade of pure republicanism. We don't see the presidency for what it is—a limited monarchy—because we have been fooled by myths about the Founding and misled by our stereotypes of what makes a king.

A Constitution of and for Its Era

The Constitution was drafted in 1787, when many leading statesmen had concluded that a stronger federal government was what America desperately needed. To understand the significance of this historical context, imagine what Article II would look like if it had been written in a radically different era. Picture a set of Framers wearing not breeches and powdered wigs but bell-bottom pants and long, hippy hair, gathered at a convention in Philadelphia in May of 1975 to draft a new constitution. Watergate, Vietnam, the Saturday Night Massacre, the secret bombing of Cambodia, Gerald Ford's controversial pardon of his disgraced predecessor—these and other searing events would have been on the minds of these Framers. What kind of executive would emerge from such a convention? Because the faults of Richard Nixon would have been front and center, Article II—the president's part of the Constitution—would look extremely different. These framers might have wrested away the pardon power, deleted the Commander-in-Chief Clause, or created a plural executive of the sort found in many states today. The backdrops of constitutional framings really do matter.

As another experiment, imagine a constitutional framing in August of 1776, eleven years before the actual event. Recall the distrust, fear, and loathing that Americans felt toward King George III, as manifested in the July Declaration of Independence: "The history of the present King of Great Britain is a history of repeated injuries and usurpations, all having in direct object the establishment of an absolute Tyranny over these States." Among other things, the signatories accused George of vetoing good laws, vexing legislators, dissolving legislatures, obstructing justice, coercing judges, cutting off trade, abridging the jury right, altering the forms of government, and waging war on America. With this indictment of executive authority serving as the background, what sorts of American executives would materialize?

Some people might assume that we don't have to conduct this second thought experiment. After all, didn't our 1787 Constitution emerge from that exact context?[4] According to this view, the Constitution, like the Declaration, was at least partly a reaction to the excesses and tyranny of the king of England. It follows that the Constitution must have been designed to tightly constrain the executive, because the British monarch was dreaded and reviled. Accordingly, the Constitution's grants to the president should be read narrowly to prevent the establishment of a monarchy on these shores. We did not oust King George III only to replace him with King George Washington of America.

But this reading ignores momentous changes in political thought. During the decade that separated the Declaration and the Constitution, Americans had acquired some sorely needed experience in self-government and constitution making. In 1787, as in 1776, executives remained part of the problem to be solved, but not because they were dominant or omnipotent. To the contrary, these executives generally were dominated and impotent: their feebleness was the problem.

FAILED CONSTITUTIONAL EXPERIMENTS

In 1776–1777, eleven states created constitutions. For our purposes, each constitution established an executive nominally distinct from the state legislature, thereby creating at least a modicum of separated powers. But the separation was more illusory than real. To be sure, these constitutions usually conveyed a general grant of "executive powers" that was refined, cabined, or limited in a number of ways. This approach was a rather familiar mode of drafting constitutions, one replicated in our Constitution.[5] Notwithstanding these seemingly significant grants, state executives were dependent, divided, and checked at every turn because the framers of state constitutions chose to so construct them. They were dependent because state legislatures often selected them, presumably favoring submissive or docile personalities. Moreover, state executives typically could serve only one year in office and during that year relied on their legislatures to supply salaries and other funds for the executive branch. They were divided because the states typically vested constitutional authority in an executive committee, meaning that someone might be styled the "governor" but enjoy little or no unilateral authority. Instead, governors often would have to secure the approval of the executive council to take meaningful action. Finally, executives were checked because state constitutions usually permitted the legislature to statutorily modify, and therefore curb, the executive's constitutional powers. One of the few governors who initially enjoyed a veto unceremoniously lost it. In 1778, the South Carolina legislature sought to eliminate the veto. Though the governor vetoed the attempt to snatch away his veto, the legislature completely disregarded his veto. This episode was emblematic of the sorry standing of most state executives, who, when push came to shove, had rather little power.[6] As James Madison put it, the state executives were "little more than Cyphers."[7]

In contrast, the state legislatures were made all-powerful and showed little hesitation in confidently asserting their authority. During the Revolutionary War, they ran roughshod over individual rights. Before and after the war, they dominated executives and the courts. Assemblies usurped executive and judicial powers, by stripping away elements of executive authority, creating docile extraconstitutional executives under their control, and reopening closed judicial cases. Such practices led Madison to describe the legislative branch as "drawing all power into its impetuous vortex."[8]

At the federal level, there was not even a pretense of separated powers. Though the Continental Congress enjoyed a handful of legislative and judicial authorities, it was predominantly an executive institution, with powers to supervise executive officers, decide to wage war, and direct foreign affairs.[9] Despite Baron de Montesquieu's warning about the evils of concentrating governmental powers, the Continental Congress had all three powers of government and was utterly anemic nonetheless.[10]

Its structure fairly ensured that it would be a feeble executive. To begin with it was a committee, an arrangement that dissipated energy and ensured sluggish decision-making. It did not meet continuously and therefore could not provide the constant supervision necessary to properly direct the subordinate executive officers, military and civilian. Its delegates typically served short stints, meaning that the group suffered from a lack of experience and familiarity with national institutions. Moreover, the Continental Congress could not unilaterally raise an army or fund it—for either of those two sinews of war it needed to plead, hat in hand, with the sovereign states. Think of the United Nations, whose dysfunctions largely mirror those of the Continental Congress: delegates whose fundamental loyalties lie elsewhere; decisions by committee, meaning often no decisions at all; rather little in the way of leadership and resolve; and only the semblance of power.

The Constitution's Creation in Context

In the Continental Congress, there were some belated attempts to fortify the executive by creating standing executive departments, each headed by a secretary. But these reforms, enacted in the early 1780s, failed because the drawbacks of a plural executive persisted. The secretaries looked to their masters in Congress and those delegates remained divided, inattentive, and uninformed. By 1787, leading thinkers came to the conclusion that stronger medicine was necessary.

In the months leading to the Philadelphia Convention, some openly called for a monarchy. Indeed, some historians believe that in 1786, the president of the Continental Congress wrote a letter asking Prince Henry of Prussia to serve as king of America. In 1787, some Americans speculated that one of the sons of King George III might serve in that capacity.[11]

The very idea of an American monarchy astounded George Washington, who noted that "even respectable characters speak of a monarchical form of government without horror."[12] Such a change, he thought, would "shak[e] the Peace of this Country to its foundation."[13] Similarly, Virginia governor Edmund Randolph argued that "the permanent temper of the people was adverse to the very semblance of Monarchy."[14]

At the convention itself, this was likely the majority sentiment—that Americans would not tolerate a monarchy. But there was some qualified support. James Wilson, a future Supreme Court justice, claimed that the size of America argued for "the vigour of [a] Monarchy" and that the "people of Amer[ica] did not oppose the British King but the parliament."[15] A Virginian said he "was not so much afraid of the shadow of monarchy as to be unwilling to approach it."[16] A delegate from New Hampshire praised advocates of a "high toned Monarchy."[17] Another delegate admitted that he "considered [a limited monarchy] as *one* of the best Governments in the world. It was certain that equal blessings had never yet been derived from any of the republican form." He added, however, that "[a] limited monarchy . . . was out of the question."[18] Whether it was beyond the pale, or not, one delegate allegedly asserted that more than twenty colleagues preferred a monarchy.[19]

The Virginia Plan, presented at the convention's outset, called for an executive with authority to execute the law, conduct foreign affairs, and direct officers (with the latter two powers stemming from a grant of "executive rights" formerly vested in the Continental Congress).[20] Beyond this, the blueprint seemed to envision a somewhat weak executive. Though the proposal called for a veto, it would be exercised in concert with judges. Moreover, the executive could serve one term only and would be chosen by its rival, Congress. Further, rather than vesting power in a single executive, the Virginia Plan left open the possibility of an executive committee.

By the convention's end, the executive had grown stronger in almost every respect. In terms of structure, Congress lacked primary authority to select the executive; instead, elite presidential electors would choose the executive, with the House of Representatives making the selection only if the initial process failed. Moreover, the delegates gave the executive a long term—four years—with repeated reelection a possibility. This framework meant that the executive could develop expertise and proficiency and be rewarded with additional terms. Perhaps most importantly, the convention decided that the executive would be a single person rather than a triumvirate or council. The executive could act with alacrity and resolve and would not be riven by factionalism. None of these structural choices were obvious and, in fact, the delegates flirted with alternatives throughout the convention.

In terms of power, the executive acquired express authority over pardons, the military, and state militias. By including the Vesting Clause of Article II, the Constitution conveyed a general grant of authority—the "executive power"—to be read in light of the limits and exceptions found elsewhere. The Constitution granted some executive power to Congress—for example, the power to declare war. The delegates evidently did not want a unitary executive on this matter, but rather a deliberative, plural decisionmaker. Other times, the delegates granted the president executive authority with a constraint, such as the requirement that the president secure the consent of the Senate to make treaties or appoint officers. Where the Constitution did not otherwise constrain the executive, the executive power rested with the president alone. Hence the president could direct and remove executive officers and could unilaterally exercise all those foreign affairs powers not vested in Congress or checked by the Senate. Moreover, the Constitution never granted Congress a generic authority to regulate or strip away the president's executive powers. Finally, the president had a qualified check on legislation, what we call the veto, and did not need the consent of anyone to wield it.

The executive faced several other constraints. He could be removed for high crimes and misdemeanors. Though far less consequential than having the president serve at Congress's pleasure, this was a check. The electoral process also served to constrain, since incumbents would generally strive to maintain sterling reputations to secure reelection. In other words, the possibility of reelection encouraged executive lawfulness and rectitude.

All federal officers had to take an oath to "support" the Constitution. At a minimum, this was a loyalty oath to the new institutions and system; beyond that, its significance was unclear. Presidents had a special oath, likely because their office would be the most distinguished and the most powerful. As the first magistrate, presidents had to take an oath to "faithfully execute the Office of President of the United States, and . . . preserve, protect and defend the Constitution of the United States."[21]

This clearly was more than a loyalty oath. The first part required the president to stay within the bounds of the office. To faithfully execute likely meant to diligently exercise the office's powers and eschew the temptation to refashion the office in order to achieve some end. The second part made it clear that the president could not violate the Constitution. He had to preserve it, not change it; protect it, not despoil it; defend it, not attack it.

Why did the executive become stronger over the course of the convention? First, as noted earlier, the fledgling nation was perceived as fragile because its national government was bereft of power. Greater legislative, judicial, and executive powers were part of the zeitgeist, for many supposed that the United States would not long remain united if it coupled a feckless central government with powerful states that could antagonize foreign states and discriminate against their neighboring states. When delegates decided not to amend the Articles of Confederation and chose instead to craft an entirely new framework, the overhaulers outflanked the tinkerers. The new Congress, infused with a host of legislative powers, including the authority to raise armies, regulate commerce, and impose taxes, was now a genuine legislature. At the same time, the multistep lawmaking process made it somewhat difficult for Congress to exercise these powers. The new, independent judiciary, which was to decide many types of cases and help standardize the operation of federal law, also had its power divided across multiple courts. By contrast, the new executive was mostly unitary and came bristling with powers. Alone among the three branches, it generally lacked the checks that flow from vesting authority in a multitude rather than in a single person.

Second, there was something of a reversion to the idea of a powerful executive. Recall that the Continental Congress was a frail, plodding, and distracted plural executive and that most state executives were dominated by the assemblies. By the time of the convention, many Founders had realized that these early frameworks had reflected a misbegotten suspicion toward executives. Such "jealousies are very apparent in all our state constitutions," Thomas Jefferson noted.[22] As James Wilson put it, executives had been the unloved stepchildren of American governments.[23] For some, the shedding of these resentments, misgivings, and fears led to a swing back toward familiar forms of executive power. This may seem astonishing, but only if we forget the context. Americans "were educated in royalism: no wonder if some . . . retain that idolatry still," said Thomas Jefferson.[24] Benjamin Franklin similarly spoke of a "natural inclination in mankind to Kingly Government."[25]

Third, the champions of a robust executive were tenacious. They pressed for unity, the ability to serve indefinitely, and significant authority; they resisted congressional selection, an executive council, and short terms of office. They often lost. But rather than accepting defeat, they regrouped and repackaged, often prevailing in the end. Proponents of a strong executive were confident and persistent, with a plan and a spirit to bring their vision to life.

Lastly, one cannot minimize the role that George Washington played in the creation of the executive. During the convention, he apparently was silent on the scope of presidential power. But he didn't have to utter a syllable. His mere presence spoke volumes. Most everyone knew that if there was going to be but one chief executive, Washington would be that man. His standing was unparalleled. Having peacefully relinquished his powers to the Continental Congress after defeating the mighty British army, Washington was seen as selfless and patriotic—the polar opposite of someone obsessed with amassing power, fame, and wealth. His integrity caused some to favor more executive authority and led others to drop their guard. As one delegate put it, executive authority "would [not] have been so great had not many of the members cast their eyes towards General Washington as President; and shaped their Ideas of the Powers to be given to a President, by their opinions of his Virtue."[26] Or as Thomas Paine said much later, the "Executive part of the Federal government was made for a man, and those who consented, against their judgment, to place Executive Power in the hands of a single individual, reposed more on the supposed moderation of the person they had in view, than on the wisdom of the measure itself."[27] Thus the widespread, healthy suspicion that politicians were unprincipled, venal, and power hungry was somewhat held in check. This was not a constitution built to curb a George III, a Richard Nixon, or a Chairman Mao. It was built to empower the virtuous, selfless, and thoughtful George Washington.

BEHOLDING A MONARCHY

The Constitution that emerged from the convention had a president with kingly powers. Many repeatedly drew the connection, especially critics. Patrick Henry observed that the Constitution "squints [inclines] towards monarchy."[28] Luther Martin of Maryland said the president was "so constituted as to differ from a monarch scarcely but in name," with the president "nearly . . . the same thing" as an elective king.[29] George Mason agreed that the presidency "will be an elective monarchy."[30] The president possessed "the powers of a monarch," said "Cato" the Anti-Federalist, and asked, "wherein does this president . . . essentially differ from the king of Great-Britain (save as to name [and] the creation of nobility . . .)"?[31] Some complained that the combination of substantial authority and the use of electors to choose a single executive meant that the Constitution created an elective monarch. The president was "a bad edition of a Polish King," said Thomas Jefferson, speaking of an elected monarch.[32] Even foreigners noted the semblance: William V, the Dutch stadtholder, declared that Americans would have "a king under the title of President."[33]

Though John Adams celebrated the Constitution's creation of "a limited monarchy," most who favored the Constitution denied any resemblance.[34] Yet as historian Max Farrand later noted, "the supporters of the new order were at a loss to defend their contention that no monarchy had been established."[35] If it looked like a duck and quacked like a duck—well, the conclusion was obvious to many.

The same impulses that led the delegates at Philadelphia to propose a formidable executive led the people, in their state conventions, to ratify a monarchical federal executive. People understood that a more powerful executive was the order of the day and that existing state executives were much too weak. And the promise of

George Washington as first president continued to play an outsized role. As Edward Larson put it, in ratifying the Constitution, the "people's delegates had ratified Washington."[36] One might say the people all but crowned him.

Bewildered by Forms

Why can't we see the presidency's resemblance to a monarchy? Probably because the Constitution lacks the trappings. There is no crown, throne, scepter, or resplendent garb. There is no mention of coronations, anointments, or majestic processions. There is no grant of immunity—nothing in the Constitution proclaiming that the "president can do no wrong" or is "untouchable." American officials take no oath to the president—they take an oath to the Constitution. Americans are not humbled "subjects" but free "citizens." And there is a guarantee of republican government to the states.

But don't be fooled by trifling omissions. To see the resemblance more clearly, imagine a different constitution, one with a presidency enjoying the exact same powers ours has under our Constitution. And imagine that this hypothetical constitution gave its president a crown, magnificent purple robes, and a scepter. Would that president be a king (or queen)? Or imagine that this constitution claimed that the president "could do no wrong," as was said of the British king, and would reside in a palace and sit on a throne. Would that executive be a monarch? I think the addition of one or more kingly trimmings in the Constitution would end our mental block quickly. Indeed, if we subtracted several clauses, like the Pardon, Treaty, and Appointments Clauses, and added one that granted a "sparkling crown," there would be no doubt that the Constitution had erected a kingly office.

Indeed, Americans often are unsophisticated when it comes to monarchies. When we think of monarchs, what often comes to mind is a single person wielding absolute power. Yet if we pause and reflect a little, we know that none of the current European monarchs exercise such authority. To the contrary, most have the trappings of power but little or no real authority. And if we consider the monarchs of the eighteenth century, many of them lacked absolute power. King George III, as despised as he was in America, was a limited monarch. He could not make or unmake any law. He could not ignore the adverse judgments of his courts. And he relied on parliament for most of his funds. Whatever his abuses in America, George was no despot in Great Britain.

Likewise, many conceive of monarchy as necessarily hereditary—that kings or queens invariably transfer their power, wealth, and titles to their first born. In fact, elective monarchies were common in the eighteenth century, and several hereditary European monarchies were originally elective. The Polish king was elected, as were at one time the Dutch stadtholder; the kings of Norway, Sweden, and Denmark; and the Holy Roman emperor. Properly understood, monarchy in no way implies hereditary succession.

Americans are also unacquainted with mixed monarchies or mixed governments. We tend to think of simple forms—democracy, republic, aristocracy, absolute monarchy. America is a republic. Britain is obviously a monarchy. After all, many people enjoyed following the royal wedding of Prince Harry and Princess Meghan. We are wholly unaware that the most famous exponent of the need for separated powers, Montesquieu, noted in the eighteenth century that Britain was a "republic, disguised under the form of monarchy."[37] What he meant was that although Britain had the trappings of a monarchy, its inner and actual workings were somewhat republican. More generally, governments can have elements of monarchy, republic, and aristocracy. A nominal republic can have certain monarchical features, and an ostensible monarchy can have decidedly republican traits. As the historian Eric Nelson astutely observes, "On one side of the Atlantic, there would be kings without monarchy

[Great Britain]; on the other, monarchy without kings [the United States]."[38]

We also overlook the office's monarchical features because the title—president—seems decidedly unregal, even pedestrian. Don't 4H clubs and softball leagues have presidents? But would we have a monarchy if the Constitution had christened the president "his highness?" If so, we almost had one in 1789, when the Senate insisted on some such title for the president.[39] Moreover, if we consult an influential dictionary of the era, we find that one synonym for "monarch" was "president."[40] This meaning is lost to us, of course. But it perhaps was not lost to some eighteenth-century readers.

What John Adams said of his era is equally true of ours. Our "Heads are most miserably bewildered about" monarchy.[41] We are ignorant about mixed monarchies and elective monarchies. And we cling to the idea that America is a federal republic. We tell ourselves we are not a monarchy, and we know we don't much care for them (except for their weddings, it seems), but we don't really know what monarchies are.

In denying the truth regarding our presidency, we have exalted form over substance. We have been deceived by the republican trappings of the Constitution and have paid little heed to its actual features. That the presidency was not to be an absolute, hereditary monarchy has no logical implications for whether it became something slightly less awesome: an elective, constrained monarchy. And the office certainly was that.

CONSTITUTIONAL CHANGE AND THE LIMITED PRESIDENT

This historical context undercuts those who would seek to illuminate the scope of presidential power by reference to what the presidency supposedly was not, namely a monarchy. As we have seen, the original presidency was certainly a monarchy, albeit a limited, republican one. Because of this context, the constitutionality of a particular presidential act cannot turn on whether it seems redolent of kingly government. Instead, the constitutionality of presidential deeds turns on a painstaking analysis of the metes and bounds of Article II.

Having emphasized the power of the presidency, we must not lose sight of its constraints. The rest of the book largely focuses on the original confines of the presidency and the erosion of those limits. For now, let's focus on the original presidency's relationship to constitutional change. In particular, could the president unilaterally alter the Constitution to expand his authority, create new individual rights, or extinguish existing liberties? The answer may seem obvious. But sometimes it is useful to demonstrate the obvious as a means of underscoring its importance. The general inquiry breaks down into two components: Was Article V meant to be the unique means of changing the Constitution? And if so, what role was the president to have in that process of constitutional change?

Article V, which specifies the means of amendment, mentions Congress, the state legislatures, and two types of conventions—drafting conventions and ratification conventions. Congress can propose amendments or, if a sufficient number of states demand a drafting convention, call one so that it may propose amendments. However proposed amendments are generated and finalized, Congress decides whether to send them to state legislatures or to popular conventions for possible ratification.

This article creates a demanding gauntlet. The procedures relied on in the past—two-thirds of each chamber of Congress to propose and three-quarters of state bodies (legislatures or popular conventions) to ratify—are exceptionally arduous. Many suppose that Article V is far too challenging. Whatever the case may be, it seems clear that there is no alternative means of changing the Constitution. Article V is not one of several options—it is the *only* method of making amendments.

We know this because when faced with the evident inadequacies of the Articles of Confederation, no one at the time suggested that the Continental Congress could ameliorate the difficulties by taking an implied amendment route. The Articles specified a very onerous means of amending itself, namely the approval of Congress and the concurrence of *every* state.[42] Had there been an alternative, a less demanding means of amending the Articles, surely someone at the time would have proposed using it.

The Philadelphia Convention, when it proposed a new constitution, consciously chose to circumvent the amendment process specified in the Articles. The convention never asserted that its proposed means for creating new law—ratification of the Constitution by nine state popular conventions (slightly less than three-quarters of the total)—was somehow consistent with the prescribed method for amending the Articles (state unanimity). The states simply acquiesced to the new formula and ratified the Constitution, leading the nation to conclude that the latter had superseded the Articles. This sleight of hand was, in a sense, a benign and soft revolution.

To be sure, there were many Founders who said that the people had an inalienable right to alter their government. But this was an extraconstitutional right of the people, meaning it existed outside any existing legal system. When the people, acting through their states, chose to create a new constitution outside the confines of the Articles of Confederation, they were exercising a revolutionary (not legal) right. Likewise, should the people today choose to create a new constitution outside the confines of Article V, they too would be engaged in a revolution.

Indeed, the means found in Article V for limited popular participation fairly presupposed that there were no other legal means for the people to act collectively. In particular, the ability of the people to participate in ratifying proposed amendments presupposes that they have no other means of participating in, or directing, the process. The Constitution's Article V grants *Congress* the power to decide whether to send amendments to the state legislatures or popular conventions. In this system, the people cannot themselves send an amendment to the states because Congress alone has that task.

Moreover, the people cannot ratify amendments that Congress never sends to the states or those amendments that Congress directs to the state legislatures for ratification. Given these limitations, it seems that the Constitution likewise does not sanction the ability of the people to amend the Constitution outside of Article V.

Put simply, while the people may have a natural right and a practical power to create and abolish governments and therefore create and abolish the constitutions that undergird them, the Constitution does not recognize this fundamental right, much less grant it legal status. Neither Article V nor anything in the historical context suggests that there are alternative lawful methods of amending the Constitution. Article V is the only legal means of altering the Constitution.

For its part, Article V does not mention presidents. Though many other institutions are mentioned, the presidency and the judiciary are not, and thus they seem excluded from the process. Now one might read the Presentment Clause of Article I as if it sanctioned presidential involvement. The clause specifies that "[e]very Order, Resolution, or Vote to which the Concurrence of the Senate and House of Representatives may be necessary" must be "presented to the President."[43] Because Congress can propose constitutional amendments to the states only if both chambers approve them (by a two-thirds vote), one might suppose that proposed amendments must likewise be delivered to the president before the amendments "shall take effect." But the first ten amendments were not presented to the first president for his signature. In fact, per Congress's request, George Washington forwarded the amendments to the states, never objecting to the lack of presentation nor attempting to sign them. When the question was first raised before the Supreme Court, the justices concluded that the Presentment Clause did not apply to amendments, and this has been the dominant view ever since. The only successful amendment to have been signed by a president was the Thirteenth Amendment. But his successor did not sign the next proposed amendment, likely because the Senate publicly insisted, in the wake of the Thirteenth Amendment, that proposed amendments were not subject to presentment or the veto.

The upshot is that the president has no formal role in the making of amendments. He or she has no vote and no veto. To be sure, the president can propose amendments, as part of the executive's right to recommend "Measures" to Congress.[44] But this authority is really no different from the right that each American has to speak his or her mind on public matters, including the amendments Congress ought to take up. On matters of changing the Constitution, the president has no more formal role than you or I do.

Remember, too, the president's peculiar obligation to "preserve, protect and defend" the Constitution. As noted earlier, the president's constitutional oath prohibits him or her from violating the Constitution. As one person put it at the time, the president is "under the immediate controul of the constitution, which if he should presume to deviate from, he would be immediately arrested in his career."[45] In addition, because neither the president (nor anyone else) has constitutional authority to change the Constitution via transgressions, it follows that the president has no authority to repeatedly violate the Constitution in hopes of changing it. Amendment-by-infringement was not an accepted method of constitutional change.

In sum, our Constitution does not explicitly or implicitly permit amendments outside of Article V. Reading Article V in conjunction with Article II, it is clear that presidents have no warrant for supposing that they may amend the Constitution, either alone or acting in conjunction with others. They can propose amendments and encourage members of Congress and others to support their proposals, but these steps are far removed from a formal role and even more distant from a unilateral authority to revise the Constitution.

Statutory Change and the Limited President

Article I of the Constitution specifies how federal statutes are made. This process consists of bicameral passage, presentment to the president, and potential veto and congressional override (a sequence familiar to generations of schoolchildren who grew up watching Schoolhouse Rock's catchy song and video "I'm Just a Bill").

The president's part in the legislative process, though limited, is considerable. He or she can cajole Congress, propose measures, and veto bills. While any American may lobby Congress and recommend legislation, the veto rests with the president alone.

May federal statutes be made some other way? No. Article I supplies the exclusive means of making federal statutes. The Constitution does not specify any alternative. Further, there is no reason to suppose that the Constitution silently permits other, unspoken means of making, altering, or repealing statutes. Another way of putting the point is that *only* Congress may enact, amend, and repeal statutes, and then only under the rubric of Article I.

Hence, under the original system, the president could not make laws unilaterally. But it is not so much that the president's "power" as the executive "refutes the idea that he is to be a lawmaker," as Justice Hugo Black once claimed.[46] After all, some eighteenth-century executives—absolute monarchs—could make laws. Rather, the president's express duty to faithfully execute the laws, coupled with a narrow role in making federal statutes, strongly implies that the president has no unilateral lawmaking authority. Why grant the president a limited, surmountable check on the making, unmaking, and amending of federal statutes—the veto—if the president could, by putting pen to paper, make (and repeal) laws on his or her own? The president's lesser power of a qualified veto signals that the executive never was meant to enjoy the greater power, namely the power to make laws unilaterally.

✳ ✳ ✳

Our Constitution, as originally constructed, created a powerful executive. The Framers crafted a presidency far more formidable than any state executive, and one more potent than several European monarchs. When the Constitution was sent to the states, many

Americans and foreigners noted that the presidency was an elective monarchy.

The original presidency was also incomparably more powerful than many current monarchies. Today, the United Kingdom has a "sovereign who reigns but does not rule."[47] In contrast, the United States created a president meant to rule by law but not "reign." The British monarch has all the title and trappings, but no power, while the American president had considerable authority, but little of the regalia.

Yet as powerful as it was, the original presidency was not meant to be all-powerful. The presidency was a limited, republican monarchy. In particular, the American executive lacked the unilateral authority to amend the Constitution or to make, amend, or unmake statutory law. The executive's sway over constitutional change was exceedingly slight and its influence over ordinary law, while considerable, had rather clear limits.

Today, this part of the original framework exists on paper and nowhere else. We no longer have a Constitution that carefully constrains the engines of legal change; instead, our Constitution and laws change in informal ways outside the strictures of Article V and Article I. The presidency's considerable powers and advantages— originally conveyed to defend against invasions and to ensure vigorous execution of the laws—are now exploited to alter the Constitution and laws through informal means. Our Constitution's "energetic executive" has channeled the office's considerable advantages to become the amending executive, both to enlarge the presidency's own powers and to remodel our living Constitution.

CHAPTER TWO

Why Presidents Amend *the* Constitution

In the Constitution's earliest days, frightful prophecies were commonplace. At the Constitutional Convention in Philadelphia, delegates such as Virginia governor Edmund Randolph predicted that a single executive would be a "foetus of a monarchy," eerily forecasting that a unitary executive would usurp power.[1] And once the Constitution was put before the people, its opponents—the Anti-Federalists—groused that the presidency would be a monarchy in all but name. Recall Patrick Henry's claim that the presidency "squints towards monarchy."[2] According to this view, the Constitution's feeble defenses and paper boundaries, meant to confine the office, would be tossed aside with ease by presidents with armies at their backs.

The howls continued after the Constitution became supreme law. But this time they took the form of attacks on America's Cincinnatus, George Washington. Critics said that Washington, and even more so his allies, were hellbent on establishing a hereditary monarchy. Washington had no children of his own, so this was a little odd. But his critics sensed conspiracies everywhere to raise the already regal office of the president even higher still. Did not some senators, and Vice President John Adams, want to call Washington his "Highness?" Did not others want the president to hold levees—formal receptions—full of obsequious curtsies and groveling glances? Did not Washington have an extra-fine coach with many attendants and glossy stallions? Did he not, in the manner of the British king, make an annual address to the legislature, aping another royal custom? Did not some say that as long as Washington was president, no one could touch a hair on his head, treating his body as an object of reverence?[3]

More than two centuries later, the howls continue unabated. Except that now, the whines and wails are justified. Many of the earlier constraints on the office of the presidency have been consigned to the ash heap of history. The elective monarch that John Adams beheld is not only far more monarchical, but also far more republican. The American presidency is more imperial because presidents have acquired vast new authority since 1789. Indeed, the office easily eclipses modern European monarchs—they have the titles, crowns, and throne, while the presidency has genuine, far-reaching authority and faces constraints that seem to continually recede. The American presidency is also more republican, in the sense that many regard presidents as enjoying a unique, direct, and almost intimate tie with We the People. A president is often regarded as the people's choice, elected by them in a quadrennial contest, with the presidential electors mere afterthoughts. Among national political figures, presidents alone are seen as representing the entire people of the United States.

Although many factors help explain the expansion of the presidential office, presidents themselves bear some measure of the responsibility. They have been willing participants in the ongoing expansion of their office. Why would presidents choose to enlarge the domain of their office, usurping powers granted elsewhere?

One reason is that presidents are human and share the foibles of the species. As William Howell notes, the Founders evinced "a universal skepticism of human nature."[4] They supposed that ignoble urges moved all politicians because politicians were human. "[T]he motives which predominate most in human affairs [are] self-love and self-interest," said George Washington.[5] The Madisonian maxim from the Federalist, "[i]f men were angels, no government would be necessary," assumed that people are somewhat devilish and posits the necessity of structuring government in order to restrain their venal impulses.[6]

Another generic reason for grasping authority is that presidents often find existing rules and structures to be too confining. They cannot do what they wish to do (or what they believe must be done) under prevailing conceptions of presidential power and existing institutional arrangements. Typically, this means that Congress (or the existing framework) is obstructing the president's agenda. Rather than simply accepting the existing legal regime and its express and implied limits, presidents create new pathways of power, ones that they may tread again and ones that their successors may ratify and rely on.

Other, more specific urges, inclinations, and compulsions underlie and explain the grasping ways of presidents. I will give each its due.

A Love of Power

One should never discount the lust for power, or ambition. The Founders agreed with an Englishman who wrote that "[t]he love of power is natural; it is insatiable; almost constantly whetted, and never cloyed by possession."[7] Benjamin Franklin argued that two passions have a tremendous influence on people: ambition (or "the love of power") and the love of money.[8] As George Washington understood, the passion for power has consequences for how governments operate. In his farewell address, he lamented the tendency of officials to usurp and consolidate government authority, which emanates from "that love of power, and proneness to abuse it, which predominates in the human heart."[9] If America's foremost renunciate thought this, a man who yielded power multiple times, it seems likely that other Founders likewise regarded it as an iron law of nature. Indeed, proponents of the Constitution anticipated that presidents would grasp for power. Anti-Federalists, too, certainly expected that presidents would try to snatch power, and their writings are suffused with feverish speculation about how presidents would establish a hereditary, despotic monarchy.[10]

Some Founders argued that the prospect of serving multiple terms would tend to defuse a president's temptation to seize authority.[11] After all, incumbents could continually prevail in presidential elections and hence would not need to overthrow the system in order to retain power. Another counter to the lust for power was the separation of powers, a system borrowed from the British. The division of governmental powers across legislative, executive, and judicial branches creates rival power centers, each with its own interests. These contending officers would inevitably try to encroach on their counterparts, but also strive to repulse the incursions of their rivals. As James Madison put it, "[a]mbition must be made to counteract ambition."[12] Members of Congress would seek to advance legislative authority, and the ambition of its members would serve to check the aggrandizement of the executive and vice versa.

Even if Madison's prediction about ambition serving to counter ambition has not been fully borne out (more on this later), the idea that presidents would seek greater power is amply proven by our lived experience. With some exceptions, presidents have generally taken care to preserve the power they have and to acquire still more.

A Hunger for Fame

Along with a lust for power comes an appetite for fame, a desire to be known as a "'great man', who stands out, who towers above his fellows in some spectacular way."[13] John Adams wrote that "[m]en of the most exalted genius and active minds are generally perfect slaves to the love of fame."[14] The Founders fully anticipated that a yearning for fame might spur executives to act irresponsibly. John Jay wrote of monarchs waging wars for "military glory" even when their nations "get nothing by it."[15] James Madison noted that "the executive is . . . most distinguished by its propensity to war" because any victory "laurels" will bedeck the "executive brow."[16]

History fairly proves that vanquishing an enemy yields considerable renown. Some of our greatest presidents—Washington, Jefferson, Lincoln, and Theodore Roosevelt—can be found on Mount Rushmore, courtesy of the sculptor Gutzon Borglum. But the three repeatedly ranked at the top by historians and political scientists are those who triumphed in great wars—Washington, Lincoln, and Franklin Roosevelt.[17] War makes it easier for "a president to achieve greatness," or so claimed John F. Kennedy.[18] Theodore Roosevelt groused that had Lincoln presided during peaceful times, "no one would know his name now."[19] One has to suppose that Teddy Roosevelt, often ranked fourth in such polls, might be higher still had he defeated a formidable enemy.[20]

Does ranking presidents make sense? Probably not. Rankings exist because they are fun to read and sell copy, not because they reflect objective truths. It is hard to evaluate a president outside of his context. John F. Kennedy once said "[n]o one has a right to grade a President—not even poor James Buchanan—who has not sat in his chair, examined the mail and information that came across his desk, and learned why he made his decisions."[21] Julian Zelizer has argued that the rankings "are weak mechanisms for evaluating what has taken place in the White House," and he is surely right.[22]

But rankings, formal and informal, matter, as do the incentives they generate. No one should doubt that every modern president has wished to be seen as a "great man." When presidents cleverly say they will let history decide such questions, they are not evincing humility or indifference. They are merely stating the obvious. And by deflecting the question as they often do, incumbents (and their predecessors) all but confirm that they wish to be celebrated as successful and consequential and ranked among the greats.[23]

The desire for lasting fame does not, by itself, necessarily generate a compulsion to amass power. But it is hardly controversial that the skillful accumulation and wielding of power helps presidents prevail in wars, navigate domestic crises, and enact their policy agendas. Lincoln is the obvious example of a wartime president who upended the constitutional order. He expended funds, raised armies, and suspended civil liberties, all without legal warrant. He sought a Unionist victory and the reintegration of the South into the Union. To achieve his worthy goals, he made unprecedented constitutional claims. But defeating the South also would bring him everlasting fame, something some scholars claim he desperately desired. He apparently wanted to be on the same plane as the Founders.[24] Thankfully, he succeeded, in both respects.

What is true of real wars is no less true for political battles. When presidents successfully wield greater authority, either constitutional or otherwise, they will prevail more often in skirmishes over taxes, spending, and social issues—and the more often they triumph in these contests, the higher they will be ranked among the greats. Successfully advancing a broad legislative and policy agenda is now a requirement for presidential greatness. For those unable to reap wartime glory, because they are blessed (or cursed) to preside over a pacific period, the domestic arena is the only battleground available for securing a shining, enduring legacy.

An Impulse to Keep Promises

The Founders were right to anticipate that presidents would covet power and fame. But since 1789, changes in politics have further incentivized presidents to aggrandize their office. One such transformation is presidential candidates making promises that they strive to fulfill once in the White House.

The original presidency was largely, though certainly not entirely, conceived of as an office focused on duty. There was some discretion, to be sure. But the principal function was executive—that is, executing the wishes of others, be they members of Congress or the Constitution's makers (the people). Presidents were to be faithful executives, as the Faithful Execution Clause and the presidential oath clearly signaled.[25] Consequently, early presidential candidates (most of whom were quite coy about their burning aspirations) did not disclose which bills they would sign or veto, or what measures they would recommend to Congress. Candidates were chosen on the strength of prior accomplishments, not on what they would do in office. Résumés mattered more than future acts. Candidates made no promises.

The first presidential promises arose in the mid-nineteenth century. Astonishingly, they consisted of vows to serve only one term. These were promises not of action, but of abstention. There were no lists of action items relating to the economy, jobs, or tariffs. Later, candidates both made promises and decried the habit of making them. In 1840, for example, William Henry Harrison praised the "old system of selecting" presidents, when candidates made no pledges and where a candidate's "whole life was a pledge of what he would do." More recently, however, America had adopted the "corrupting system of requiring pledges" of aspirants. "The Presidency hath been put up to the highest bidder in promises, and we see the result." Yet Harrison himself went on to make several pledges. He would not fight an impossible battle for a lost cause.[26]

The trend continued as candidates began endorsing party platforms. If the party was going to nominate a candidate for president, the least he could do was endorse the party's agenda. Candidates then began to deviate, here and there, from those planks. Eventually, they came to influence, and finally, help dictate party platforms, which became, in part, a *presidential* platform.[27] As platforms grew longer and more specific, it became harder for presidents to satisfy all of the planks, and it became more difficult for voters to discern the core from the periphery.

By the twentieth century, independent will had become paramount in a presidential candidate and duty was relegated to something of an afterthought. The modern president is not some mere law enforcer. He is not akin to an FBI agent or a US attorney. Indeed, many regard attorneys general of the United States as the nation's chief law enforcers, a curious turn of events given that attorneys general have no constitutional authority over law enforcement (the Constitution never mentions the office). Writing in 1908, Woodrow Wilson questioned whether presidents should even be regarded as executives at all, especially in light of their vital role as party leaders, their burgeoning influence in the legislative process, and their sweeping power in the international arena.[28]

Rather than a law enforcer, a modern president must be a law reformer and must exhibit the zeal, impulse, and energy of a crusader for renovation and transformation. He must be, in the words of Bill Clinton, a "change agent."[29] He must promote an ambitious policy agenda, filled with promises about jobs, health care, and the environment. If candidates lack a laundry list of promises, they will get taken to the cleaners come election time. Voters expect promises, even if they know that presidents will not keep all of them.

Take the 1988 campaign of Michael Dukakis. He ran as a technocrat, promising not "ideology" but "competence."[30] This approach might have made sense in the early years of the nineteenth century, but his opponent, George H. W. Bush, had a better grasp of modern expectations. As he put it, candidates need to "understand the magic of the machine" and recognize that the election is about "the beliefs we share, the values that we honor and the principles we hold dear."[31] Any candidate who comes across as offering to make the trains run on time will not prevail, because voters expect far more than a tinkerer or a law enforcer. Making the trains run and catching lawbreakers are the province of a pure executive, and presidents are no longer solely, or, for that matter, even principally, executives. Policy innovation, not superior implementation, is the coin of the realm for candidates and presidents. In other words, what matters are subsidies, tax breaks, and legislative and regulatory change. One of the most memorable quasi-promises was attributed to Republicans stumping for Herbert Hoover: a chicken in every pot and a car in every backyard. That has been the pattern ever since.

With the rise of promises, presidents could be evaluated by whether they stayed true to them. Not every promise will be carried out in its entirety. But presidents who keep few or none of their campaign promises will suffer at the polls and in history. When George H. W. Bush ran in 1988, he promised, "Read my lips: No new taxes," then conspicuously raised taxes once in office.[32] This shattered promise no doubt played a role in the rise of Ross Perot as a third-party candidate, Bush's defeat at the polls, and Bill Clinton's election.

Consider a recent example, where a president kept his promise, in a manner of speaking. In 2008, Senator Barack Obama "guarantee[d] that we will have, in the first year [of my presidency], an immigration bill that I strongly support."[33] Despite a Democratic Congress in the first two years of his presidency, that first year came and went with no such bill. Upset with this inaction, elements of Obama's coalition demanded that he halt deportations. Facing a drumbeat of sharp criticism, the president gave a civics lesson. He was neither "king" nor "emperor." He had no "magic wand." Rather, he had a duty to "execute laws" until Congress changed them.[34]

In 2011, however, President Obama adopted a more flexible mindset. A new slogan—"We Can't Wait"—heralded a pivot to a unilateral "pen-and-phone" strategy.[35] By 2012, though he still lacked a magic wand, he discovered the pen's magic, and wielded it to remake the immigration landscape, bypassing and sidelining Congress. The first magical use came in the form of DACA—Deferred Action for Childhood Arrivals—a program that shielded from deportation those illegally brought to the United States as children. In 2014, administration lawyers found still more discretion, deferring deportation for parents of American citizens—DAPA. Neither program stopped all deportations. But President Obama's deferred actions were momentous and, in many ways, groundbreaking, for he essentially promised millions of illegal immigrants that they would not be deported, albeit for a limited period of time. He also dangled the prospect that future presidents might renew these promises indefinitely. The president would supply the legal reforms that Congress would not. While these reforms were not as useful as legislation, they were a good start and they had the effect of changing the status quo.

We will return to this episode later. For now, two lessons come to mind. The first is that those pushing for action shook loose a reform from a hesitant president, a breakthrough that any interest group seeking a change in the status quo will long remember. If our interpretation of the law can change as circumstances or preferences change, then the meaning of the law often will change when enough pressure is brought to bear. The second is that advocates of reform decided that if President Obama was not on the edge of breaking the law (or beyond the edge), he was far too passive and was not truly dedicated to their agenda. In the language of sports, "If you ain't cheating, you ain't trying." The president heard that message and acted to placate his allies in the summer of an election year.

My general point is that the desire to keep promises and thereby satisfy an electoral base often causes presidents to strain and stretch. If Congress will not pass legislation implementing their promises, presidents must seek other ways of keeping them. Those methods sometimes require presidents to transgress existing norms, be they constitutional or statutory. Given the choice of breaking a promise or breaking the law, presidents occasionally will choose to break the law to fulfill their electoral pledges. Fulfilling vows may help them

to secure reelection and climb up the charts of presidential greatness, while caution, passivity, and unfulfilled promises generally lead
in the opposite direction. Few today will say of a president, "he was
great because, rather than breaking the law, he chose to break his
promises."

A NEED TO FULFILL HEROIC EXPECTATIONS

We expect too much from our presidents, in part because we demand
that they make promises during their campaigns and fulfill them
while in office. But outsized expectations also arise from the president's status as the single most famous and recognizable American
politician. The president is, after all, our nation's de facto chief of
state. Because the federal government is rightly perceived as powerful
and because the president personifies the government, presidents are
seen as formidable. They are thought to embody the government
and all its capacity for doing good. Little wonder that Americans
demand from our presidents robust economic growth, full employ-
ment, and wage increases—all of which must be realized with low
inflation and interest rates. We insist that our presidents maintain a
peerless military, with the finest aircraft, vessels, and body armor
that money can buy. We expect that the president will safeguard the
nation from threats, foreign and domestic, and ensure that terrorists
do not strike American soil. We seek presidential solutions to drug
epidemics, sky-high college tuition, the incarceration crisis, and even
the dearth of "livable communities." And we simultaneously clamor
for low taxes, greater spending, and balanced budgets.

When did we develop these superhuman expectations of our presidents? There were heroes who became president (Washington) and
presidents who became heroes (Lincoln). But when did we first expect all of our presidents to be heroic problem-solvers? Michael
Genovese and Todd Belt argue that the "myth of the president as
a national savior who could be powerful and purposeful, could

overcome the roadblocks of the separation of powers, and govern" emerged in the twentieth century, with Franklin Roosevelt.[36]

Regardless of when they started, the ludicrous expectations placed on the executive have led some, including Jeremi Suri, to lament that we have an "impossible presidency."[37] Presidents cannot succeed because far too much is expected of them. In his view, the American electorate is akin to the unrealistic and irrational tiger mom who demands of her children straight A's, concert-level piano recitals, and unmatched athleticism.

Suri overplays his fine point. Serving as president is stressful, tiresome, and draining. Presidents enter office with exuberance and energy and leave haggard and gray. But the office of the presidency is not "impossible." If we judge departing presidents by their polls, many leave with decent ratings. Some assessments reveal improved poll numbers after they leave office.[38] Nothing makes a former president look better than comparing him to his successors. If many citizens have fond views of some former presidents, that strikes me as a success, even if those citizens also realize that these presidents did not meet every single public expectation.

Nonetheless, Suri is on to something. Unrealistic public expectations generate extreme pressure. Presidents are aware that in addition to fulfilling their explicit promises, they will be held responsible for all manner of events beyond their control. Presidents generally do not run on a platform of aiding the victims of a natural disaster. They may not promise to battle inflation or cut interest rates. They may not even discuss terrorism. But they are expected to help victims, check inflation, cut interest rates, and crush terrorists. Presidents know full well that the privilege of occupying the Oval Office comes freighted with unexpected and unreasonable expectations.

How do presidents navigate this minefield of inflated expectations? Sometimes they grasp for new authority and cut corners to get things done. Presidents generally prefer that Congress alter the law to endorse presidential policies because this approach gives the policies greater stability and avoids the stench often associated with executive unilateralism. But waiting for Congress is often like waiting for Godot. Congress, aware that it does not owe a new president a honeymoon package of legal reforms, frequently does not enact the legal change that a president believes is necessary or the policies a president imagines that the public demands.

As noted earlier, presidents who are too reliant on Congress run the risk of being perceived as overly cautious. No president can expect much praise for being law-abiding. The opposition certainly will not give a president credit for following existing laws. Indeed, critics will decry many presidential actions as illegal, regardless of whether there is merit to the charges. And on the other side, the president's base often will condemn their leader for being insufficiently aggressive. Better to have a president lean forward than bend over backward to be law-abiding. Cheating—stretching and bending the law—sends a strong signal that the president is trying hard to satisfy the base.

Take the 2008–2009 auto bailout. During the financial crisis in 2008, George W. Bush decided to save the domestic auto industry. He did not want to be blamed for Detroit going belly-up on his watch, since there would have been many eager to jump on the president if any of the automobile manufacturers went bankrupt. Perhaps tens of thousands of jobs would disappear, with many localities devastated by unemployment and despair. The legal problem was that there was no appropriation, no congressionally sanctioned funding, that could be drawn on to rescue General Motors or Chrysler. There was, however, a much-criticized bailout law for financial institutions.[39] Though neither manufacturer was a financial institution, Bush used some of the funds intended for financial institutions to prop up the two firms. In this case, the fervent desire to avoid blame, prevent the demise of major manufacturers, and avert hundreds of thousands of layoffs led to a violation of our Constitution. Facing identical constraints, President Obama made the same choice for the same reasons. Both presidents spent money from the Treasury without an appropriation, something the Constitution expressly forbids. They did so in part because they knew full well that if they did nothing, they would be pilloried for standing by as the car companies collapsed. Facing these incentives and pressures, they concluded that unlawful action was better than lawful inaction.

If Americans are prone to blame presidents for feeble responses to events, many of which are unpredictable and beyond their control, presidents often will seize the power to successfully navigate those crises. Likewise, if in times of tranquility we demand that presidents fulfill our policy wishes, they often will snatch the authority they need to fulfill our overblown expectations.

There is an old adage that with great power comes great responsibility. For presidents, it sometimes appears very much the converse: with great expectations and responsibility must come great power. They occasionally act as if their power must be expansive enough to tackle the outsized responsibilities placed on their shoulders. Or to borrow from a saying attributed to Napoleon, presidents often suppose that the tools must belong to those who will be vilified for not using them.

An Appetite for Sound Policy

Presidents are not just bent on power and fame. Nor do they merely respond to what the public demands and expects. Sometimes presidents merely wish to do the right thing. In other words, presidents often seek to advance their genuine policy preferences about immigration, gay marriage, and the environment. They typically have opinions about ideal policies and the reform of current practices. Presidents run on a reform platform not only because people expect action from them; they also want to transform various aspects of the federal government.

For instance, President Ronald Reagan had strong preferences about federalism, an issue that was probably not on the radar of most voters in 1980. In keeping with his sincere preferences about sound national policy, he wanted to shrink the influence of Washington and send authority back to the states. Similarly, Reagan touched the third rail of American politics—Social Security—lived to tell of it, and secured reelection. He succeeded despite the absence of a groundswell in support of an overhaul. No large cohort of voters clamored for higher taxes and reduced benefits. The reform succeeded because Reagan had a vision and brought the country together by cajoling Congress and compromising with the loyal opposition.

Likewise, I assume that when President Obama allowed certain illegal immigrants to remain in the country, he was not merely satisfying his base and bolstering his reelection chances. He also was advancing his views about sound public policy and the immorality of deporting longstanding migrants. In the case of his deferred actions, Obama hit a trifecta. He furthered his own preferences on immigration, partially fulfilled a campaign promise, and acquired more fame. His decision, in retrospect, seems almost overdetermined. Facing an inflexible Congress, he flexibly interpreted his legal authorities and bypassed Congress. In the process he created a new legal status quo that his successors must navigate at their peril.

How Pursuing Short-Term Ends Generally Furthers the Presidency's Long-Term Interests

Strengthening the presidency is not typically the goal of executive stretches and usurpations. Rather, presidents push the boundaries of executive power—by funding a priority, going to war, or bending a law—principally as a means of doing the right thing, fulfilling a promise, achieving greatness, or satisfying public expectations. That is, when presidents grasp for more power, they often are keen to advance sound policy and make themselves great and powerful; the long-term effects on the presidency are secondary.

For instance, in refusing to defend the constitutionality of the Defense of Marriage Act (DOMA) in court, President Obama made a small adjustment to existing conceptions of how executive duty relates to the defense of congressional laws. In the past, executive officials had proclaimed an ironclad "duty to defend" the constitutionality of statutes if any reasonable defense of them might be mounted.[40] To help undermine DOMA, President Obama's administration weakened the longstanding practice of defending Congress's laws from constitutional challenge. Specifically, Attorney General Eric Holder endorsed an artificial distinction between reasonable arguments and plausible ones. Holder said that while there were plausible arguments in defense of DOMA, there were no reasonable arguments. By adopting this specious distinction, the Obama administration made it easier for future presidents to decline to defend the constitutionality of congressional laws, thereby increasing executive discretion and power.[41] Yet in modifying the "duty to defend," Obama likely did not seek to expand presidential power. Rather, the dominant motivation was certainly a desire to see the courts declare DOMA unconstitutional, in keeping with his views about same-sex marriage. The slight expansion of presidential power was simply a means to that end.

In fact, one might go so far as to say that most incumbents are not intrinsically interested in the presidency's long-term expansion or its health. Occasionally president-watchers assert that an incumbent has made the presidency weaker principally because he pushed claims of presidential power too far, in the sense that the courts and Congress successfully resisted his advances. Some critics said as much about President Clinton's claims regarding presidential immunity from private lawsuits and his assertion of a novel "protective function privilege" that barred testimony by the Secret Service. Because he made such claims and lost in court, Clinton was said to have weakened the presidency.[42] Maybe so. My point is that most presidents are far more interested in their own power and standing and probably care rather little about the long-term well-being of their institution. Only two sons have followed their fathers into the office, and there likely is little genuine sense that presidents must leave some sort of bequest of a stronger presidency. To be sure, a stronger presidency helps both the incumbent and successors. But a president's reasons for favoring a stronger presidency have nothing to do with the long-term health of the office. If presidents believe that they personally can gain some advantage via some strained legal argument, they often will make the argument even at the expense of the presidency. In the case of President Clinton, the privilege claims he made served his immediate interests (or so he thought), and from his perspective, his political fortunes were paramount.

To be clear, I am certainly not claiming that presidents are uninterested in advancing presidential power. They hunger for power, as do all politicians. But they crave power and influence for themselves. They do not care much about whether the office they occupy is made more powerful. We can see this most clearly when presidents compromise their office's authority for political gain. Occasionally, the desire to advance personal goals (fame, fulfilling promises, satisfying the public, and policy reform) may cause some presidents to sacrifice the office's power. If a president can secure immigration reform or single-payer health care, or garner assistance for some action that vaults him or her into the ranks of presidential greats, he or she may be willing to make concessions on matters of presidential power.

✶ ✶ ✶

Presidential candidates promise the world—tax cuts, balanced budgets, and more guns and butter—and voters respond by expecting them not only to keep their promises, but also to take responsibility for events and crises outside their control. Presidents navigate these absurd expectations by using their existing set of authorities and by occasionally reaching beyond them. When you add a lust for power, an intense yearning for fame, and a sincere desire to advance their own policy preferences, it is no wonder that every modern president since Jimmy Carter has been unable to resist the temptation to expand presidential power. This is especially so since the alternative, consistently playing by the rules, means risking being seen as a feckless failure. No president wants to be the next James Buchanan, who fiddled while the Union was collapsing.

CHAPTER THREE

How PRESIDENTS AMEND *the* CONSTITUTION

A s we have seen, the imperialism of modern presidents—their tendency to usurp the powers of others and alter the existing constitutional order—reflects a number of motivations and impulses. One reason for the imperialism is that those who crave the highest office of the land are, by their nature, prone to seeking greater power and fame. Another is that the public places enormous expectations on their shoulders and essentially requires candidates to make and fulfill outlandish promises. A final factor is that presidents have sincere policy preferences about which policies are best for America. To further these goals, some lofty and others base, presidents are willing to push, bend, and break the existing legal order.

How do presidents pull off the remarkable and seemingly impossible feat of amending the Constitution, particularly their role in it? They benefit from the legacies of the Founders, including the gaps and seeming ambiguities in the founding document and its structural limitations on rivals. They also capitalize on modern circumstances and conceptions, such as the unstinting support that presidents receive from co-partisans.

WINDFALLS FROM THE FOUNDING

The Founders made a number of design choices for the new government, each backed by sound reasons. They chose a single executive to energize decision-making. They drafted Article II using relatively general terms in part because that was the tradition in the states. They divided Congress as a compromise between the large and small states. And they greatly strengthened federal judicial power without making the courts the perpetual censors of governmental conduct. What they could not foresee, however, were the unintended consequences of these choices: an overly energetic executive; a capacious Article II capable of misconstruction; the possibility of debilitating congressional division; and judicial inaction.

An Energetic, Unitary Executive

Generals are often fighting the last war. So too constitution makers; frequently they craft a document meant to better fight old battles. As Chapter 1 recounted, the Constitution was in part a response to the prevailing model of feeble and divided executives. Those pathetic executives, in turn, were made weak because they were meant to avoid any semblance to America's earlier supposed problem, a British king.[1]

One crucial ingredient of the Founders' robust presidency was "energy." Over and over again, they praised the presidency's potential energy. The most famous exposition is in *Federalist*, no. 70: "Energy in the Executive is a leading character in the definition of good government." For a "feeble Executive implies a feeble execution of the government. . . . [A] government ill executed, whatever it may be in theory, must be, in practice, a bad government."[2] Alexander Hamilton was unquestionably right. Without a vigilant executive, one always on duty, the nation is more vulnerable to attack. A legislature, often recessed for weeks or months, may be unable to respond in the immediate aftermath of an invasion or rebellion. Similarly, absent a vigorous executive, laws would be mere pageantry—no more meaningful than the "National Wear Red Day" and "National Pi Day" resolutions that the chambers of Congress routinely pass.

The indispensable condition for energy was and is unity. "Decision, activity, secrecy, and despatch will generally characterize the proceedings of one man," said Hamilton. Because an individual need not secure the consent of others, he or she can act rapidly. In the pursuit of a well-executed government, a single executive can quickly gather information, weigh differing views, and implement the chosen option. In contrast, groups often enervate rather than energize. No one has ever supposed that the best way to decide and act promptly is to form a committee. After all, "bitter dissensions" often plague committees. Moreover, a committee would "lessen the respectability, weaken the authority, and distract the plans and operation" of the executive.[3]

Understandably, Hamilton chose not to dwell on the drawbacks of an energetic executive. Alas, we don't have the same luxury. Energy not only enables the executive to fulfill presidential duties and exercise the office's assigned powers; it also proves tremendously advantageous in *any* executive endeavor or adventure. That is, an executive built for energy neither guarantees any particular outcome (such as vigorous execution of the laws) nor implies a deep commitment to the Constitution's sanctity. Rather, energy merely creates a context in which the executive can decide quickly and act decisively.

Though Hamilton ignored the potential dangers of an energetic executive, others did not. Edmund Randolph, the Virginia governor, told the convention that a single executive would continually push for greater power.[4] The delegations rejected Randolph's plan for a triumvirate, presumably imagining that internal clashes would end in indecision or, worse yet, despotism, much as the infighting between Pompeii, Marcus Crassus, and Julius Caesar eventually led to Caesar's dictatorship.[5]

Randolph was right; executive unity did pose a risk. While none of the changes made to the executive after the Framers had implemented their plan were in any way foreordained, a unitary executive made the accumulation of power more probable. A single executive can be more aggressive, nimble, and resolute in advancing its interest, and in the process, bolstering presidential power.

Whether an energetic executive chooses to act consistently with the law depends on factors that are wholly unrelated to energy. In a regime where the executive is tightly bound by custom and is expected to obey existing laws, the executive will tend to use its energy in lawful ways. In a context where citizens do not demand constitutional and legal changes from the executive, the executive will more likely act within the system.

But in an environment where the executive can alter the Constitution and laws by violating both, presidents will tend to break the law in order to advance their own policies and interests. Likewise, in a context where citizens demand policy innovation from their presidents, these presidents are more apt to gratify such demands even at the expense of the law.

Our modern constitutional system is the latter sort. As a matter of text, the Constitution requires the president to "take Care that the Laws be faithfully executed" and to "preserve, protect and defend the Constitution."[6] But in reality, our contemporary regime permits presidents to change statutory and constitutional law. In this sort of system, an energetic executive is a weaponized one. The executive, because it can act quickly and repeatedly, is primed to play the preeminent role in legal and constitutional change. The unitary executive president can set the reform agenda, take quick action, change policies, and through a flurry of actions keep the other two branches off balance.

We can, of course, make too much of executive unity. We speak of presidents and the powers and influence they *personally* wield. But in fact, the presidency is both singular and plural, both a "he"— or "she"—and a "they." At the very top is a president whose singularity can help advance a presidential agenda. But the modern presidency is certainly more than one person. To fully exercise their constitutional and statutory authorities, modern presidents rely on more than a thousand people within the Executive Office of the President and a couple of thousand senior officials scattered throughout the executive branch. These aides—from cabinet secretaries to the lowest political appointees—act in many ways like the president's extra eyes, ears, mouth, arms, and legs. Yet because they are hardly automatons, many of these people also may act to thwart the president, via leaks and political sabotage. In our government, this longstanding practice dates back to Secretary of State Thomas Jefferson's sponsorship of a newspaper that consistently abused the Washington administration.

Nonetheless, the executive is certainly far more unified than the House, the Senate, or the federal courts. Harry Truman once claimed that when Dwight Eisenhower got to the Oval Office, he would be stymied: "He'll sit here . . . and he'll say, 'Do this! Do that!' And nothing will happen. Poor Ike—it won't be a bit like the Army."[7] But this was exaggeration. Presidents invariably encounter bureaucratic resistance, some more than others. But if they focus on a handful of items that they regard as significant and doggedly insist on their preferences, they should prevail over recalcitrant bureaucrats. Unity at the apex genuinely does generate energy and action, even if the unitary executive consistently requires the cooperation of many, many others.

A Capacious Article II

In every rule-bound system, there is the problem of legal drift over time. The longer it has been since some rule or system was enacted, the more the shared meanings and assumptions underlying that rule or system erode. This is no less true for the presidency. Implied limits on the office that were once unquestioned can, with the passage of time, be doubted and ultimately tossed aside. Aggressive actions that were unthinkable become imaginable in the messy cauldron of politics, where one's views on the content of law are often shaped by the immediate dispute. We cannot help but see the Constitution through a modern lens, and that lens often distorts the contours of the original Constitution.

The Constitution's delineation of the presidency—found mostly in Article II—exacerbates this problem. The first sentence of that article—which decrees that the "executive Power shall be vested in a President"—reflects a common strategy in drafting such documents, namely to grant a general authority and then list a host of restrictions.[8] As James Madison noted, "Nothing is more natural nor common than first to use a general phrase, and then to explain and qualify it by a recital of particulars."[9] But this approach has its perils. A general phrase, because it is more capacious, is more prone to acquire new meanings.

Although the Constitution granted limited executive powers—the authority to carry out laws, some foreign affairs powers, command of the military, and control of the executive bureaucracy—in modern times the Article II Vesting Clause has come to encompass so much more. Though it was meant to be a limited catchall, it is today capable of *catching all*. Almost a century ago, Charles Thach said the Vesting Clause stands as a constitutional "joker," a wild card ready to be cited as a legal basis for any executive action.[10] This prospect has not waned since. To the contrary, executive privilege, emergency authority, the taking of private property in time of war—all of these and more have been ascribed to the Vesting Clause, even though none of them are traceable to the original understanding of "executive power."[11]

Even specific Article II clauses can become incubators for constitutional innovation. The Commander-in-Chief Clause is widely read to grant far more power today than it conveyed in the past. Today, it is common to suppose that the commander in chief can command the military to do almost anything. After all, the president is the commander, right? Many read the clause, misunderstand its eighteenth-century context and import, and invest the commander in chief with the kind of military and emergency authority that the Founders neither intended to grant nor, in fact, conveyed.

It didn't have to be this way. The Founders might have exhaustively cataloged executive authority in much the same way they did for Congress. Imagine an Article II that enumerated the following powers (and still others): serving as the principal organ of foreign communications, recognizing foreign nations and governments, concluding minor international agreements, and directing and removing executive officers, both civilian and military. In that world, there would have been no need for a potentially protean grant of "executive power" because all that it encompassed would be exhaustively specified. The Founders might have safely omitted the Article II Vesting Clause.

Additionally, the Founders might have added explicit restraints on the presidency. Imagine an Article II, section 5, one that somewhat mirrored Article I, section 9 (a list of constraints on Congress), except that the restrictions explicitly limited presidents: "The executive shall never use force or wage war except by virtue of law," "The executive shall never make treaties or equivalent international agreements except with the consent of the Senate," "The executive shall never alter the Constitution." At the time of the Founding, there were famous examples of express limitations on executives. The English Bill of Rights contains a number of such constraints, most prominently its prohibitions on executive suspensions and dispensations. State constitutions likewise contained specific restrictions on executive authority.[12]

Adoption of one or both of these strategies would not have wholly eliminated the possibility of changed constitutional conceptions and misreading. Nothing can truly prevent constitutional drift and interpretational errors. But they would have made them less likely because specificity generally makes it harder for readers to inadvertently or willfully misconstrue legal documents. Few readers of the Constitution suppose that some states may pass ex post facto laws or that Congress may create a national religious establishment. That is because the Constitution contains explicit rules against these outcomes. Similarly, if the Constitution exhaustively listed presidential power and simultaneously declared that presidents could not amend the Constitution, start wars, or evade the Treaty Clause, presidents would have found it far more difficult to push the boundaries of their office.

Houses Divided

The Framers assumed that Congress would be the strongest branch. In state after state, the legislature had proved to be what Madison called an "impetuous vortex," swallowing up the powers of executives and judges.[13] The Framers seemingly did little to quiet fears of an overly strong Congress, giving it considerable legislative authority, control over war, and complete power over taxes and spending. Moreover, the original Constitution contained rather few express protections of individual rights. No wonder that most complaints about the proposed Constitution centered on Congress and the threat it posed to state authority and civil liberties.[14]

A momentous side effect of Congress's structure went largely unnoticed. At the Constitutional Convention, states with small populations had demanded a unicameral legislature where each state would have an equal voice, as had been the case under the Articles of Confederation. Heavily populated states disagreed, arguing that seats in Congress should be apportioned by population. With the creation of two chambers (the Great Compromise), both factions got half a loaf. In the Senate, every state would have an equal voice (two senators), while in the House, the distribution of representatives would be based on population.

The unintended consequence of the Great Compromise was an increased likelihood of internal fracturing. Prior to the Civil War, Abraham Lincoln presciently warned that a house divided cannot stand.[15] He was speaking of the Union, but what he said is no less true for Congress. A Congress divided cannot stand up to the president. The very division of Congress into two chambers makes a clash between the two parts more likely and weakens Congress in any interbranch disputes. One branch may try to oppose or thwart executive overreach while the other cheers it. Indeed, sometimes people refer to the two chambers of Congress as distinct branches of the government precisely because it is easy to see that while they are both part of a broader entity, they often have divergent interests and policy perspectives.

The divisions in Congress do not stop there. Each chamber is internally divided by partisanship, sectional interests, and ideological preferences. Should alleged executive overreach agitate some legislators, others may fervently support the action, leading to skirmishes within the House or the Senate. Given its cast of hundreds and its many internal divisions, Congress finds it difficult to consistently deter and punish executive misdeeds. Presidents and their minions are fully aware of these divisions within Congress and regularly take advantage of their immobilized, divided counterpart.

Bicameralism also created a more demanding lawmaking gauntlet, with bills having to emerge from both chambers, rather than from one chamber as was true under the Articles. The presidential veto made enacting laws even more challenging. The veto pen could be wielded not only to protect the executive from congressional encroachment, as the Founders fully expected, but also to thwart attempts to constrain and beat back executive invasions of congressional turf. The Founders seemed not to have imagined that the veto pen might be used to erode, if not destroy, Congress's capacity to check the presidency.

Though impeachments and impeachment trials cannot be vetoed, the threat of the process has scant effect on the executive. An impeachment requires a House majority, a daunting task. Convicting a president is all but impossible because it requires that two-thirds of senators present find "Treason, Bribery or other high Crimes and Misdemeanors."[16] After all, 40 percent (or more) of the Senate often will be the president's co-partisans. Knowing that a Senate conviction is essentially out of the question greatly dampens the House's interest in the process. Why dust off the impeachment machinery if the Senate will not convict? Impeachment is largely a pathetic "scarecrow," as Jefferson derisively called it.[17]

Some may demur and point out that the House has impeached several presidents. But one must bear in mind that, despite repeated presidential usurpations across centuries, the House has impeached only three presidents (Andrew Johnson, Bill Clinton, and Donald Trump). Moreover, it took a crime of the highest order (obstruction of justice) to oust the only president who left office prematurely and in utter ignominy (Richard Nixon). Jefferson's claim about the impotence of impeachment remains true to this day.

In essence, the Founders both strengthened Congress (by granting it greater legislative authority) and hobbled it. The sheer multiplicity of views within both chambers often means that Congress will be paralyzed. In particular, the obligation to present legislation to the president means that most attempts to limit presidential power through legislative strictures will founder. Imagine what the modern presidency would look like if Congress consisted of one chamber, rather than two, and if the president could not veto legislation. Imagine the contours of the modern executive in a world where Congress could oust officers with a bare majority in either chamber. My point is not to endorse such possibilities. Rather it is that our modern presidency is in part a byproduct of an internally divided, and externally checked, Congress and an impeachment process that is more illusory than real.

An Irregular Judicial Check

When we think of the courts, we envision an institution dedicated to maintaining and upholding the law. That is their peculiar province, in the sense that it is their only function and mandate. Moreover, the president cannot fire federal judges, for they have tenure "during good Behaviour," meaning that they must misbehave if they are to be ousted.[18] Given these features, judges seem tailor-made for curbing the executive. Though there is nothing in the Constitution expressly requiring executives to enforce judicial judgments, everyone at the Founding understood that when judges issue judgments, it is the (implicit) duty of executives to see them faithfully executed. Any other answer would mean that judges did not actually decide who won (and lost) cases and controversies.[19]

As compared to Congress, it is far easier for courts to check the executive. At trial, a single judge can hear arguments and decide whether the executive is acting contrary to law or the Constitution. When a judge concludes as much, the executive invariably complies with this ruling. Of course, the executive can appeal, which means that sometimes multiple judges must jointly conclude that the executive has gone off the rails. If a case reaches the Supreme Court, five justices might be necessary to constrain the executive. But securing two judges on a three-judge appellate court or five Supreme Court justices is generally easier than relying on Congress to check the president.

Yet the federal courts were not built to check all executive wrongdoing. Under our system, courts do not decide the many hundreds of thousands of legal questions that executive officials must answer to do their jobs properly. To the contrary, the vast majority of questions about the meaning and application of federal law—both its enforcement and implementation—are decided by the executive branch alone. Part of the reason for this stems from the federal judiciary's reliance on the aggrieved to sue. If no one brings a case to the courts, our judges cannot resolve the underlying questions. Not all judicial systems work this way. For instance, the courts of India essentially have a roving commission to investigate legal violations, including executive abuses. They do not need someone to file suit.[20] Our federal judges don't believe they have this license.

Another reason why the executive is often the final arbiter of federal law is that the federal courts suppose they cannot resolve certain disputes, even when brought to the courthouse by eager plaintiffs. For instance, federal courts will not judge some legal questions on the grounds that the Constitution leaves them to the political branches—Congress and the president. This is why federal courts will not decide what is an impeachable offense: that is something that each chamber must decide for itself. Moreover, federal courts will not hear a case unless the party bringing it has suffered a personalized and concrete injury. For example, if a president raids the Treasury and spends money without congressional approval, it may well be that no court will opine, simply because the courts may conclude that no one has suffered a personalized and concrete injury. A desire to see the executive comply with the Constitution and federal laws, however genuine and deeply felt, does not grant a plaintiff the right to invoke a federal court's judicial authority.[21]

As a result of such rules, and others, judicial review of executive action is asymmetric and limited. If the executive harms people in concrete ways—by detaining them, seizing their property, or regulating them—then those actually harmed can seek judicial relief. But if they don't sue, then the courts can say nothing. Moreover, if the president violates the law or the Constitution but harms no one in a personal, particularized way, the courts will steer clear. This means that one of the easiest and most inexpensive means of resolving questions about the legality of executive action is often unavailable. In sum, the courts are often on the sidelines of legal and constitutional disputes involving the presidency.

Again, imagine a different regime. Picture a system where the courts could decide all legal questions involving executive authority, where any party dismayed by the executive's legal or factual claims could march into court and have a disinterested judge decide the matter. One does not have to endorse such a system to recognize that it would have radically different consequences for the presidency. In essence, we have a judicial system that acts as only a partial, fitful check on the executive, and the weakness of the check has consequences for the actions the executive is willing to take. When the executive knows that the judicial watchdog cannot (or will not) bark, much less bite, it will be more willing to take aggressive legal stances. This is not a comment on the executive in particular; rather it is a comment on human nature.

Windfalls from Modern Attitudes and Politics

A quartet of revolutions in thinking and practice also help account for the expansion of presidential power. Presidents wield a mandate from the people, using it as a sword. They exploit their position as party leader to draw sustained public support. They use tools of influence and party affiliation to weaken an already divided Congress. Finally, they have a phalanx of executive officers predisposed to advance presidential power.

A Mandate for the People's Choice

Chinese emperors claimed a mandate from heaven.[22] If people believe the assertion, this is a rather meaningful mandate. In a secular democracy, however, the best mandate is one from the people, and modern presidents have been eager to claim it. This is such a familiar part of our political discourse that we might be tempted to pass over it. But the claim is critical and, as we shall see, has profound consequences for presidential power.

We forget that assertions of a popular mandate rest on a profound revolution in thought, one that occurred decades after the Constitution's creation. We also forget that the claim has no constitutional foundation. To get a sense of the once revolutionary nature of the claim, picture something wholly implausible. Suppose that the chief justice asserted that "the Supreme Court is the direct representative of the American people." Many would be dumbstruck. We the People do not choose justices. The invocation of the people might seem a scheme to intimidate or subdue the other branches. After all, the claim that one acts on behalf of the people has a whiff of usurpation and demagoguery. It is what authoritarians perpetually proclaim.

Now imagine if a president declared that he was "the direct representative of the American people." Few Americans would flinch. This seems obvious to our ears. Yet at the Founding, presidents claimed no such link to the people. The Founders did not establish a popular vote for candidates. Rather the Constitution provided that elite electors, chosen pursuant to state legislative rules, would elect the president. The Founders assumed that the electors would exercise independent judgment, not merely parrot the collective sentiments of the people or anyone else.[23]

In the first presidential election, only four states had their citizens exclusively select presidential electors. In the other six states participating (not all states took part), legislatures appointed at least some of the state's electors. In 1800, ten of sixteen states used legislative selection. As late as 1820, nine states used that method. The use of legislative selection ended with the election of 1860, when one state legislature (South Carolina) handpicked its electors. Thereafter, all states have continuously relied on the popular selection of electors.[24] Though this change was consequential, the rest of the system remained untouched. Even with the uniform use of popular elections to select electors, We the People still don't vote for president. Although we discuss voting for this or that candidate and although we are usually unaware of the personalities and policy preferences of the presidential electors, we actually vote for electors who shortly thereafter cast votes for candidates. We still vote for people who vote for presidents.

Of course, whatever the Constitution might formally state, a modern president may seem to represent the people. Electors are often regarded as obliged (whether legally or morally) to vote for particular candidates, and when they violate these expectations, some are dismayed by the sheer presumption. "Do I chuse Samuel Miles [a Federalist elector] to determine for me whether John Adams or Thomas Jefferson shall be President? No! I chuse him to *act,* not to think!" or so one Federalist voter groused in 1797 when Miles crossed party lines to cast his vote for Jefferson.[25] This attitude continues today. Indeed, attempts to convince presidential electors to exercise genuine choice will stir up anger, at least among those who imagine that their favored candidate "won" on election day and who regard the casting of electoral votes as a formality. Voters generally demand that presidential electors serve as automatons and cast the expected vote. In this environment, Americans can be forgiven for supposing that We the People, not "They the Electors," elect the president.

Moreover, modern Americans can hardly be blamed for concluding that presidents uniquely represent the people. But originally this too was far from obvious. It took our seventh president, Andrew Jackson, to usher in this reconception of the office. Like Napoleon Bonaparte, who had the cheek to place an emperor's crown on his own head, Jackson publicly anointed himself "the direct representative of the American people."[26] This claim caused a firestorm. The silver-tongued Daniel Webster noted that the Constitution in no way designates the president a representative of any people. "I hold this, Sir, to be mere assumption, and dangerous assumption. If he is the representative of *all* the American people, he is the only representative which they all have. . . . And if he may be allowed to consider himself [thus,] . . . then I say, Sir, that the government . . . has already a master."[27] Webster was arguing, prophetically as it turned out, that if Jackson successfully laid claim to be the people's representative, presidents would dominate the other branches.

What in 1834 was a brash assumption is now an uncontested verity. Modern presidents revel in the assertion that they uniquely symbolize and embody the American people. In Charlottesville,

Virginia, where I live, people vote for two federal senators and a representative of a far smaller constituency. Neither my Virginia senators nor my district representative is a representative of the people of the United States, because the people of Maryland or Oregon have no electoral say in who serves in these positions. If my federal legislators purported to speak on behalf of the entire people of the United States, many would rightly scoff at the conceit. But given that people think they vote for the president, that candidates stump for their votes, that electors almost invariably mimic the election returns in their state, that presidents claim that the people have chosen them, and that no other federal elected official can claim to represent the entire United States, there is a good deal of sense underlying the modern intuition that the president is the direct and sole representative of the people.[28]

By itself, this singular status substantially strengthens presidential sway. "The people choose me," presidents insist, "so other officials should heed me." But modern presidents claim much more. Not content with serving as the people's sole representative, presidents also lay claim to a "popular mandate," meaning that We the People have commanded the other branches to implement the president's agenda. "The people have spoken," say winning presidential candidates, and the subtext is "now you, the legislators and the courts, must heed their wishes to adopt my program." In this way, presidents-elect and recently installed presidents hope to convince legislators and judges that the people have just endorsed every jot and tittle of their domestic, military, and foreign policy agendas.

This mandate does not merely aid passage of a legislative agenda before Congress. Presidents can also cite the people to give them a certain constitutional and legal license. According to this modern idea, when the people endorse a president, they not only endorse his or her agenda; they also can be seen as granting that president warrant to see those plans through, whatever the Constitution or laws provide. In other words, the concept of a popular mandate helps soften or dissolve seeming legal obstacles to those plans. From a certain perspective, this way of thinking makes sense. If the people, rather than the Constitution or the laws of Congress, are the ultimate foundation of all legitimacy and power, then the people can authorize their favored agent, the president, to transgress (or modify) the existing legal rules in order to implement the people's agenda as reflected in the president's program.

Though he never used the phrase, Andrew Jackson seems to have been the first to claim a popular mandate. His reelection campaign became, among other things, a referendum on the Bank of the United States. In 1832, the bank's supporters sought to renew its charter, a full two years before the expiration of the existing charter. Jackson vetoed the recharter attempt, arguing that the bank was unconstitutional, corrupt, and too powerful.[29] Daniel Webster declared that Jackson's veto "place[d] the question . . . fully before the people" and that voters would pick the next president based on this issue.[30]

Although Jackson had claimed that he might support a reformed Bank of the United States, his opposition to any national bank soon became implacable. He saw his reelection in 1832 as a vindication and a solid mandate to wage full war against the bank. In a document read to his cabinet, Jackson wrote, "The President has felt it his duty to exert the power with which the confidence of his countrymen has clothed him" against the bank. More than that, the president "considers his reelection as a decision of the people against the banks."[31] Jackson cited the people's mandate as the basis for his controversial decision to withdraw Treasury funds from the Bank of the United States.[32]

Also during the Jackson presidency, the idea emerged that popular mandates can be deployed to dissolve existing legal constraints. In particular, some critics understood Jackson as promoting a novel reading of the Constitution to further the agenda of the people and their tribune. According to detractors, Jackson believed that his contested reading of presidential power—that he could order federal funds withdrawn from the bank—was justified for no other reason than that the people had reelected him.[33] Whether his opposition properly characterized his legal claim is irrelevant. What is clear is that subsequent presidents have supposed that the people can bless their attempts at constitutional restoration, reformation, and transformation.

While some academics distrust the claim of a presidential mandate, they are a stock-in-trade of every new (or renewed) presidency.[34] Jimmy Carter asserted a mandate after defeating Gerald Ford with just 50.1 percent of the popular vote.[35] And although Donald Trump lost the popular vote by almost three million, some of his prominent supporters, including Paul Ryan, then speaker of the House, claimed a mandate for the president-elect's agenda.[36]

The idea of a popular mandate, which became a fixture by the late nineteenth century, persists because it is simply too beguiling to abandon. The public often focuses on who won the presidency, not the size of the margin in the electoral college or even who won the popular vote, and many expect that there will be a "honeymoon" in which the president, with the assistance of Congress, will implement his or her platform. One nineteenth-century commentator complained that the Founders should have "foreseen that the election by the people of a set of men to vote on a particular question would result in a popular mandate" for the prevailing candidate.[37] But this was more than a little unfair, because the Founders did not know that every state legislature eventually would settle on the popular election of electors. Nor did the Founders imagine that electors would rubberstamp voters' preferences. A Jacksonian popular mandate exists only because of these two enduring and unanticipated practices.

Whether we like it or not, we have what political scientist Theodore Lowi has called a "plebiscitary presidency."[38] While some monarchs of old relied on the divine right of kings, modern presidents routinely insist that their right to rule and their right to a healthy measure of interbranch deference rests on the "popular right" of presidents—a power conveyed by the people's choice.

A Party Chief

Because they failed to predict the rise of political parties, the Framers couldn't anticipate the effect that parties would have on the Constitution's allocation of powers or on the presidency in particular. Our party system has the effect of bolstering presidential power for a simple reason: any president is the de facto leader of a party and, while in office, will enjoy some level of continuing, unstinting support for almost any act or stance.

Early on, two parties developed, the Democratic-Republicans and the Federalists. The Federalists supported President Washington, while the Democratic-Republicans harshly criticized what they saw as the monarchical and nationalizing tendencies associated with his tenure. Over the decades, the creation of party machinery and newspapers solidified the burgeoning inclination to adopt a partisan perspective.

Some parties have come and gone, and others have arisen to take their place. What has remained constant is the tendency to view presidents though a partisan prism. Today, partisans are apt to oppose presidents from another party out of conviction, habit, and self-interest. They are prone to supporting presidents of their own party for much the same reasons. The depth of their support can be seen during crises. Days before he resigned, Richard Nixon's overall job approval rating was at 24 percent and his disapproval rating was 66 percent.[39] But among Republicans, *his job approval rating was 50 percent.* This latter figure was relatively low—he had hit a high of 91 percent Republican approval in 1973. But 50 percent was sky high compared to his job approval numbers among Democrats

(13 percent) and Independents (22 percent).[40] Ordinary Republicans wanted to support their president and found ways of doing so despite Nixon's entanglement in Watergate.

Similar gaps existed during the Monica Lewinsky scandal, except that in that scandal, Democrats stood by their man through thick and thin. They eventually settled on a "condemn the sins but don't toss out the sinner" approach. President Bill Clinton and his advisers cleverly reframed a scandal about perjury and obstruction of justice into an "us versus them" partisan brawl. In that utterly familiar contest, Democrats (the "us") knew they had to stick together against "them"—Republicans bent on ousting Clinton.

Why do partisans generally stand by a president of the same party? Because presidents embody their party. Modern presidents profit from their "extraconstitutional role as party leader."[41] Rank-and-file members often look to them for direction, especially because it is easier to take guidance from one person than a multitude. Federal legislators are also more apt to support a policy or a bill when a president of the same party endorses it. Over the years, too, alternative power centers have become much less influential. While some early twentieth-century House speakers were referred to as "czars," signifying their tight grip, modern speakers hold less sway, especially when the president is of the same party.[42]

Presidents can even reshape their party's platform. Because the president is the party's leader, the rank-and-file will often endorse the president's agenda, even when it deviates from established patterns. After a long association with the KKK and a reactionary and revanchist South, for example, the Democratic Party became a party of equal rights before the law because Democratic presidents made that a priority. Republican presidents, too, helped change a party of tariff supporters to one supporting free trade.[43] For these and other reasons, Sidney Milkis and Michael Nelson have described our modern system as "executive-centered partisanship," with presidents the focal points of our politics.[44]

Partisan support, moreover, generates consistent and useful backing for contested presidential policies and actions. Co-partisans will tend to resolve uncertainties in the president's favor and expediently ignore inconvenient facts. Skillful presidents will exploit these tendencies and frame their critics and accusers as being part of a partisan cabal to thwart or undo an election. Indeed, nothing better taps into the instinct to defend a president of the same party than witnessing rabid zealots from the other party launch overwrought, abusive, and one-sided attacks on your party's undisputed leader. In real wars, soldiers often rally round the flag or standard and this is no less true during political battles, with the party faithful coming to the defense of their standard-bearer. When Hillary Clinton spoke of a "vast right-wing conspiracy" during the Lewinsky affair, she helped rally the Democratic faithful to her husband.[45] Donald Trump did much the same in the midst of the Russia investigation and his impeachment ordeal.[46]

These tendencies apply no less to legal disputes. When presidents take potentially unlawful or unconstitutional measures with respect to war, the economy, or even something as prosaic as appointments, their co-partisans will be primed to endorse, if not parrot, the president's constitutional and legal claims. Much like family members will circle the wagons and support relatives in a crisis, co-partisans will be inclined to support even a president who has been accused of shredding the Constitution.

This bedrock support means that with respect to almost all constitutional disputes, presidents will have the support of something approaching 35 percent of the public for their constitutional stance. Clearly, presidents would like support north of 50 percent. But support by 35 or 40 percent of the public on a constitutional matter may be enough for the president to persist in a public stance that his or her acts are entirely lawful.

Presidential acts that advance a party's existing policy agenda will garner even greater partisan support. A Democratic president who negates a pro-life provision found in federal law on grounds that it is unconstitutional can expect almost unanimous support from pro-choice co-partisans, almost without regard to the measure's legality. And a Republican president who asserts that an existing federal policy insufficiently respects the freedom of religion will find a base champing at the bit to endorse this assertion. Co-partisans will have little difficulty or hesitation aping constitutional and statutory claims that advance their policy agendas, whatever the legal merit of those assertions.

A Congress Further Compromised

As noted earlier, James Madison wrote that "[a]mbition must be made to counteract ambition." He continued, "The interest of the man must be connected with the constitutional rights of the place." Madison imagined that under the Constitution, federal politicians would identify with where they sat, seek to maximize their branch's authority, and defend their institutions from incursions by their rivals.[47]

Yet it is also clear that politicians sometimes may better further their ambitions by *conceding* the "constitutional rights of the place." For instance, legislators may cede considerable discretion to the president in return for some policy concession. Senators might yield sweeping authority over the military or foreign affairs if they can secure a president's support for sharply higher spending in their states. Representatives may agree to halt an investigation into possible executive misdeeds in return for the president's promise to sign some bill. Because the institutions have things to trade, both may gain from bargaining, including by making concessions regarding their constitutional powers.

These bargains can occur at the individual level, too. For instance, modern presidents repeatedly have appointed the spouses of legislators to the executive branch, a move that likely suppresses the willingness of those lawmakers to criticize the president and bolsters their inclination to support an incumbent's agenda.[48] Presidents can curry favor with individual legislators in other ways as well, including by extending prized invitations to extravagant state dinners, offering tickets to the presidential box at the Kennedy Center, and hosting congressional fundraisers.[49] They withdraw these extravagances and favors when members prove obstreperous.[50]

The other cross-branch tie that blunts institutional competition is by now familiar: partisan affiliation. Just as some voters give the president the benefit of the doubt when they are of the same party, some legislators resolve every uncertainty in favor of their party's leader in the White House. As Daryl Levinson and Rick Pildes observe, parties help bind the branches together, thus partially undoing the separation of powers and independence that the Founders had counted on.[51]

In fact, there has long been a close, almost incestuous, relationship between Congress and the presidency. In the early years, party caucuses within Congress anointed candidates, meaning that early presidents likely felt a little beholden to legislators. That system broke down in the 1824 presidential contest, however, when so-called Democratic-Republican voters rejected the nominee of the congressional caucus. After experimenting with state legislative caucuses, parties moved to more popular systems.[52] With the turn toward party conventions in 1832 and then primaries and popular caucuses, presidents owed far fewer debts to federal legislators because members of Congress are no longer responsible for selecting them as a candidate. In a way, the selection of nominees mirrored the selection of presidents, with both regimes moving toward popular systems.

Technically, when no candidate secures a majority of the electoral votes, the House selects the president. But that happens only once in a blue moon. The selection was thrown to the House three times in the nineteenth century, but never since.[53] As long as the United States has only two major parties, the House is unlikely to decide who shall serve as president.

If Congresses once helped pick nominees and presidents, it now seems that presidents, as de facto and undisputed party leaders, have some influence over who serves in Congress. Franklin Roosevelt's attempts to purge conservative Democratic legislators from Congress supposedly were unsuccessful, in part because his primary challengers almost uniformly failed to oust conservative Democratic incumbents.[54] Yet it may be that he lost the battle but won the war: Roosevelt may have scared some legislators into endorsing his legislative goals, including labor legislation. Moreover, in the long run, Roosevelt's party became a liberal party of big government, just as he wished. It took time, but conservative Democrats were a fading faction, albeit a powerful one due to congressional seniority norms.[55]

Over his limited tenure, Donald Trump has denounced some Republicans and endorsed their primary opponents. Some members of Congress, like Senators Jeff Flake and Bob Corker, did not seek reelection, in part because they recognized that they might lose the party primary to a pro-Trump Republican.[56] One critic, Representative Mark Sanford, lost his primary race after Trump endorsed his opponent and denounced Sanford.[57] The dominant trend has been for Republican officials to walk back or downplay previous criticisms of Trump in the hopes of appealing to his supporters.

The general aversion to criticizing a president of the same party signals that presidents wield great influence within their party's legislative caucuses. Legislators too critical of their party's standard bearer run the risk of inviting a primary challenger who will run as the president's loyal ally. Recognizing the president's strength, many congressional incumbents will seek the president's favor and wish to be seen as a supporter. This phenomenon further increases the tendency that co-partisan legislators will endorse the president's programs or actions. Federal legislators have ideological *and* personal reasons to stay on the president's good side, through thick and thin.

An Army of Enablers

We have but one president at a time. But as noted earlier, a single person cannot execute the laws, receive and confer with foreign ambassadors, negotiate and make treaties, repel invasions, suppress rebellions, pardon individuals, propose measures, and read and assess Congress's bills.

The Framers knew this. They understood that the executive branch would be more than just one person. The Constitution mentions "heads of departments" and "principal officers in the executive departments," and it contemplates that the president will direct these officers. As our first president put it, the "impossibility that one man should be able to perform all the great business of the State, I take to have been the reason for instituting the great Departments, & appointing officers therein, to assist the Supreme Magistrate in discharging the duties of his trust."[58] Washington's supervisory authority over the executive bureaucracy extended to communications and negotiations with foreign governments; deciding which Americans to prosecute; directions to tax collectors; and other matters, trivial and important.[59]

While the Constitution mandates a president and demands a presidential salary, it does not require that Congress create subordinate executives. The Constitution does not compel the establishment of an army or a navy, much less an attorney general. Congress creates all offices and departments and, in the process, specifies their jurisdictions and duties. Similarly, Congress is under no obligation to fund these offices. In the eighteenth century, some chief executives enjoyed a "civil list"—a guaranteed annuity to cover expenses and salaries.[60] But the Framers did not compel Congress to fund a civil list for the executive branch.

In choosing to create and fund a civilian executive force of almost two million employees and officers and a military 1.3 million strong, modern Congresses further their own agendas. Congress writes laws that it generally wants enforced. It also supplies personnel and coin to the executive to ensure the execution of its laws and to safeguard our national security and overseas interests.

Yet staffing and funding the executive is a double-edged sword. Because of Congress's largesse, every president has plenty of staff to help flex constitutional powers and, potentially, encroach on Congress's turf. This possibility for executive encroachment has ballooned in modern times, so that today, congressional funds are often used to thwart, or evade, the will of Congress.

We can divide the executive bureaucracy in several ways. About four thousand workers are temporary political appointees serving at the president's pleasure. Almost all of them serve a handful of years, with those confirmed by the Senate serving on average a little over two years. The rest of the executive is composed of the civil service, which is almost two million. Like permafrost, this latter set of executives never really goes away.

Both the political appointees and the civil service have reason to back the enlargement of executive authority. Political appointees generally favor executive expansion because it is almost always undertaken to advance policies that they favor, namely their president's agenda. For example, if a president seeks to revamp health care and immigration policies, and expansion of presidential power serves such purposes, the president's political appointees will tend to favor the enlargement of executive authority.

The upper echelons of the civil service favor the growth of executive authority for a different reason. In some cases, they actually may disagree with many aspects of the incumbent's policy agenda. Yet they favor broader executive authority because their power largely tracks the power of the presidency. For instance, if the presidency wields more authority over war and military, the bureaucracy of the Department of Defense gains at the expense of Congress and the courts. After all, the department can cite the president's constitutional prerogatives as a reason to ignore statutes and urge the courts to keep out of war and military matters. Indeed, an assertion that

Congress cannot intrude into certain war and military affairs may strengthen the bureaucracy more than it does the current president. How? First, presidents often will not meaningfully exercise the discretion afforded by the constitutional claim; instead Defense Department officials, including civil servants, will enjoy the autonomy of the constitutional stance. Second, the bureaucracy's gains are longer lasting and thus more valuable. Though the incumbent president will leave office in four or eight years, the permanent defense establishment will enjoy the advantages of greater executive autonomy for decades to come. Every time a president chooses to ignore some congressional directive on constitutional grounds, the bureaucracy is likely to acquire greater autonomy.

There is also a tiny cadre of elite lawyers who provide legal cover and exoneration for executive aggrandizement. The most prominent of these are in the Office of Legal Counsel (OLC) in the Department of Justice and the Office of White House Counsel. The OLC provides legal advice to executive branch institutions, serving as counsel for the attorney general and outside counsel for other executive branch entities, including the White House. The White House Counsel provides legal advice to the president on constitutional and legal matters, along with assistance navigating federal ethics laws. Lawyers in both offices regard themselves as defending the institutional interests of the presidency, with lawyers in the Office of White House Counsel more closely identifying with the incumbent's favored policies. Both offices were created in the mid-twentieth century using authority derived from Congress.[61]

Each office has become a power center in its own right. The Office of Legal Counsel is the most elite group of lawyers within the executive branch, and the White House Counsel provides legal and political advice to the president. Of the two, the OLC is more respected by outsiders for its comparative willingness to opine that certain proposed executive acts would be illegal.

Yet even if both occasionally tell the president "no," they are far more apt to say "yes" than are lawyers outside the executive branch.

The reasons are simple. Because both identify with the executive, they are more apt to see the wisdom of expansive readings of presidential power. Both are headed up by political appointees who will tend to regard the incumbent as responsible, patriotic, and wise. These lawyers would not be the first to closely identify with their client. Nor would they be the first inclined to tell the client what he or she wished to hear. This tendency afflicts all lawyers, from mob lawyers, to public interest lawyers, to corporate counsels. Though no lawyer worth her salt will sign off on every scheme, it is equally true that no lawyer wishes to be a repeated naysayer, continually telling the president that a favored plan is illegal.

John Brennan, a director of the Central Intelligence Agency (CIA) during the Obama administration, once said: "I have never found a case that our legal authorities, or legal interpretations that came out from that lawyers group, prevented us from doing something that we thought was in the best interest of the United States to do. . . . Is there a right answer? Truth is elusive—as is 'right.'" Apparently, Brennan spoke too soon: though the Obama administration wanted to move a prisoner from Iraq, they did not when lawyers said the law forbade the transfer.[62] Yet if there were only a handful of such situations during the Obama administration, which took pride in its willingness to wrestle with legal questions and abide by the law, it seems that lawyers do less to constrain presidents than one might have imagined.

It is no surprise that for decades both offices have faced intense criticisms. During the Clinton years, William Safire of the *New York Times* said the White House Counsel was a "cancer" in the presidency.[63] Back in the George W. Bush presidency, OLC readings of executive authority were roundly criticized, with some calling for drastic reform. Bruce Ackerman argued that the OLC had a "one-sided culture" because it saw itself as an advocate of the presidency and the incumbent.[64] He had a point.

During the Obama administration, the OLC sometimes told the president "no," with mixed results. Sometimes the "no" was welcomed because the administration could trumpet it as evidence that the administration was law-abiding. In one case, the Obama administration decided to request and release an OLC legal opinion that declared that the executive could not do something because the "no" was politically expedient.[65] Adherence to the resulting OLC opinion would supposedly signal a fidelity to legal constraint. This was a cynical move, even for Washington. Other times, the OLC "no" mattered little because other lawyers said "yes." When asked whether President Obama could bomb Libya without regard for the time constraints on hostilities laid out by the War Powers Act, the lawyers came to a split decision. OLC said "no," while the White House Counsel said "yes."[66] Because the OLC has no right to bind presidents on legal matters, Obama could side with the "yes" lawyers—the White House Counsel.

This supposed "opinion shopping" by Obama was heavily criticized, on both the Left and the Right. But for centuries presidents have received conflicting legal advice and then acted on one of those opinions and not the others. The Constitution in no way forbids this: it states clearly that the president "may require the Opinion, in writing, of the principal Officer in each of the executive Departments."[67] Whatever the opinions of others, the choice, and the responsibility, are the president's alone. When George Washington sought out multiple opinions on the proposed Bank of the United States, he received conflicting advice and chose to disregard counsel that it was unconstitutional. Washington was not accused of acting in bad faith merely because he asked for several opinions. No one at the time thought that a president would shop for a legal opinion to justify a decision already made, without regard to the law or Constitution. In other words, multiple opinions, by themselves, are not a problem. The difficulty arises if one supposes that presidents seek them in order to skirt the law and its constraints.

Consider another problem with the content of OLC opinions. Recall that the executive branch believes that practice can add a gloss to the executive's power and thereby diminish legislative power.

What about the converse? Can practice enlarge the scope of legislative power and, in so doing, circumscribe executive power? Apparently not. The OLC has a philosophy of "heads the President wins, tails the Congress loses." Although the OLC endorses the living Constitution when presidential power expands, it denies that Congress can also acquire authority at the president's expense. In 1989, the OLC opined that "usage alone—regardless how longstanding and venerable—cannot validate a practice that clearly violates constitutional principles."[68] This approach seems right. Yet as we will see later, the OLC has blessed the acquisition of novel powers by the president even when the practices clearly violated the Constitution. Apparently, presidential powers are clear and can never be curtailed, while congressional powers are rife with uncertainties and ambiguities and hence subject to acquisition.

Essentially, the OLC has an expansionist mindset, favoring a sort of Brezhnev doctrine for the executive. Soviet president Leonid Brezhnev insisted that while communism should expand into new nations, it could never be allowed to recede.[69] Likewise, though OLC helps expand executive power, it will stoutly oppose any rollback.

The point of this discussion is not to criticize executive officers or executive lawyers in particular. Rather it is that Congress supplies all these dedicated executives and legal eagles to its adversary. This level of assistance to an institutional rival is extraordinary. It brings to mind the saying attributed to Vladimir Lenin that "the capitalists will sell us the rope we will use to hang them."[70]

* * *

The presidency has all the tools it needs to acquire additional constitutional authority. It has internal unity as well as Article II, with its apparent capacity for constitutional expansion. It faces institutional rivals that are divided and constrained. Alone among the branches, the executive has a plausible claim to speak for We the People and is thought to enter office with a powerful popular mandate. As party chieftains, presidents receive the loyal backing of their party's rank-and-file. For similar reasons, presidents also command the support of a sizable chunk of congressional legislators and hence can expect at least some support from Congress for their policies and power grabs. Finally, they have the backing of thousands of officials who generally regard the presidency's interests as aligning with theirs.

Any institution backed by this extremely advantageous balance of forces will be prone to advance its power, prestige, and influence at the expense of its rivals. Because our current system seems tailor-made to generate executive growth, we should not be surprised that the American presidency has grown by leaps and bounds.

Even reformist pols succumb to these temptations. Senator Obama zealously ran against presidential aggrandizement. But by the end of his presidency, he had become what he had detested: a great aggrandizer of the office. He had become, if not George W. Bush, something of a facsimile. It brought to mind the scene at the end of George Orwell's *Animal Farm,* when the farm animals could not tell the tainted pigs from the humans whose behavior and mannerisms they had adopted.

In jest, President Obama made light of his use of executive power in a way that perhaps signaled his actual views: "After the midterm election, my advisers asked me, 'Mr. President, do you have a bucket list?' And I said, 'Well, I have something that rhymes with bucket list.' Take executive action on immigration? Bucket. New climate regulations? Bucket. It's the right thing to do."[71] The last line telegraphed Obama's motive for wielding as much executive power as possible. If an act is "the right thing to do"—however defined—then constraints must be skirted, reimagined, or bucked.

The modern presidency brings to mind a line spoken by the voluptuous Jessica Rabbit from the live-action animation film *Who Framed Roger Rabbit?* At one point in the film, femme fatale Jessica Rabbit says, "I'm not bad, I'm just drawn that way."[72] Each modern president can truthfully say, "I'm not bad. I just can't help doing what some people expect me to do." Given the contemporary presidency's enormous institutional advantages and the internal and external pressures that presidents face, it seems that modern executives cannot resist using legal legerdemain to advance their personal and policy goals.

CHAPTER FOUR

The LIVING PRESIDENCY
in A LIVING CONSTITUTION

Since Arthur Schlesinger Jr. first published *The Imperial Presidency* in 1973, countless people have denounced our "imperial presidency."[1] Indeed, if there is but one constitutional principle that unites those on both the Left and the Right, it is their sincere conviction that modern presidents are far too kingly and that the imperial presidency is a blot on our republic. The only hitch in this consensus is that the two factions tend to believe this at different times. Republicans were quick to see Barack Obama as a rampant, lawless monarch who defied Congress, cowed the courts, and despoiled the Constitution. And Democrats, when beholding George W. Bush, saw King George IV, the unworthy successor to the tyrannical George III.

These modern criticisms share a similar foundation. Only a few critics assert that the presidency was poorly constructed or that the Founders made some fatal error. After all, everyone knows that the Founders did not want a king and did not create one, or so the argument goes. Rather, the objection is that presidents have perfidiously expanded their office in order to create a regal, imperial presidency, and in the process have breached the Constitution. Because the fault lies not in our Constitution, but in the hearts of our presidents, the obvious solution in this scenario is to undo the damage and return to the Constitution's modest presidency.

As we shall see, both sets of critics are only fair-weather friends of the original Constitution and its more modest presidency: they tend to fall silent when a co-partisan acts imperially. But two other sorts of faithlessness are afoot. First is fickle originalism—when someone who proclaims fidelity to the Constitution's original meaning somehow manages to find a soft spot for some imperial aspects of the modern presidency. Maybe it is an eager acceptance of executive war powers. Perhaps it is an embrace of the plebiscitary presidency, the theory that voters grant the executive a mandate to implement campaign promises.

Second is fickle living constitutionalism—when someone who applauds all manner of informal constitutional change simultaneously exalts the original presidency and excoriates the living presidency. With respect to the presidency itself, many living constitutionalists would have us believe that the Founders got it right on this one point alone. Living constitutionalists also have failed to consider the advantages the presidency has in a living constitutional system. Those who favor a constitution that changes with relative ease should realize that one consequence of such a system is that presidents will wield the greatest influence over the ongoing transformations of that mutable Constitution. Presidents will not only renovate their constitutional office, making it more powerful; they also will wield outsized influence on matters of federalism and individual liberties. In other words, living constitutionalism systematically privileges the presidency.

Article V and Constitutional Change

As discussed in Chapter 1, the Constitution was not meant to be impervious to change, and Article V specifies a means of amending—a demanding, two-step process. Congress, by a two-thirds vote in both chambers, can propose amendments. Alternatively, if two-thirds of the states apply for a constitutional convention, Congress must call one and that convention may propose amendments. Once the amendments are proposed, by either Congress or the convention, they go to the states. To complete the process, three-fourths of the states must ratify the amendments, either by legislative vote or via special state popular conventions.[2] A little more than two dozen formal amendments have navigated this onerous process. Ten of those were ratified within the first three years after the original Constitution was signed. Over the two centuries or so that followed, only a little more than a dozen have made it through this ordeal. As you can tell, formal constitutional amendments are exceedingly rare.

Compared with state and foreign frameworks, the Constitution ranks as one of the most difficult to formally amend. I am far from alone in thinking that Article V erects obstacles to formal constitutional change that are too demanding. Yet the opinion that the process is too burdensome, and so may thwart needful amendments, reflects a modern sensibility. From where the Philadelphia Framers sat, the Constitution was a marvelous improvement over the Articles of Confederation, which permitted amendments only via *unanimous* agreement.[3] Every state legislature had to agree to amend the Articles, a requirement that proved impossible to meet. Though proposed amendments to the Articles surfaced from time to time, none were successful.

This daunting process influenced the Founders to bypass the Articles and its unanimity requirement. Article VII of the proposed Constitution declared that it would take effect when a mere nine states—not all thirteen—ratified it.[4] Aware that they were dodging the existing framework's rules, the Framers also provided that only the states ratifying the Constitution would be bound to it.[5] This was a weak sop to holdouts, for if nine states ratified the Constitution, the waverers would join to avoid being the outsiders looking in at a more perfect (and powerful) union. Early holdouts (North Carolina and Rhode Island) made the rational choice.

Just as the Articles were unsuccessful in channeling all alterations through a rule of unanimity, so, too, the Constitution failed to funnel all amendments through Article V. In particular, we have had many informal amendments to the Constitution. In his book defending the living Constitution, David Strauss recounts how many of our Constitution's most momentous transformations came via informal changes to understandings and conceptions.[6] Among these are the enlargement of freedom of speech and the vast expansion of congressional power.[7] Though these radical alterations in thought never yielded a formal amendment to the Constitution, they nonetheless should be ranked as amendments, albeit of a different sort.

The Fickle Originalist

Originalists decry this living constitutionalism and the informal amendments that are made (or imposed) outside the formal, exacting procedures of Article V. The theory of originalism asserts that the meanings of words, phrases, and sentences are fixed by the particular context in which people used them. As applied to the Constitution, originalism insists that when the Founders ratified the Constitution, they not only adopted a complicated set of marks on a page (the Constitution's text); they also ratified and incorporated a particular set of meanings—the original meanings of those words and phrases. These meanings are as much a part of the Constitution as the marks on the page and, in fact, are far more important than those symbols. The letters strung together to make words, and the words linked together to make sentences, are but devices to convey the far more significant meanings. Lawmakers do not make laws without meanings and, in fact, it is those meanings that actually matter.

Originalists further insist that if we choose to abide by the original Constitution—the document generated at the Philadelphia Convention and ratified in the states—it makes little sense to simultaneously claim that we will decide what those words mean based on our needs and preferences. In other words, originalists say that if we are going to follow this law (the Constitution) made by those men (the Founders), then it would be rather silly to suppose that this law—the Constitution—means whatever we wish it to mean. Originalists point out that a commitment to a set of rules made by others is meaningless if we do not also commit to the particular meanings those others sought to adopt.

For originalists, the modern presidency is legitimate only when it conforms to the Founders' presidency. If the best originalist reading of the Constitution is that presidents cannot authorize military trials of civilians because the Constitution never conveyed that power to the office in 1787, then modern presidents cannot impose military trials on their own. If the best originalist reading is that the president must veto a bill in its entirety and cannot object to a portion of it and allow the rest to become law, then presidents may not read the Constitution's grant of a veto power, found in Article I, section 7, as if it also conveyed a line-item veto.

Conservatives tend to profess allegiance to originalism and the original Constitution, and to repudiate the idea that new meanings should arise from its unchanged text. This makes sense, because conservatives are predisposed to conserve existing traditions and practices. Conservatives are often especially upset when the courts take language from the Constitution—often from the Bill of Rights or the Fourteenth Amendment—and attach a newfangled meaning that advances a progressive political agenda. For instance, originalists are fond of insisting that the Founders did not mean for the Fourteenth Amendment to further the progressive cause du jour, be it reproductive liberties, welfare rights, or the fundamental right to suicide. When courts press the Fourteenth Amendment into service for such purposes, conservatives are apt to say that the courts are amending the Constitution in the guise of applying it and that the Constitution never granted the courts such license.

But when it comes to the presidency, it sometimes seems that originalists apply different rules. For instance, some originalists imagine that the Founders created a presidency meant to enjoy almost plenary authority over foreign affairs, with presidents exercising a free hand in the international arena. These originalists repeatedly cite modern practice and underplay the limits of the original scheme. Some of them suppose that in foreign affairs presidents can circumvent the Treaty Clause's strictures and make international agreements that override state constitutions and laws. The original Constitution does not sanction any of these assertions, let alone make presidents supreme in foreign affairs (more on this in Chapter 7).

The more obvious disconnect is in war powers. There are originalists who will regularly invoke the Founders but also insist that presidents can use military force overseas because they are commanders in chief. As we shall see later, this is a decidedly nonoriginalist claim that lacks any basis in the original Constitution. Instead, it is grounded on modern practices. The Founders vested Congress with the power to decide to wage war and the president with a partial check—the power to veto a bill declaring war by stating objections to it.[8] Absolutely no one at the Founding—not one person—said that the Constitution gave presidents the power to decide to wage war.

The stark dichotomy between prominent features of the modern executive and the original presidency poses a problem for some originalists. Which commitment will prevail? Will originalists give up their preference for presidents with sweeping powers in foreign affairs, including the power to wage war, because these readings run counter to the Constitution's original meaning? Or will their general commitment to originalism collapse, given their desire for a muscular presidency empowered to advance the long-term interests of the United States? The questions remain unanswered in part because many originalists have yet to confront the contradiction between their constitutional principles and their perception of America's real-world needs.

FAITH IN THE LIVING CONSTITUTION

Living constitutionalists suffer from even greater contradictions. As noted earlier, living constitutionalists argue that though the Constitution's text has stayed relatively fixed, its meaning and application properly change over time. Perhaps this was best explained by Woodrow Wilson when he wrote, "All that progressives ask or desire is permission—in an era when 'development,' 'evolution,' is the scientific word—to interpret the Constitution according to the Darwinian principle."[9] In other words, the Constitution's meaning should evolve with the times to fit modern needs and events.

More than a century later, Wilson's allies no longer ask for permission. All three federal branches—and a sizable portion of the public—generally favor an evolution in constitutional meaning because such mutability allows for greater constitutional change. Today's task is to defend the prevailing Darwinian principle, to fend off the originalist counterattack mounted by the likes of Robert Bork, Antonin Scalia, and Clarence Thomas. In 1985, Justice William Brennan gamely responded to the incipient originalist resurgence:

[T]he ultimate question must be: What do the words of the text mean in *our time*? For the genius of the Constitution rests not in any static meaning it might have had in a world that is dead and gone, but in the adaptability of its great principles to cope with current problems and current needs. What the constitutional fundamentals meant to the wisdom of other times cannot be the measure to the vision of our time.[10]

In the same public address, Brennan spoke of the need for courts to periodically revise their constitutional views, lest "the Constitution fall[ ] captive, again, to the anachronistic views of long-gone generations."[11] Apparently, both the Founders and old judicial opinions must be discarded lest the dead control the living.

Clearly, living constitutionalism is a theory that prizes modern values and needs over older ones. Many imagine that the arc of history bends toward justice, and lo and behold, living constitutionalism helps justify the creation of new individual rights that help bend history toward that progressive vision of justice. In fact, many liberal scholars insist that the Constitution would be absolutely intolerable without the reformative influences of living constitutionalism, that is to say, without the many informal amendments that mark our Constitution as it is understood and enforced today. The Constitution, they contend, embodies legal rules and principles that were crafted by dead white men, many of them slave owners, and the overall framework seems suitable only for the primitive, agrarian economy of the eighteenth century. The constitutional amendments of the nineteenth century likewise reflect a cramped and backward sense of federal power and constitutional rights. It is no exaggeration to suppose that many liberals imagine that living constitutionalism saved our Constitution, by liberating us from some of its most retrograde features. After all, without these informal reformations the Constitution might have been junked long ago. In turn, our current version of the imperfect, living Constitution can be redeemed and saved only through further creative and reformative reinterpretation, each such change reflecting the evolving principles of political science, economics, and morality that reflect the progress of a maturing, progressing society.

In area after area, living constitutionalists praise change. Consider Congress. While Congress was meant to have far more power than its predecessor (the Continental Congress), it was nonetheless designed to have but limited legislative authority. Under the Constitution, Congress has the "legislative Powers herein granted"—meaning only those powers enumerated or implied.[12] After all, one ordinarily does not list and grant more than two dozen powers (see Article I, section 8 and elsewhere) if these powers are not meant to be exhaustive. In the early decades under the Constitution, there were fierce debates about whether Congress could charter a national bank, assume state war debts, and build various public works like roads and canals. Almost no one thought that Congress had general legislative power across the entire nation. For instance, no one argued that Congress could criminalize murder nationwide or regulate a state's internal commerce. As Chief Justice John Marshall put it, "[t]he enumeration presupposes something not enumerated," that is, areas of life outside the reach of Congress.[13]

From the perspective of living constitutionalists, these early debates are of only historical interest because both the express and implied limits on legislative authority have been almost wholly obliterated. Our Congress routinely regulates matters over which it has no enumerated or implied authority, like abortion and manufacturing.[14] Living constitutionalists generally praise this transformation of congressional authority because the welfare and regulatory state they favor rests on a profound expansion of legislative power. Without it, there would be no Social Security Administration, Environmental Protection Agency, or Department of Labor.

Or consider the courts. Alexander Hamilton predicted that the courts would be frail. The courts would have "no influence over either the sword or the purse; no direction either of the strength or of the wealth of the society; and can take no active resolution whatever. It may truly be said to have neither FORCE nor WILL, but merely judgment."[15] His prophecy has proven false. Modern federal courts command the purse and direct the strength of society. If a single federal judge declares that a government must spend funds to rectify some wrong, the Congress and the president both honor this command. Likewise, when a federal judge issues a judgment in a case, the executive stands ready to use force to implement the judgment. This very much seems like the courts directing society's strength.

To be sure, when the executive loses, it often appeals the adverse judgment. But this appeal proves the point. The executive appeals the judgment because it will otherwise obey it. Appealing to a higher court, rather than appealing to the people or ignoring the opinion of a court, bespeaks a profound respect for, and deference to, the judiciary. By way of contrast, the executive seldom bothers to respond to a legal scholar's opinion, let alone take the time to consult a panel of academics. (I am quite confident that this book will not receive a rebuttal from the executive.) In sum, the courts are all that Hamilton confidently said they would not be.

Likewise, the relationship between the states and the national government—what we call "federalism"—is strikingly different today. James Madison predicted that the vast majority of legislative powers would remain with the states. "The powers delegated by the proposed Constitution to the federal government are few and defined. Those which are to remain in the State governments are numerous and indefinite. . . . The powers reserved to the several States will extend to all the objects which, in the ordinary course of affairs, concern the lives, liberties, and properties of the people, and the internal order, improvement, and prosperity of the State."[16]

With the colossal expansion of both the Commerce Clause's reach and the federal power to spend, Madison's description is entirely topsy-turvy. Federal power today is close to "indefinite" and reserved state powers are now "few," defined as whatever isolated and uncertain pockets remain outside the purview of the federal government's tremendous grasp. Moreover, every state government is utterly reliant on federal funds, the receipt of which requires the adoption of federal programs or rules. Because the federal government vacuums up vast amounts of money from all US residents, the states feel pressure to dance to federal tunes lest other, more cooperative states receive a disproportionate share of federal subsidies.

Finally, the original Constitution's express protection of rights was comparatively weak. The few express rights against the states and federal government are found in sections 9 and 10 of Article I. Today, federal constitutional rights have been transformed beyond the wildest dreams of anyone at the Founding. A handful of rights, like the Contract Clause, have been virtually read out of the Constitution because the states regularly impair the obligations of contracts and the courts sanction these violations.[17] But far more rights have been exalted and stretched to new realms. The First Amendment that did not prevent the passage of an act making it a crime to criticize federal officials (the 1798 Sedition Act) now partially safeguards nude dancing and the urging of unlawful action.[18] The Sixth Amendment's Right to Counsel, a rule clearly meant to prevent the government from barring the use of private counsel, now requires governments to supply legal assistance.[19] The Fourteenth Amendment, birthed in an era of prudery, now guarantees a somewhat general right of sexual liberty. The list goes on and on.

Living constitutionalists celebrate each of these changes and credit their theory for them. In their view, living constitutionalism helps infuse the seemingly static Constitution with a healthy dose of progress. Without a living Constitution, they assert, we would lack all these cherished rights, as well as benefits of the modern regulatory state. Cass Sunstein, in his engaging book *Radicals in Robes,* argues that whereas originalism leads to an undesirable Constitution that permits all sorts of governmental oppression (like segregated schools) and private misconduct (for example, racial discrimination by private companies), our actual lived Constitution—which arises because of our willingness to ascribe new meanings to the old Constitution—generates truly wonderful results.[20] David Strauss makes the same point in his thought-provoking book *The Living Consitution.*[21] For living constitutionalists, the mantra is simple: while originalism spawns a woeful, outdated Constitution, living constitutionalism yields a wonderful, updated version.

THE FAITHLESS LIVING CONSTITUTIONALIST

Living constitutionalism tends to laud four constitutional reformations: the creation of new individual liberties to better constrain the federal and state governments; the profound expansion of congressional power, primarily to regulate industry and establish a national welfare state; the diminution of state authority and autonomy, which occurs primarily as a byproduct of a dominant Congress and enlarged individual rights; and the exaltation of the courts, especially federal courts, as the oracles, architects, and guardians of the new and improved Constitution.

What do living constitutionalists think about the living presidency? Some say little, preferring to gloss over it. In *The Living Constitution*, which continually celebrates informal constitutional change, Strauss stays rather mum about the undoubted expansion of presidential power.[22] This is a little awkward. But Strauss faced a choice among multiple embarrassments. For many living constitutionalists, quite a few of whom loathe the idea of expanding presidential powers, the living presidency is akin to the crazy uncle in the attic: the less said, the better. But one cannot properly evaluate living constitutionalism as a theory of beneficial constitutional change if one averts one's gaze from one of the most momentous constitutional transformations: the metastasizing presidency.

One might have supposed that Arthur Schlesinger Jr. was steadfast in his opposition to a living presidency. In his opus *The Imperial Presidency*, he generally suggests a deep antipathy to an evolutionary reading of presidential power. But he also declares that "what the Constitution 'really' meant . . . only practice could disclose."[23] He also favorably notes Woodrow Wilson's admonition to construe the Constitution "in the spirit of Darwin." "It was," he writes, quoting Wilson, "'a vehicle of life,' and its meaning was determined 'not by the original intentions . . . but by the exigencies and the new aspects of life itself.'"[24] These formulations make it clear that the meaning of the Constitution was not fixed, once and for all time, at the Founding. Rather, Schlesinger clearly believed that meaning comes from practice and that constitutional meaning could and should evolve to take into account "new aspects of life." This was in keeping with his embrace of a broad reading of congressional authority, where successive practices and evolving conceptions led to the accretion of federal legislative power at the expense of the states.[25] Schlesinger was a living constitutionalist at heart who, late in life, loathed what the presidency had become. He opposed an imperial presidency, it seems, but he did not oppose either an imperial Congress, or a living, organic presidency.

Other modern progressive critics fit the same template. In the wake of the administration of George W. Bush, Bruce Ackerman decried a "runaway presidency" and "presidential unilateralism."[26] But elsewhere he has written about how Franklin Roosevelt, unbeknownst to most Americans either then or today, informally amended the Treaty Clause during the New Deal.[27] Roosevelt did this via repeated practice, and in this way he satisfied Ackerman's theory of informal constitutional change.[28] Ackerman's scheme of informal amendments is quite interesting and complicated, and I don't wish to get into the details here. The theory is controversial because it supposes that presidents can generate legitimate constitutional change by, in part, prevailing in an electoral contest where constitutional change was somehow part of the campaign. Ackerman uses his theory to attempt to justify, and hopefully legitimate, among other events, the vast expansion of Congress's legislative powers during the New Deal.

The difficulty is that the public chooses among presidential candidates, and few of the votes for a single candidate can sensibly be understood as an endorsement of all their policies, much less their supposed push for the implicit ratification of informal constitutional amendments. I can assure you that I would vote for a socialist for no other reason than that I hate the fascist or Maoist opposing him or her. My eager vote for the socialist would not mean that I support state ownership of the means of production even if that were the only plank of the candidate's platform. Nor would my vote for a socialist signal that I would endorse an informal constitutional amendment that required the state to own the means of production or allowed the state to take private property without providing just compensation.

This limitation on the information a vote conveys has long been understood. Henry Clay, responding to President Andrew Jackson's broad claim that the people approved of his agenda, thoroughly mocked the assertion. "Sir, the truth is, that the re-election of the president proves as little an approbation by the people of all the opinions he may hold . . . as it would prove that if the president had a carbuncle . . . they meant, by re-electing him, to approve of his carbuncle."[29] Clay later would say that electors take a candidate "as a man takes his wife, for better or for worse" with no endorsement of the "bad opinions and qualities which [the candidate] possesses."[30] Hence while it is true that voters back candidates, it is manifestly not true that those casting ballots for the winning candidate mean to endorse every policy wart of the winner.

In any event, according to Ackerman's account of constitutional change, presidents can acquire new powers if they satisfy his complicated checklist. Under his theory, we might not, in fact, have a "runaway presidency" if Presidents Truman, Johnson, Nixon, or Reagan had acquired the authority to wage war by placing it on the electoral agenda (in much the same way that Franklin Roosevelt supposedly did in order to make international agreements without satisfying the Treaty Clause). Because Ackerman's test is laden with uncertainty, individuals may look at the same set of events and disagree about whether there has been a moment when We the People amended the Constitution. A disciple of Ackerman with a different perspective on the presidency could claim that the modern presidency is not out of control but is instead entirely constitutional, a product of the public's repeated (if implicit) endorsement of presidents enamored of power grabs and unilateral action. After all, modern presidents have repeatedly pushed the boundaries of their office outward and the public has repeatedly reelected them. For instance, Presidents Reagan, Clinton, George W. Bush, and Obama used military force without congressional authorization, and each served two terms.

Or consider Peter Shane, a respected specialist in presidential powers who penned a book, *Madison's Nightmare*, largely on the George W. Bush presidency.[31] The thesis is that James Madison would have detested what the presidency has become. Fair enough and certainly true. This framing of the issue makes sense coming from an originalist. But Shane is no such thing. He endorses aspects of the living presidency.[32] This stance is confusing, because it is inconsistent with the book's general thrust. For example, why shouldn't readers be just as agitated by Madison's nightmares arising from the executive innovations that Shane favors? Moreover, Shane embraces a Congress that has far broader legislative powers than at the Founding. Why, then, shouldn't we be equally concerned about Madison's (imaginary) nightmares about an imperial Congress vacuuming up legislative powers? Finally, does anyone doubt that Madison would also have regarded the modern judiciary as a bad dream, given its proclivity to remake the Constitution? If we are going to wonder what Madison would say about today's Constitution and government, we have plenty of night terrors to haunt us.

Ultimately, it seems that living constitutionalists have a grave difficulty with openly embracing one of the most signal features of the living Constitution, the living presidency. Indeed, for a host of reasons it seems as if the modern presidency is a rather discomfiting feature of our living Constitution. In particular, why some contemporary features of the presidency are unconstitutional and others constitutional, even welcome, is often a mystery. Additionally, why any presidential violations of the existing constitutional order should ever be condemned as unconstitutional when they can help generate valid, if informal, constitutional amendments is likewise something of a puzzler. After all, if judges and Congress can amend the living Constitution by transgressing existing norms, surely presidents can do the same.

One suspects that opposition to a living presidency often tracks the partisan proclivities of the scholarly essayist or the speechifying politician. When a Republican is in the Oval Office, living constitutionalists often become enamored with the Founders, using them to scold the incumbent. There are laudable exceptions, as when Ackerman rebuked President Obama for starting a war against Libya.[33] Likewise, while Shane reserves his fiercest reproaches for Republican presidents, he never quite absolves their Democratic counterparts.[34] Still the dominant trend cannot be wished away by pockets of commendable consistency. Living constitutionalists love constitutional change, except when it involves the presidency—and then their opposition to a mutating presidency seems to change with the political seasons.

THE UNBALANCED PRESIDENCY

At this point, a living constitutionalist might assert that the difficulty lies not with a living presidency, but rather with an *unbalanced* executive, one where the presidency is too strong relative to the other two branches. Think of a scale with three (rather than two) weighing pans, with one—the executive tray—brought low by a weighty object. A living constitutionalist might say that too much presidential power destabilizes the scale and disrupts any prospect of balance.

Balance is a beguiling separation-of-powers metaphor. One finds it everywhere, likely because it is visually arresting. But it is a useless trope. When someone earnestly says that the balance among the branches is out of whack because the president has too much power, they are simply expressing a preference for less presidential power.

They are not expressing some fact about balance or equilibrium, since there is no actual balance or scale to evaluate the relative power of the branches.

Moreover, balance was never a constitutional goal. The Founders created a powerful legislature, a formidable executive, and a relatively weak judiciary. There was no attempt to make the three equally powerful. There were curbs to be sure—for instance, the Senate's check on treaties. There were balances, such as the House and Senate counterbalancing each other with respect to impeachment, a point that Alexander Hamilton made.[35] But the Constitution neither established an interbranch balance nor authorized the branches to reallocate or usurp powers in a bid to generate or maintain balance.

If we must use the balance metaphor because we simply cannot escape its allure, some may well conclude that the three-branch scale is now *closer* to balance than at any time in the past. The weaker branches are stronger. Both the president and the courts wield far more authority. The strongest branch, Congress, has lost some authority to the other branches. Some might argue that such changes in relative power may have been needed to generate the elusive interbranch balance. In other words, a living presidency may be necessary to achieve the balance that the Founders never sought but some modern scholars prize.

The Unchecked Presidency

A living constitutionalist might also claim to oppose the frightening specter of an utterly unchecked presidency, favoring the existing set of presidential power grabs but nonetheless opposing any further expansion. Fair enough. Yet we are far removed from this dire possibility of a truly unfettered executive. And agonizing over it is somewhat akin to fretting about our sun blowing up billons of year from now.

Anyone with a passing familiarity with our presidency knows that each occupant of the White House faces a range of legal duties and constraints. As noted earlier, modern presidents are rather submissive to the courts. Executives invariably honor judicial judgments, even when they clearly disagree with the legal opinions and factual findings that undergird those judgments. Every day, courts force the president to release the accused, to grant benefits, and to honor and enforce Congress's laws. The executive complies with such judgments because for two centuries presidents have consistently supposed that judges decide who wins and loses a case, with the executive obliged to enforce and honor those judgments. The handful of exceptions, such as Abraham Lincoln's refusal to honor Chief Justice Roger Taney's constitutional opinion in *Ex parte Merryman* (Lincoln ignored Taney's conclusion that the executive was illegally holding John Merryman), force us to take notice.[36] But these exceptions do not detract from the more universal pattern: when it comes to court judgments, the executive is an obedient poodle.

Likewise, presidents honor almost all congressional laws; again the spectacular violations and disobedience are what grab our attention. Although these brazen acts have multiplied over time and may grow worse in the future, they are still rare. Every day while in office, presidents, via their minions, enforce and implement a slew of laws, many of which they mildly oppose. Presidents also tend to honor the restraints, both express and implicit, of the laws that Congress enacts. If Congress appropriates $100 million for tanks, presidents generally will not spend $110 million on them. If a criminal law imposes a ten-year prison term for an offense, the executive will not keep a convict in jail for twenty. Should Congress grant welfare to a class of people, no president will withhold those benefits merely because he disagrees with Congress's policy.[37]

I admit that some regard the separation of the legislative and executive authority as unnecessary or unwise. The more such sentiments are expressed publicly, the more likely presidents are to usurp greater legislative power, for it will appear that they are reacting to a clamor for reform. In 2016, William Howell and Terry Moe provocatively argued that the Constitution was a "relic" precisely because of its separation of legislative and executive functions.[38] They endorsed a shift to a parliamentary system, where the legislature and executive would be one and the same.[39] Woodrow Wilson made the same diagnosis more than a century ago.[40] The immediate impetus for the Howell and Moe suggestion, and others that bad-mouthed the separation of powers, may have been the sense that Republicans in Congress were unduly obstructing President Obama's legislative agenda. But despite the periodic expression of such views, we are not close to a situation where presidents are about to seize all legislative power. Instead, as we will see in Chapter 8, we have a creeping—and hardly complete—executive usurpation of legislative authority.

To be clear, the separation of legislative and executive functions has many fans, and I am one of them. The separation makes government tyranny less likely and creates rival power centers that will occasionally clash over momentous issues, both legal and political. These battles can be quite helpful in the defense of liberty. My point is that despite the presidency's undoubted inroads into the legislative realm, we are far removed from any real prospect that the presidency will completely swallow Congress.

Finally, as Eric Posner and Adrian Vermeule observe, there are plenty of political constraints on what presidents may do.[41] While I disagree with their claim that there is an absence of effective legal constraints and that political constraints are sufficient to keep the presidency in check, they are absolutely right that, given the plebiscitary nature of the presidency, executives do feel hemmed in by what the public favors and opposes. Presidents feel constrained by public opinion because they want to avoid undermining a considerable source of their strength, which can help advance other parts of their agendas. Hence no president will try to eliminate parental rights or refuse to disburse Social Security because today's public would not stomach policies so outside the political mainstream.

In sum, because a wholly unchecked presidency is not a real possibility in the foreseeable future, it is a mistake for living constitutionalists to try to justify opposition to further additions to the executive office merely because of this hazy fear. This is like dreading a sip of water for fear of drowning in it.

THE CONFUSING RHETORIC OF LIVING CONSTITUTIONALISTS

The rhetoric against the "imperial presidency" often tends to focus on its legality and on the Founders. Many living constitutionalists wail about the unlawfulness of presidential aggrandizement and point to what the Founders wanted in 1787. They seem almost morally offended that presidents would seek more power. But when they talk this way, they are contradicting their own first principles, for a living constitutionalist, by definition, can have no foundational objection to informal constitutional change. And that attitude must apply no less to the executive than to Congress or the courts regardless of which of the three is the primary agent of such constitutional reformation.

We must disentangle two distinct points. First is the question of the legitimacy or lawfulness of informal constitutional change. Either informal constitutional change is lawful or it is not. It cannot become illegitimate merely because one happens to dislike the particular constitutional change at issue. No one denies that amendments that have gone through Article V are legitimate, even if some may oppose one or more of those formal amendments. Similarly, if the Constitution can change by informal means, presidential attempts to expand their office cannot be unconstitutional merely because presidents attempt to use informal methods. Some living constitutionalists might say that particular processes of informal change are impermissible, but there is no consensus among living constitutionalists about the proper way of ushering in constitutional change.

Given this lack of accord, outsiders can be forgiven for concluding that living constitutionalism makes it possible for one branch to unilaterally change the Constitution. After all, a bedrock feature of most (but not all) theories of living constitutionalism is that one should not be too formal or demanding about the mechanisms of informal constitutional change.

Second is the question of the desirability of particular informal constitutional changes. Living constitutionalists are free to oppose any particular innovation on the grounds that it would be a mistake for the executive to enjoy a particular power, by means of informal amendment or otherwise. But this opposition would be grounded on policy concerns, not on a general opposition to informal constitutional change or a faux reverence for the Founders. Whatever else they may believe, living constitutionalists support the idea of informal constitutional amendments. Similarly, living constitutionalists should shun arguments about the Founding Fathers because making such arguments contradicts their anti-Founding first principles. When living constitutionalists invoke the Founders, it is akin to an atheist invoking the divine.

FORMAL AMENDMENTS: THE PRESIDENCY'S FRAILTY

As noted in Chapter 1, presidents have no role in the passage of formal constitutional amendments. More particularly, Congress need not present amendments to the president prior to sending them to states.[42] In fact, the only successful amendment to be signed by a president is the Thirteenth Amendment, a practice not repeated by any of Abraham Lincoln's successors.[43] None of them insisted that Congress must present amendments to them for their consideration.

To be sure, presidents can play a limited role in the process of formally amending the Constitution. They can campaign on a platform of supporting an amendment, as Lincoln did when he supported the abolishment of slavery in 1864; they can propose amendments to Congress, as Ulysses Grant did when he asked Congress for a line-item veto; they can jawbone Congress, the states, and the public, hoping to galvanize official sentiment and public opinion, much as Lincoln did by securing votes in the House for the Thirteenth Amendment. Finally, presidents may help decide whether the states have properly ratified a proposed amendment. In 1992, the executive branch concluded that the states had legitimately ratified the Congressional Pay Amendment, which had been proposed over two centuries before.[44] This legal judgment helped pave the way for the widespread sense that the pay proposal from 1789 should be regarded as the Constitution's Twenty-Seventh Amendment.

Informal Amendments: The Presidency's Forte

A single-minded focus on the executive's role in formal amendments unduly minimizes presidents' influence on the development of constitutional law. We must expand our inquiry to include informal amendments. Doing so enables us to see that the presidency's role is second to none. How do presidents shape informal constitutional change? Presidents can reshape constitutional policy through their appointments to the federal bench, in keeping with the adage "personnel is policy," in this case constitutional policy. The most obvious examples are nominations to the Supreme Court. Dwight Eisenhower admitted that he had made mistakes in appointing Earl Warren and William Brennan to the Supreme Court, presumably because he disliked some of their constitutional decisions.[45] Other presidents revel in the transformative effect of their appointments. Franklin Roosevelt must have been delighted that his Supreme Court justices—surprise, surprise—upheld his vigorous expansion of federal legislative power. Only slightly less important are the nominations to the district and appellate courts. Because the Supreme Court hears only a fraction of all cases, most cases involving questions of constitutional law are decided by lower courts, which, in practice, have great discretion in how they interpret and apply the Supreme Court's constitutional doctrines and the Constitution itself. Further, presidents can advance what we might call a restrictive constitutional agenda and use it to constrain Congress. That is, they can buttress existing prohibitions on legislative action or attempt to create new limits on Congress. Presidents can voice constitutional objections to bills before they receive them and can veto those bills on constitutional grounds after presentment. Unlike the courts, which rule on the constitutionality of only a handful of provisions in but a fraction of all laws, presidents collectively see *every* bill before it becomes law. For instance, Andrew Jackson used constitutional objections to the 1832 Bank Bill in an attempt to reorient constitutional law away from John Marshall's expansive reading of federal legislative power.[46] He was hardly the last president to use his veto messages to convey and promote particular constitutional theories.

Bill Clinton took advantage of one presidential innovation—the issuance of signing statements to assert that a new law contains unconstitutional provisions—to successfully advance his vision of equal protection of the laws.[47] In 1996 Clinton signed into law a bill that required the automatic discharge of all military personnel with HIV. But he simultaneously objected that the new law was unconstitutional, claiming that it advanced no legitimate government purpose while ousting many soldiers and sailors perfectly capable of serving their country.[48] The next year, Congress left out the provision, apparently to accommodate his objections. In objecting to the HIV provision, Clinton certainly nudged constitutional law in a particular direction.

Well after a bill becomes a law, presidents may disregard that law on the grounds that it is unconstitutional. This practice dates back to Thomas Jefferson, when he refused to enforce a Sedition Act that he regarded as unconstitutional.[49] This practice has accelerated in modern times, with presidents especially willing to ignore laws that attempt to constrain presidential authority. Both George W. Bush and Barack Obama ignored a law that touched on Israel's claim to Jerusalem because each supposed that the law infringed on their constitutional authority over foreign affairs.[50]

Should a president elect to enforce a law he or she believes is unconstitutional, that president may nonetheless urge the courts to declare it unconstitutional, a stance that may influence some judges. Clinton vowed to take this approach—enforce yet undermine—with respect to the HIV provision. Likewise, as noted earlier, Obama chose to enforce the Defense of Marriage Act (DOMA) while simultaneously decrying it as unconstitutional before the courts.[51] While it is impossible to say whether Obama's stance influenced any of the justices who ruled DOMA unconstitutional, it is easy to imagine that over the run of cases some justices might be swayed by a president's decision to vigorously denounce (rather than defend) a federal law.

Even after the courts rule that a law is constitutional, the president retains the ability to pardon federal offenses. For instance, if the courts decide that the Constitution permits Congress to imprison Americans for marijuana possession, a president may pardon all those convicted on the grounds that, whatever the courts might say, the executive regards the law as unconstitutional. Indeed, in issuing a blanket pardon the president may declare that the courts utterly misread the Constitution. Thomas Jefferson did something like this when he pardoned all those found guilty of violating the Sedition Act. Judges had said the act was constitutional; Jefferson thought them mistaken and acted on his opinion. Today most scholars agree that the Sedition Act was unconstitutional, a stance arguably influenced by Jefferson's firm stand against it.

Presidents can also push in the opposite direction, advancing what we might call a permissive constitutional agenda by arguing that a law is constitutional. If several presidents have claimed that a law is constitutional, judges may well be moved by this consistent practice. In upholding the constitutionality of the Bank of the United States, Chief Justice John Marshall observed that the arguments in favor of the original bank's constitutionality had "convinced minds as pure and as intelligent as this country can boast."[52] Among these fine minds was George Washington, who, after considering the constitutional doubts, had signed a bill creating the Bank of the United States. Marshall went on to note that a former opponent of the bank had eventually endorsed its constitutionality, referring to President James Madison.

In these two cases, the presidents were not seeking to influence future litigation about the bank. But sometimes presidents do take stances designed to pressure the courts to uphold legislation. Franklin Roosevelt's court packing plan—a scheme to increase the number of justices and thereby render obstructing justices irrelevant—is thought by some to have caused one justice to switch his vote on the constitutionality of New Deal legislation. Whether true or not, the story certainly has surface plausibility. Likewise, some speculate that Barack Obama's repeated public warnings to the Supreme Court that it must not strike down the Affordable Care Act (ACA) may have influenced Chief Justice John Roberts's vote to uphold the individual mandate as a tax. Even if the president's admonishments had no effect on any justices, one can imagine future presidents drawing a lesson from Obama's cautionary threats, and future justices concluding that sometimes submission to executive pressure is the better part of valor.

Presidents also shape constitutional law by going after perceived constitutional violators. Andrew Jackson's firm stand against South Carolina's nullification of federal tariffs helped establish a now venerable principle of constitutional law, namely that the states have no constitutional right to nullify federal law within their borders.[53] In the wake of the Civil War, many now suppose that secession is illegal, in part because the North defeated the South. If there is a person most responsible for this constitutional judgment, it is not any justice of the Supreme Court, but rather Abraham Lincoln. Another president, say, James Buchanan, might have let the South slip away. But Lincoln thought that secession was unconstitutional, and had no compunction about deploying Union forces to advance that constitutional conviction.

Through word and deed, presidents steer the future course of constitutional law regarding the separation of powers, federalism, and individual rights. To influence the courts, they rely on appointments, court briefs, and public suasion and pressure. To sway Congress, they issue veto messages and craft constitutional arguments designed to attract their partisan allies in the two chambers. Hence a president can wield more influence on the shape of constitutional change than any other single person, even a justice of the Supreme Court. Indeed, it seems fair to say that the influence of certain powerful presidents on the shape of constitutional law—think Washington, Lincoln, Roosevelt—has far eclipsed that of their contemporaneous Supreme Court.

THEORIES OF PRESIDENTIAL POWER AND CHANGE

However influential presidents are with respect to federalism or individual rights, they have the greatest ability to reshape the contours of presidential power. The underlying question—whether presidents can amend their own constitutional powers via practice—surfaced as early as Andrew Jackson's presidency. As discussed in Chapter 3, Old Hickory saw himself as the people's steward and as their sole and direct representative. Jackson's critics argued that the president was using this status to rewrite the Constitution in a way that expanded executive power. In particular, Henry Clay imputed to Jackson the belief that his reelection to the presidency had granted him *additional* constitutional powers. Though Jackson never claimed to have acquired any new powers, Clay is worth quoting at length because he foreshadows our predicament:

I am surprised and alarmed at the new source of executive power, which is found in the result of a presidential election. I had supposed that the constitution and the laws were the sole source of executive authority; that the Constitution could only be amended in the mode which it has itself prescribed; that the issue of a presidential election, was merely to place the chief magistrate in the post assigned to him; and that he had neither more nor less power, in consequence of the election, than the Constitution defines and delegates. But it seems that if, prior to an election, certain opinions . . . are known to the people, these loose opinions, in virtue of the election, incorporate themselves with the Constitution, and afterward are to be regarded . . . as parts of the instrument.[54]

Whigs like Clay and Webster believed that Jackson had repeatedly violated the Constitution and laws (as they understood them). They supposed that Jackson had justified his illegal acts on the grounds that if the people sought some end, any acts in pursuance of that end were necessarily constitutional.[55] Whether their understanding of Jackson was right, the basic idea that presidents could cite the public to alter constitutional principles has only grown in importance.

Abraham Lincoln successfully advanced a different evolutionary concept, one tied to emergencies. Lincoln had cut his teeth in Clay's Whig Party, a party dedicated to limiting what its members saw as the regal pretensions of Andrew Jackson and his party's successors in the White House. But when Lincoln was faced with a rebellion on both sides of Washington, DC, he leapt into action, taking a series of illegal steps, at least according to prevailing readings of the Constitution. He suspended habeas corpus, spent millions of dollars without an appropriation, and raised armies.[56] Later he ignored congressional statutes relating to trials and habeas corpus and freed millions of slaves.[57] As justification for many of these acts, he resorted to a novel claim: presidents may do whatever is necessary to save the nation.[58] The seventy years leading up to the Civil War provided no basis for this remarkable assertion, for despite fighting foreign enemies on domestic soil and suppressing rebels, not one of his predecessors had ever claimed such authority. To the contrary, despite its undoubted appeal during emergencies, Washington, Jefferson, and Madison had repeatedly and utterly disclaimed this sort of argument.[59]

Even though Lincoln was helping to change the Constitution, he never saw himself as amending it. Despite the serious flaws in his arguments, they were grounded in old-fashioned materials. He was making claims about what he felt the Constitution always meant. He did not conceive himself as a living constitutionalist. Nonetheless, Lincoln succeeded in forever changing constitutional thought. It is now conventional wisdom to suppose that the Constitution itself grants presidents some measure of emergency authority. That change in thought and perception is largely due to Lincoln, his successes, and our affection for the Great Emancipator.

Woodrow Wilson, the professor, advanced numerous constitutional theories. In his *Congressional Government,* he lamented that the Article II presidency was too weak and argued that we ought to unify the executive and legislative under a parliamentary system.[60] In *Constitutional Government,* however, he adopted an entirely different approach. He argued that eighteenth-century theories about checks and balances were not incorporated into the Constitution. To the contrary, the "actual provisions of the Constitution" were extremely flexible, because, after all, "our government is a living, organic thing."[61] The Constitution's malleability granted the presidency tremendous elasticity. In Wilson's view, the president's "office is anything [the incumbent] has the sagacity and force to make it."[62] Indeed, "[t]he President is at liberty, both in law and conscience, to be as big a man as he can. His capacity will set the limit."[63] Both statements suggested that law was largely irrelevant and that only politics constrained the presidency.[64] Strong presidents could (and should) reshape their office.

Wilson was eerily prophetic at times, yet he could not wholly escape certain orthodoxies of his era. For example, other portions of *Constitutional Government* made clear that the executive was to execute the laws and could not merely reinterpret them or displace them by executive fiat.[65] It took a Rough Rider to try to run roughshod over this long-established principle. After he left the presidency, Theodore Roosevelt enunciated an astounding theory of executive power that apparently reflected his time in the Oval Office:

> My belief was that it was not only [the president's] right but his duty to do anything that the needs of the Nation demanded unless such action was forbidden by the Constitution or by the laws. . . . I did not usurp power, but I did greatly broaden the use of executive power. . . . I acted . . . whenever and in whatever manner was necessary, unless prevented by direct constitutional or legislative prohibition. . . . The course I followed [was] of regarding the executive as subject only to the people, and, under the Constitution, bound to serve the people affirmatively in cases where the Constitution does not explicitly forbid him to render the service.[66]

Because the Constitution never "explicitly forbid[s] him to render the service" (as discussed in Chapter 3, there are no provisions declaring "The president shall never . . ."), this theory has the potential to transform a limited executive to an untrammeled tribune of the people.

Although William Howard Taft subsequently denounced Roosevelt's theory, more recent presidents have tended to eschew either articulating or condemning theories of presidential powers. Modern presidents have wisely left the theorizing to the theorists. But one does not need to propound a theory of constitutional change to take actions in service of one. In general, Democratic presidents and their administrations have embraced the idea that the Constitution's meaning should change over time, while Republican presidents have not. In fact, Republican administrations often have waged a feeble rear-guard action against living constitutionalism.

Presidents of both parties, however, have been united in favoring a living presidency. In the modern era, Democratic and Republican administrations have resolutely defended the existing frontiers of presidential power, wherever those borders happen to be at the moment. Further, both eagerly cite practices that advance the immediate policy interests of the incumbent and that simultaneously expand presidential authority. Sometimes this presidential creep—pushing the frontiers of executive power outward—arises in the statutory context, meaning that executives are bending or modifying federal laws. Other times, presidents amend the presidency.

To be sure, no president has ever admitted that he has amended the Constitution by virtue of his election or otherwise. Likewise, no chief executive has ever confessed that his constitutional office can be as big as he can make it, primarily because the assertion remains to this day jarring to the ear (how long that will remain so is unclear). Finally, contra Theodore Roosevelt, no sitting president has yet said that he can do anything he pleases unless there is a specific prohibition against it. The closest any president came to making such a claim was Richard Nixon. After resigning, he once said, "If the president does it, then it's not illegal."[67] But Nixon's assertion may have been limited to national security, an attempt to hide behind Lincolnian precedents. Nixon was no Lincoln, of course, but was relying on the powerful intuition that the scope of presidential power cannot vary by reference to the incumbent's character or reputation.

PRESIDENTIAL PRACTICES AMEND THE PRESIDENCY

It is quite likely that virtuous Lincoln will forever be exploited by his less-worthy successors, in emergencies and otherwise, as a means of justifying presidential action and executive grasping. Indeed, acts of prior presidents are habitually trotted out, reinterpreted, massaged, and even distorted to prop up the actions of incumbents. When someone claims that the president has done something amiss, the executive (and its allies) stand ready with precedents, a version of "executive whataboutism": if past presidents have done something similar, however remote the resemblance, then the current occupant's acts simply must be constitutional.

Justices of the Supreme Court have supplied more than a patina of respectability to executive whataboutism. In *Youngstown Sheet & Tube Co. v. Sawyer*, Justice Felix Frankfurter ruled against President Truman.[68] Nonetheless, as discussed earlier, his opinion supplied a rather rough roadmap for presidential aggrandizement:

> It is an inadmissibly narrow conception of American constitutional law . . . to disregard the gloss which life has written upon [the words of the Constitution]. . . . [A] systematic, unbroken, executive practice, long pursued to the knowledge of the Congress and never before questioned, engaged in by Presidents who have also sworn to uphold the Constitution, . . . may be treated as a gloss on 'executive Power' vested in the President by § 1 of Art. II.[69]

Frankfurter is not the only justice to ever make such a claim about the import of gloss or practice. But his is the most famous of such assertions.

There is a certain wisdom in Frankfurter's view, especially when the gloss dates back to the origins of the relevant constitutional text. The requirements that the practice be systematic and unbroken seem to cabin a president's ability to alter his or her own constitutional authority. The conditions that Congress know of the practice and that no one has questioned it also constrain the ability of presidents to covertly gloss or expand their constitutional powers.

Yet the argument is also disquieting. Frankfurter himself recognized the perils of the position, or at least its rather awful optics.

Just before this quoted excerpt, Frankfurter declared that "[d]eeply embedded traditional ways of conducting government cannot supplant the Constitution."[70] In a previous case, too, Frankfurter had said that "[i]llegality cannot attain legitimacy through practice."[71] Other justices have said similar things. Writing for the entire Court, Chief Justice Earl Warren asserted, "[t]hat an unconstitutional action has been taken before surely does not render that same action any less unconstitutional at a later date."[72]

But these platitudes, however sincerely felt, often do little work. First, the Court conveniently ignores them when it sanctions practice-based alterations of the Constitution. That is, when the Court chooses to treat the Constitution as an "organism," as Oliver Wendell Holmes once described it, things once unconstitutional actually can "attain legitimacy through practice."[73] No one familiar with the Court's jurisprudence could deny this. Second, these statements are occasionally made in cases where the court sanctifies the use of practice to change the Constitution. Although Frankfurter ruled against President Truman's claim of authority in *Youngstown,* his theory clearly contemplated that, had previous presidents taken more acts akin to Truman's seizure, those "deeply embedded" practices would "supplant the Constitution." Declaring that practice cannot change the Constitution while clearly admitting that it can is remarkable. It is the hypocrisy that one living constitutionalist—Frankfurter—paid to the virtues of constitutional fidelity and stability.

Other parts of his theory of constitutional change are rather hazy. To begin with, what is a "systematic" practice? Frankfurter denied that three analogous events were enough.[74] But how many would be? He never said. Whatever yardstick he had in mind, lawyers are quick to argue that if something has been done before, even once, that lends great legitimacy to the practice. Politicians steeped in the ways of the real world have long warned that even one act of usurpation may alter the Constitution in practice. Complaining of transgressive acts by General Andrew Jackson in 1819,

Henry Clay cautioned that a "single instance fixes the habit and determines the direction of governments."[75] In other words, while more is better, sometimes once is enough to change habits and to change the Constitution.

There is the related matter of what counts as an analogous act. There is no neutral or obvious way of characterizing or tallying executive acts. If I want to know whether presidents can start a foreign war without congressional approval, should I consider every time that presidents have unilaterally waged a general war against another country? Or should I sum up every time presidents have used any amount of military force, no matter how small, in a foreign nation? The first will yield fewer instances and the second far more. One can easily guess which set of practices executive advisers will tend to emphasize.

Somewhat ironically, the actual "practice" of practice-based arguments is far removed from Frankfurter's description. Neither politicians, nor lawyers, nor courts hew to Frankfurter's many requirements. In part this reflects the context in which the gloss is typically invoked. This sort of argument is typically trotted out to justify a pro-executive innovation in the law by those hoping to stretch presidential power. In that context, the fewer the requirements the better.

For instance, consider the requirement that the practice be "never before questioned." This is rarely, if ever, taken seriously. When executive lawyers make a practice-based claim, they tend not to delve into the reactions or responses, in part because there likely were members of Congress or the public (including scholars) who questioned, even denounced, the practice. Precious few practices actually can meet the "never before questioned" standard.

Moreover, Frankfurter noted that presidents take an oath to uphold the Constitution.[76] It is hard to know what to make of this point. Are we to suppose that the only practices that should count are those where presidents sincerely believe them to be constitutional? How would we know whether their convictions were sincere? What if presidents don't even consider the constitutional question and instead focus on factors like expediency, which seems likely in most cases? Many times, presidents leave legalities to the lawyers. If the lawyers give the green light to an executive act, presidents often do not give the constitutional questions any thought.

Sometimes courts and scholars consider other factors that Frankfurter never mentioned. For instance, some scholars tack on an extra requirement for a gloss to take hold—that the constitutional text be susceptible to multiple meanings.[77] That is, practice counts only when the text is unclear. But such arguments are often driven by the preferred ends of those applying the constraint. For instance, as noted earlier, executive lawyers have argued that Congress cannot curb executive authority, despite the existence of contrary practice, where the Constitution supposedly clearly favors executive authority. "[U]sage alone—regardless how longstanding and venerable—cannot validate a practice that clearly violates constitutional principles. The Constitution, not history, is the supreme law."[78] To underscore the point, the executive lawyers cited a Supreme Court opinion: "It is obviously correct that no one acquires a vested or protected right in violation of the Constitution by long use, even when that span of time covers our entire national existence."[79]

Yet executive lawyers (and their principals) are rather unwilling to apply the same rule when it comes to presidential accretions. Even text that clearly favors Congress will not bar executive aggrandizement. Even practices that do not span the entire nation's history will nonetheless coalesce to form a new legal principle and convey a new right to the presidency. Where creep is at issue, constitutional clarity protects the presidency, but not Congress. And practices can bestow new powers on the president, but generally not Congress.

Consider, in this regard, Justice Stephen Breyer's opinion in a case involving the Recess Appointments Clause (which authorizes presidents to make appointments during the Senate's recesses).[80] Because the justice concluded that the clause was susceptible to multiple readings, he claimed that it made sense to look at practice to decide how best to read the clause today. But to support this claim of uncertainty, he cited the existence of a practice that departed from prior readings. According to this logic, deviant practices can generate ambiguity where there once was none, and that uncertainty, in turn, can help sanctify the once deviant practice, making it seem like an entirely reasonable reading of the now ambiguous text. Rare is the case where a deviant practice fails to contribute to the sense that the text is fundamentally unclear.

Another factor that plays a powerful role in practice-based arguments is the practice's perceived utility. The more useful an executive action is perceived to be, the more likely it is that a court will uphold it. For instance, in the Recess Appointments case just mentioned, the Supreme Court majority recognized that many in Congress had questioned a longstanding executive practice.[81] Indeed, some of those doubting the pro-executive reading were high-ranking executive officials, essentially a telling admission against interest.[82] Yet the Court nonetheless upheld that disputed practice. The "most natural" (and the early) reading of the Recess Appointments Clause was shunted aside in order to endorse a functionally superior reading.[83] Again, if the executive innovation seems beneficial enough to a president, his lawyers, or a reviewing court, other considerations are given short shrift.

Frankfurter's beguiling practice-makes-perfect theory of constitutional change largely skipped—one might say glossed over—all the hard and interesting questions. Because his theory was so underspecified, perhaps it was inevitable that an opinion trumpeting the virtues of practice would itself be superseded by subsequent practice. In modern times, whether the courts will recognize the legality of a dubious practice turns on a hodge-podge of especially manipulable factors, some of which Frankfurter never mentioned: the clarity of the constitutional text, the utility of the challenged practice, and the number of deviant practices. The presidential oath is almost certainly irrelevant, as is the stipulation that the practices must never have been questioned before. Although practice-makes-perfect is an established mode of constitutional argumentation, it seems quite likely that the means by which practice alters the Constitution will itself continue to change over time as practices further change. If you live by practice, you can rest assured that your theory of practice will someday die at the hands of practice.

One final note about the appeal and perils of practice and executive whataboutism. During the Obama presidency, there was an internal clash over whether Congress could prevent the executive from trying alleged terrorists in Article III courts. Congress wanted the accused to be tried in military courts, far from our shores. Some administration lawyers argued that Congress could impose such a constraint and others insisted that such a law would invade core executive powers. (For the record, I agree with the former group.) In response to the argument that if President Obama declared his unwillingness to honor any such limit he would be "acting too much like Bush," Harold Koh, the State Department legal adviser, "repeatedly argued in meetings: Democrats get to be president, too."[84]

What Koh meant by this, I'm not precisely sure. But someone in his situation could be forgiven for supposing that if President Bush took some action, President Obama must have the same authority as Bush; otherwise Obama would occupy an inferior, second-class version of the office. What is crystal clear is that those favoring a president's agenda will rarely shrink from pointing out that if one or more presidents have taken some step or act, the incumbent absolutely must be able to do the same. Every president must be able to do what previous presidents did, or else we have an asymmetric and one-sided contest, where some presidents advance their agenda by the constitutional rules and others promote their programs by flouting those rules. Hence almost every supporter of the incumbent will fervently believe that the current president must "get to be president, too."

This understandable and sensible short-term strategy has the long-term effect of creating a one-way ratchet, where no president, and few of the president's supporters, would be willing to step back and reassess what the presidency has become, and will become, if every incumbent gets to be all that every predecessor has been, and more. The mantra that my guy or gal gets to be president too, a rallying cry that, by itself, does not grapple with legal claims but instead trades on principles of fairness and symmetry, has proven too enticing and powerful. Yes, everyone who is the president gets to be president. But it hardly follows that the president can (or should) do whatever any previous holder of the office has been able get away with.

* * *

Living constitutionalism privileges presidents in two ways. First, it massively amplifies the presidency's influence over the constitutional system writ large. As a general matter, mechanisms of informal change favor those who are most influential, and no one can match the reach and sway of a president. Presidents claim a popular mandate, enjoy the bully pulpit, and can make decisions quickly. They promiscuously assert that the public fully endorses their (re)understanding of the existing constitutional order. They loudly proclaim and spread that vision before Congress, in their weekly radio addresses, and on the campaign trail. And they can more easily reach a decision on matters of constitutional law because they need not parley and compromise on their vision. They can declare that equal protection demands governmental recognition of same-sex marriages. They can proclaim that the First Amendment bars forced contributions to labor unions. They can argue that the Constitution does not protect the modern understanding of birth-right citizenship. This is not to say that the views of presidents will invariably prevail. Far from it. But they don't have to always get their way in order for them to have the biggest voice under our living Constitution.

Second, living constitutionalism enables presidents to remake the presidency with relative ease. Rather than navigating Article V—a rather arduous, almost impossible process—presidents rely on informal mechanisms using the amendatory powers of practice. Presidents thereby alter the existing set of principles and rules that are meant, in part, to constrain them. While in the reminder of the book I focus on this second aspect of living constitutionalism—presidents' transformation of the office they occupy—no one should doubt the presidency's considerable influence on other areas of constitutional law, like the scope of congressional power or the direction of equal protection practice. We must never forget that in a regime of living constitutionalism, a sitting president can wield the most influence over the future contours of constitutional law. No other actor comes close.

CHAPTER FIVE

From CONSTITUTIONAL DEFENDER *to* CONSTITUTIONAL AMENDER

Formidable though limited. Independent but checked. These descriptions fairly encapsulate the original presidency. They also describe our early presidents, whose critics routinely accused them—even George Washington, who always put country first—of being despots or worse. In truth, our early presidents almost invariably acted within the confines of the original presidency's contours. Constitutional deviations tended to be minor, temporary, and unintentional. While there were complaints about imperial behavior—of transcending the bounds of their office—these were mostly overreactions and partisan smears.

In many ways, the presidency of the twenty-first century looks much the same. We continue to call our federal executive the "president" and not "dear leader" or "highness." Likewise, the executive Constitution—Article II—is still largely unchanged, save for some minor alterations to how presidents are elected, when they take office, how many terms they may serve, and how to remove them if they become incapacitated. Despite these modifications, no formal amendment has grafted new powers onto the presidency.

Furthermore, our lived experience emphatically corroborates Alexander Hamilton's prediction that presidents would be energetic and reinforces why many in the eighteenth century thought the executive was the "moving force of a government."[1] At its best, Congress solemnly resolves and enacts. At their best, federal judges carefully opine and judge. The executive vigorously acts. It *does*. That was true at the Founding and it remains so today.

Nonetheless, the handful of surface continuities are eclipsed by scores of more fundamental differences. The modern presidency is a radically different office. Where the early presidency was weak, it is now strong. Where the original presidency was strong, it is generally stronger still. Formerly, presidents could not start wars; now they can and do, with astonishing frequency. In the past, presidents could merely veto bills; now they can make laws on their own and, not infrequently, ignore the laws that Congress has made. Under the original regime, presidents took a grave oath to defend the Constitution; now they mouth the oath but go on to periodically defile it as they amend the Constitution.

This last transformation in the presidency is a momentous one because it helps explain and illuminate the others. It is worth exploring what the presidential oath to defend the Constitution meant at the Founding and why and how it is drained of meaning today. If we can grasp how an oath has lost its meaning, we can better see what has transpired elsewhere.

A Meaningful Ritual, an Empty Vow

Every four years, presidents take an oath on the west front of the US Capitol in Washington, DC. The vow, traditionally administered by the chief justice of the Supreme Court and taken from Article II of the Constitution, is freely given before a massive crowd and to the nation via radio, television, and the internet. While past presidents merely swore to abide by the oath after someone else read it, modern presidents prefer to recite the oath's actual words: "I do solemnly swear (or affirm) that I will faithfully execute the Office of President of the United States, and will to the best of my Ability, preserve, protect and defend the Constitution of the United States." Though federal and state officials take an oath to "support" the Constitution, the Constitution does not specify that oath's precise wording. The presidential oath is unique, in keeping with the office's singularity.

The recitation of the presidential oath is the high point of a happy day, for two reasons. First, it symbolizes the peaceful, democratic transition of power. Departing presidents attend even when their successor has promised to undo their signature achievements and policies. Second, and even more significantly, the new president's oath underscores, in a public way, a seeming commitment to the rule of law. Presidents are conspicuously vowing to honor the foundational law—the Constitution—that creates, empowers, and limits their high office.

But in no small measure the ceremony is bunkum. It is true that our presidential contests generally replicate a democratic outcome in the sense that the candidate with the most popular votes tends to win the presidential contest. Since 1900, the candidate with the most popular votes has won the White House twenty-eight out of thirty times (two candidates secured a majority in the electoral college alone).[2] It is also true that presidents occasionally get tossed out of the White House and thereby lose the levers of executive authority—the considerable patronage, the incomparable prestige, and the unrivaled power.

When I say that the ceremony is hogwash, I refer to the oath and its beguiling promise. Modern executives take the presidential oath in a transformed system that empties the oath of any meaning. Presidents today enjoy the rights to change the Constitution unilaterally, via practice, and to assist others when they seek to informally amend it. Under this curious scheme, where presidents may change that Constitution via their transgressive acts, a pledge to preserve the Constitution has little import. When someone vows to honor laws that he cannot unilaterally alter, that oath has at least the *potential* for genuine constraint. But when the oath taker may unilaterally amend the law that she is pledged to honor and execute, the oath is a farce.

Origins

It was not always so. At the Founding, the presidential oath to preserve, protect, and defend the Constitution had real bite because in the Constitution's early years, there was no recognized, legitimate category of informal constitutional change.

To see the constraints, let's unpack what the obligation to "preserve, protect and defend the Constitution" originally required of a president. First, presidents could not violate the Constitution themselves because doing so would certainly be inconsistent with their oath to "preserve [and] protect" it. Firefighters have an implied duty not to moonlight as arsonists; likewise, constitutional preservationists and protectors have an obligation to avoid breaching the Constitution themselves. The idea that presidents must honor, and therefore not breach, the Constitution was widely accepted at the Founding. One Federalist noted that the "power of the President is still guarded further" because he takes an oath to "defend the constitution."[3] Another observed that the oath placed the president "under the immediate controul of the constitution, which if he should presume to deviate from, he would be immediately arrested in his career, and summoned to answer for his conduct before a federal court."[4] Though the claim about arrest was perhaps hyperbole, the basic point was not. Presidents were not permitted to violate the Constitution that legitimated, empowered, and constrained them.

George Washington's remarkable admission of culpability captures the spirit of this constraint. After concluding that his nominee to the Supreme Court was constitutionally incapable of serving, Washington publicly confessed his error. He said it was his "*duty* . . . to declare" that his nomination was "null by the constitution."[5] One must add that this remarkable declaration seems to have no modern equivalent. When was the last time a president confessed to misreading federal law, much less to a constitutional error?

Second, presidents had to "defend" the Constitution, presumably from the onslaughts of others. While assaults might come from foreign invaders seeking to dislodge the constitutional regime, they also could come from Congress, the courts, or rogue factions of the people. If the hazard came from Congress or one of its chambers—for example, if Congress attempted to enact unconstitutional laws—there was a quick and easy corrective: not judicial review, but the presidential veto. Thomas Jefferson referred to the veto as "the shield . . . to protect against [congressional] invasions."[6] He was right. While the courts cannot judge the constitutionality of all laws, Congress must send *all* bills to the president for review. Indeed, when early presidents vetoed bills on constitutional grounds, they often cited their constitutional duty as justification. For instance, upon concluding that a public works bill was unconstitutional, James Madison said that he had "no option" but to veto the bill and voice his objections.[7] His successor, James Monroe, declared that he had been "compelled to object" to the passage of a bill on the grounds that it was unconstitutional.[8] Andrew Jackson, too, spoke of his "duty" to decide whether bills were constitutional and to veto those he believed were not.[9] Early presidents apparently felt they had no choice but to veto bills they believed were unconstitutional. Allowing unconstitutional bills to become law was akin to permitting a foreign enemy to invade and ravage the country.

The veto was hardly the only means of defending the Constitution. Sometimes defense might be grounded in presidential *inaction*.

Recall Thomas Jefferson's belief that his obligation to defend the Constitution positively barred him from enforcing standing laws that were, in his opinion, unconstitutional. When he ordered prosecutors to halt enforcement of the Sedition Act—an act that criminalized the criticism of government officers—Jefferson cited his oath to "protect the constitution" as justification.[10] In a similar vein, George Washington refused the House's demand for certain papers: in his view, "a just regard to the Constitution and to the duty of my office . . . forbids a compliance" with the House's call for his treaty instructions to John Jay.[11] Both presidents choose inaction on the grounds that the particular actions sought would violate the presidential oath.

The courts also may undermine the Constitution. For instance, they may lend a judicial imprimatur to unconstitutional federal laws. Andrew Jackson's veto of a bill rechartering the Bank of the United States can be seen as a less-than-veiled criticism of the Supreme Court's opinion in *McCulloch v. Maryland*. In that case, the Supreme Court upheld the bank's constitutionality against the claim that Congress had no power to charter a national bank.[12] Jackson's lengthy veto message to Congress served as a rebuke of the Supreme Court's broad reading of federal legislative power.[13]

As noted earlier, President Jackson also played a starring role in defending the Constitution against desecrations by the states. In 1832, South Carolina denied that federal tariffs were constitutional and planned to "nullify" them within its borders.[14] Jackson issued a stern warning. He cautioned that it was his "[s]trict duty" to "preserve the Union by all constitutional means."[15] That is, because the president was bound to preserve the Constitution, he would not only enforce the tariff laws, but also crush any attempt to secede from the Union.

Other times the constitutional threat came from an unlikely source, a segment of We the People. For instance, in September 1791, gangs of citizens attacked excise collectors in Pennsylvania, marking the beginning of the Whiskey Rebellion. By 1794, President Washington had assembled a militia to put down the insurrection, thereby fulfilling, as he put it, his "engagement" to preserve, protect, and defend the Constitution.[16] Washington understood that attacks on government officials and refusals to pay federal taxes could lead to a full-blown rebellion and that he had a duty to suppress those trying to obstruct the federal government's writ. Even if We the People were sovereign, a fractious faction had no right to obstruct the operation of constitutional laws. As Abraham Lincoln would put it more colorfully during the Civil War, rebels "have no oath registered in Heaven to destroy the Government, while I shall have the most solemn one to 'preserve, protect, and defend it.'"[17]

Early presidents recognized that they were not to violate the Constitution themselves or help amend it by informal means. They also understood that they were obliged to fend off threats to the Constitution, whether those menaces came from the halls of Congress, the bench of the Supreme Court, the state legislatures, foreign invaders, or groups of rebellious citizens.

THE AMENDING EXECUTIVE

Modern presidents are strikingly different and seem unbothered by quaint notions of duty. From time to time, they may cite "duty" to preserve, protect, and defend the Constitution. But the invocation often seems insincere because it is typically raised only as convenience suits, when the president opposes some congressional law and is eager to declare it unconstitutional. Moreover, it is disingenuous because presidents occasionally seek to revise the Constitution to pursue some cherished or needful objective with respect to war powers, individual rights, and public policy. In sum, presidents do not act as if there is a meaningful, authentic duty to oppose constitutional innovations. In this context, speaking of a presidential duty to preserve, protect, and defend the Constitution seems rather hollow.

As noted earlier, Americans have come to expect modern presidents to make and keep promises, including promises related to the Constitution. Indeed, many Americans expect a president's agenda to involve altering existing constitutional conceptions. Recent Republican presidents have advanced a pro-life, pro-business, and pro-gun Constitution because their partisans demanded as much. These presidents (and their administrations) openly called for adjustments and corrections to how the Constitution is implemented in practice. Sometimes this Republican vision was said to reflect the original Constitution. Other times it merely reflected a desire for a better state of affairs or, if you will, a more perfect Constitution. For their part, Democratic chief executives have promoted an updated Constitution that insists on greater equality and that sanctions vast federal legislative power to better the condition of ordinary Americans. The precise agendas and visions have varied over time as society, parties, and presidents have changed. For instance, Richard Nixon's push to roll back innovations in criminal procedures is no longer a prominent component of Republican rhetoric. Likewise, Democratic ardor for religious liberty has greatly diminished in recent years as progressives have come to see the freedom of religion as a regressive barrier to their vision of social progress.

On balance, Democratic presidents have been more open about their desire to make constitutional law more progressive than Republican presidents have been about their own agenda for the Constitution. But for our purposes, what is important is that presidents, at our behest, often seek to supplant orthodox readings of the Constitution, current constitutional practices, and prevailing judicial doctrines. When we expect presidents to advance a constitutional vision and praise them for doing so, we also expect them to try to counter, undermine, and replace existing constitutional norms. In effect, a good portion of the public demands that candidates and presidents be agents of constitutional change.

The pull of the oath and the push of modern politics create an incongruous situation. "[P]reserve, protect, and defend . . . the Constitution," the oath tells our presidents. Yet our politics tells our presidents to "disrupt, violate, and amend the existing, living Constitution." We cannot see the incongruity because we are so tribalized and focused on our own narrow constitutional preferences. Gun-rights advocates believe that theirs is the proper understanding of the Constitution. Backers of the legal recognition of same-sex marriage believe the same. Though such goals often require a change in existing doctrine or conceptions, from the point of view of ardent activists, the Constitution's "true meaning" is on their side. They insist on the president's support for their reform agenda, whatever the presidential oath might seem to require.

Picture telling a bright child, "Always do what your parents say." But imagine also telling her that she can alter those parental rules by violating them—and better yet, that the more often she violates them, the greater the chance the rules themselves will change. Finally, envision telling the child that she should try to informally change the rules by breaking them because that is what her parents *actually* want. What will happen? This clever child will seek to change the rules to advance her agenda. And she will feel wholly justified in doing so because her parents are daily urging her to break, and thereby reform, the existing set of rules.

Presidents and their minions take away the same lesson. Presidents take the oath to defend the Constitution. But they also see the Constitution change in practice and they see a Supreme Court and Congress that amend it. The Supreme Court does so in its decisions, via small and large changes in doctrine, while Congress changes the Constitution when it enacts laws that transgress existing limits on the scope of legislative power and modify prevailing conceptions of rights. Chief executives, too, see special-interest litigants (such as the Chamber of Commerce and the American Civil Liberties Union) pushing novel theories in a bid to alter the Constitution, and they face pressure from activists to adopt these activists' constitutional agendas. Finally, every president knows that the office they occupy is no longer the one held by Washington, Lincoln, or even Reagan. Every incumbent comes to realize that their predecessors have transformed the office over time.

When faced with all this evidence of informal and momentous constitutional change and the continuing clamor for still more, why would presidents stay their reformist impulses? Why be the only one to refrain from violating (and thereby amending) the Constitution? As compared to special interest groups, presidents advance what they perceive as the nation's interests. As compared to the courts and Congress, the presidency is the only federal institution whose occupant is elected by a process that spans the entire nation. As compared to these two rivals, presidents may rightly suppose that they are far closer to the people's sense of what the Constitution is, or more importantly, what it ought to be reinterpreted or reimagined to become. Indeed, it would be downright bizarre to imagine that present and future presidents would remain consistent and resolute constitutional defenders when so many others have been persistent and forceful constitutional amenders.

Consider their roles and stances before they become president. Prior to entering the Oval Office, many presidents likely endorsed evolving conceptions of what some provision in Article I means or what an amendment in the Bill of Rights forbids. For instance, senators likely have favored constitutional changes related to the scope of federal legislative power and individual rights. Governors may have supported expanding some doctrinal features of the First or Fourteenth Amendments. These patterns of behavior are unlikely to disappear merely because a person becomes president. Those who have favored informal constitutional change for a lifetime will not, upon taking the presidential oath, instantly become opposed to all constitutional innovation. Old habits of constitutional thought die hard.

Is it any wonder, then, that presidents vigorously advance a multilayered approach to constitutional change? In the court of public opinion, they push a reformed Constitution. In the actual courts, they skillfully advocate for informal constitutional changes that might be impossible for them to realize unilaterally, like a change in abortion rights or free exercise liberties. They appoint judges who they hope and predict will endorse and implement their reform visions of constitutional law. Finally, they violate the existing constitutional order to advance their personal and policy agendas and thereby expand the powers of the presidency itself.

DISAPPEARING DUTIES

Where there was once an obligation to fend off attacks on the Constitution and thwart violations, there is now discretion. Presidents need not defend against, much less oppose, the constitutional violations of others. In deciding whether to oppose a particular constitutional innovation, presidents will take into account the politics of the situation, what else is on their crowded policy agenda, and whether they oppose the potential constitutional amendment on policy grounds. Presidents generally will not attempt to thwart transgressions and innovations when they imagine that they might help usher in a new and improved constitutional order. For instance, a modern president who favors getting tough on crime likely will not oppose a Congress that seeks to alter existing conceptions of what the Constitution requires in terms of criminal investigations, arrests, and trials. To the contrary, the more a president supports a constitutional innovation, the more he is apt to laud the innovator and, in this way, facilitate changes to the existing constitutional order. To be sure, presidents may employ some shrewd window dressing, insisting that the innovation is not something invented or created at all but, in fact, actually vindicates the Constitution's *genuine* meaning. But anyone attentively following the constitutional dispute and not politically invested in the alteration can see through the ruse. Like many others pushing for constitutional transformation, such presidents are merely using the rhetoric of constitutional law as an instrument of constitutional change.

Where there was once a duty on the part of presidents to never trespass against the Constitution, there is now a presidential power to modify it. When modern presidents are the prime movers, pushing to reform constitutional conceptions and values, they are essentially calling for a change to the Constitution itself. For instance, presidents who stump for the repudiation of *Planned Parenthood v. Casey* (abortion rights) or *Citizens United v. Federal Election Commission* (the intersection of corporate speech and campaign finance) are attempting to modify the Constitution, at least if we use current practice as the baseline.[18] Again, presidents, in conjunction with their allies, will insist that they are defending the Constitution's true meaning. But their rhetoric does not match reality. Typically, presidents seek constitutional change merely for reasons of policy and politics and are not actually seeking to vindicate some true meaning. Pro-choice presidents are pro-choice first and constitutional vindicators second. Pro-life presidents are not meaningfully different, save for being on the opposite side of the policy question.

That is why presidents no longer act as consistent and resolute reclaimers and protectors of the original constitutional order. That is why presidents do not even serve as dependable defenders of the existing constitutional order. And that is why the oath taken on the steps of the Capitol is something of a farce.

THE LIVING PRESIDENTIAL OATH

But perhaps I have been too harsh and, crucially, too wedded to original understandings of the oath. There are radical possibilities that we should not discount. First, perhaps the modern Constitution actually *authorizes* presidents to change the Constitution via unilateral acts. If true, the president, when committing these seemingly transgressive acts, neither does violence to the Constitution nor breaks the presidential oath.

We can draw a parallel to Congress. As a matter of federal law, representatives and senators must take an oath to "support and defend the Constitution of the United States" and "bear true faith and allegiance to the same."[19] We can safely conclude that in taking this pledge, federal legislators vow not to violate the Constitution. Furthermore, because the Constitution clearly sanctions an amendment process, one where the senators and representatives can vote to send a formal amendment to the states for approval, neither set of lawmakers does anything wrong when they try to amend the Constitution that way.[20] Whether they can informally amend the Constitution via their legislative enactments is a more controversial proposition. But what is crystal clear is that their oath to support the Constitution does not categorically bar their efforts to amend it, for they are bound to a framework that sanctions at least some attempts to alter it.

From the perspective of a living constitutionalist, something similar is true regarding our Supreme Court justices. Justices take the same vow that federal legislators take.[21] Yet living constitutionalists certainly do not regard the Supreme Court's successful constitutional innovations as simultaneously breaching judicial oaths. No living constitutionalist commends a justice for updating the Constitution but criticizes that justice for violating a judicial oath. Moreover, living constitutionalists do not treat unsuccessful attempts to alter the Constitution's meaning any differently. That is, an attempt to alter the Constitution via changes to judicial doctrine is not deplorable and unconstitutional if it fails, but somehow laudable and constitutional if it succeeds. Living constitutionalists either regard the judicial oath as irrelevant (made so by practice) or suppose that its meaning was radically transformed sometime in the twentieth century. Apparently one can support, defend, and exhibit true faith and allegiance to the Constitution while informally amending it.

Similarly, one might say that in a regime where presidents enjoy the power to alter the Constitution via practice, they do no violence to the Constitution when they attempt to change it by transgressing the existing legal order. In other words, though it may seem to the untutored as if modern presidents are violating their oath when they alter the Constitution, we instead can regard them as exercising a *lawful* option to informally amend the Constitution via their transgressions. They are no more blameworthy than judges who usher in constitutional change.

Going further, one might say that just as practice has transformed much of the Constitution, so too has practice transformed the presidential oath. Practice has changed the presidential oath to such an extent that a crabbed focus on the text will unduly distract us from its modern import. In other words, those who endorse practice-based means of constitutional change might say that whatever the historical meaning of the presidential oath, times have changed—and given modern conventions and understandings, presidents do not violate it when they seek to amend the Constitution via transgressive practice or otherwise. Presidents may fail or succeed, but they no more violate the presidential oath than do members of Congress transgress their oath when they vote for legislation inconsistent with prevailing understandings of the Constitution, or than Supreme Court justices do when they add (or attempt to add) glosses to the Constitution.

In short, we might say we have a living presidential oath that ought to read something like: "I do solemnly swear to preserve, protect, and defend the Constitution, except that I may amend it through the transformative practice of serial transgressions, and I may support others who attempt to change it via other informal means."

THE POLITICS OF A LIVING PRESIDENCY

I do not assert that Americans have embraced the idea that an initial presidential transgression of the existing constitutional order is always legal. Far from it. We can be fairly sure that the incumbent's opponents will often be quick to denounce the initial act (and subsequent ones) as a constitutional violation. Does this routine denunciation mean that a living presidency is inconsistent with our existing constitutional order?

Not for a living constitutionalist. We see the same rhetoric when judges amend the Constitution; initially, such judicial moves are often denounced with little consequence for their eventual acceptance, however grudging or halting. Moreover, we must distinguish political rhetoric from the constitutionality of presidential acts that violate the existing constitutional order. Everyone recognizes that presidents can take actions that are fully constitutional but nonetheless confront unreasonable critics who will denounce those actions as unconstitutional. Similarly, from the perspective of a living presidentialist, executives who attempt to amend the Constitution via practice can expect severe, withering criticism. But such denunciations in no way signal that presidential attempts to amend the Constitution, via violations or otherwise, are somehow improper. Constitutional change, of whatever sort, will often raise the ire of some, particularly those who see themselves as the likely losers.

* * *

In some versions of Hindu cosmology, there is a trimurthi, a trinity that includes Brahma, the creator of the universe; Vishnu, the preserver and maintainer of it; and Shiva, its destroyer. Under the original Constitution, the president was meant to be the Constitution's

Vishnu, its preserver. The presidential oath, as originally understood, signaled that presidents could neither make new constitutional rules nor destroy the existing constitutional order.

Modern presidents are all three—Brahma, Vishnu, and Shiva. They are creators, preservers, and destroyers. They create new constitutional law via their practices and utterances; they strive to maintain cherished elements of the existing constitutional order; and they seek to destroy constitutional features that they disdain. They switch between these roles to suit their personal and policy interests. In adopting creative or destructive avatars, they help usher in significant informal amendments to our Constitution, particularly with respect to the expansion of executive power and the diminishment of Congress.

Given this revolution in presidential power, a living constitutionalist must be open to the possibility that practice has radically transformed the import of the presidential oath. First, we must consider the prospect that the living Constitution authorizes presidential transgressions of the existing constitutional order, at least when the president is trying to amend that order. In other words, seeming offenses against the Constitution may be wholly constitutional because we can so easily rationalize them as lawful attempts to exercise an unstated constitutional option available to every president: amending Article II (and the Constitution) by violating it. Second, we must consider whether the presidential oath has been transformed by practice. If the living Constitution authorizes presidents to amend (and help amend) the Constitution, perhaps we ought to reconceive of the presidential oath as a mutable, living oath, one that changes with the times and implicitly permits presidents to amend the Constitution via transformative violations.

This remarkable transformation in the oath was made possible, in part, by the rise of living constitutionalism, whose underlying ideology grants presidents and their enablers the license to acquire new powers, both constitutional and statutory. For an acquisitive presidency (which is the only kind we have had for more than a quarter century), living constitutionalism justifies continual increases in executive authority and signals that presidents do nothing wrong when they grasp for more. In fact, because presidents are among the leading proponents of constitutional change, grasping presidents are exemplars of living constitutionalism.

CHAPTER SIX

From FIRST GENERAL
to DECLARER *of* WARS

O ur commander in chief is a powerhouse. At beck and call are
more than a million of the world's finest warriors, an annual
military budget of almost 700 billion dollars, and earth's most
destructive and sophisticated weaponry.[1] Occupants of the Oval
Office, from Harry Truman on, have gone on a military acquisition spree, securing for presidents the authority to wage war where
and how they please. Meanwhile, Congress, though it retains ves-
tiges of its authority to declare and direct war, is but a faint
shadow of its 1789 version and poses little resistance to executive
usurpations.

In no other realm have the humbling of Congress and the aggrandizement of the presidency been as comprehensive. Parts of the
story are familiar. Others will be a revelation. As a people, we have
forgotten what it means to declare war and the scope of congressional power over wars. For instance, many imagine that if Congress
has not passed a formal declaration, it has not declared war. Likewise, many assume that commanders in chief simply must enjoy tremendous autonomy over the military or else they would not be
genuine *commanders*. These modern notions of the power to declare

war and of the commander in chief would astonish and dismay the Founders.

The Commander-in-Chief Clause has long mystified people. As Justice Robert Jackson noted in *Youngstown* more than fifty years ago, the clause has "given rise to some of the most persistent controversies in our constitutional history. Of course, [the clause's words] imply something more than an empty title. But just what authority goes with the name has plagued presidential advisers who would not waive or narrow it by nonassertion yet cannot say where it begins or ends."[2] Needless to say, we have a major problem if the president's legal advisers do not know where the commander in chief's power begins or ends. Jackson's observation was no ordinary critique. It was, in part, an admission that the clause baffled him. In his former life, Justice Jackson had been Franklin D. Roosevelt's attorney general. As one might expect, Attorney General Jackson had read the seemingly nebulous clause expansively in order to favor his superior.[3]

Justice Jackson made his veiled admission in a case about whether President Harry Truman could seize steel mills. The seizure was supposedly meant to ensure supplies for the Korean War. The president's lawyers insisted that the commander in chief could do whatever was needed to prevail in that war. But to Jackson, and to several other justices, this was sheer chutzpah. You see, Truman had unilaterally thrust the United States into a terrible land war. Using that constitutionally irregular decision as a shaky foundation, Truman further resolved to do whatever he thought necessary to triumph in his war, including seizing private property thousands of miles from Korean shores.[4] This was a particularly egregious form of legal bootstrapping.

Truman's unilateralism serves as a microcosm of the modern era. In fact, his actions did much to usher in our current predicament, which is marked by a marginalization of congressional authority and a mushrooming of presidential power. Though Truman lost the steel seizure battle and his war ended in a stalemate, his successors have largely won the battle over the conduct of warfare and the scope of the Commander-in-Chief Clause. In particular, modern presidents assert constitutional authority to wage war, a right to ignore legislative regulation of the military, and autonomy in the conduct of war. While presidents face a more difficult time invading civil liberties during wartime, they have little difficulty invading Congress's constitutional powers and ignoring Congress's laws.

This vision of unchecked presidential powers to start and wage wars has received a significant boost from the most unlikely of sources: Congress. Since the Korean War, the United States has been in a state of perpetual military readiness because Congress has funded an enormous standing army, along with a massive navy, air force, and marine corps. This permanent and highly potent military apparatus is at the beck and call of every president, ready to wage war at the president's discretion. While "[w]ar [may be] in fact the true nurse of executive aggrandizement," as James Madison warned, Congress is the true sustainer of wars that have aggrandized the presidency.[5]

Truman's theory of war powers represented a sharp break with the Founding. The original Constitution had installed a belt, suspenders, and rope approach, with almost everything in it designed to both empower Congress and enfeeble the unitary executive. First, war could be waged only after Congress sanctioned it by law. The Constitution provides that Congress enjoys the power "[t]o declare war."[6] This included the power to start a war, for to "declare war" was, among other things, to decide to wage it.[7] Moreover, the allocation of the declare-war power to Congress was universally understood to mean that presidents could not take the nation to war.

Second, under the original scheme, Congress had constitutional carte blanche over the armed forces, with the power to create, disband, and regulate almost every aspect of the military. Congress decided whether to have an army and a navy, the size of both, and where to station those forces. Relatedly, Congress could dictate the proper uses of the army, navy, and state militias, in peace and in war.[8]

Third, the commander in chief was subordinate to Congress. Though the president could command the army and navy, those directives had to conform to the standing laws. If Congress decreed that a militia could be stationed in one location, the president lacked the constitutional authority to deploy it elsewhere.[9] If Congress dictated that the navy could attack only certain enemy ships, those ships were the only lawful targets.[10] Commanders in chief were but the "first [meaning topmost] General and admiral," as Alexander Hamilton put it.[11] They certainly were not autonomous generalissimos because Congress could command the commander in chief.

Fourth, Congress had complete control over the Treasury and could draw the purse strings closed in order to halt a war or starve a military establishment that imperiled the government or civil liberties. Because many of the Framers thought a standing army posed a greater threat than a permanent navy, the Constitution expressly states that Congress cannot appropriate funds for the army beyond two years.[12]

Since Truman, presidents have remodeled the War Constitution. They have managed to all but expunge the Declare War Clause from Article I. Every copy of the Constitution still lists the clause, but it now has little consequence, in much the same way that after the Thirteenth Amendment emancipated millions of slaves, a clause about fugitive slaves no longer had any significance. Presidents have also grafted onto their office a parallel power to declare war. (Don't bother reading the Constitution to find out whether this is sanctioned—it's not.) And last, presidents have gradually acquired greater autonomy over the military, including the authority to disobey congressional laws related to the military and its use. In short, when it comes to waging war and control of the military, modern practices have layered such a thick, opaque gloss on the Constitution that one can barely make out its original features.

Origins

The Constitution's scheme had its origins in Great Britain. Formally, the Crown could declare war. But in the late eighteenth century, British monarchs would not declare war without first securing parliamentary approval. The reason was simple: money. Kings did not have enough to wage war successfully. Without considerable funds from Parliament, no war could be won.[13] Knowing this, no wars were begun without Parliament's consent.

In those days, the power to declare war was in part the authority to decide when and whether to wage it. When one nation attacked another, the assault was a declaration of war; it was the equivalent of a formal declaration.[14] Indeed, attacking another nation was the most common declaration of war. As one British prime minister put it, "of late most Wars have been declar'd from the Mouths of Cannons, before any formal Declaration."[15] Dozens of others, including Americans, concurred. During the Revolutionary War, for example, John Adams claimed that Britain had "sufficiently declared [war] by actual hostilities in most parts of the world."[16]

Why did countries use naval armadas or invasions to declare war? Because formal declarations often gave advance notice to the enemy and thus eliminated the element of surprise. If a nation could declare war by simply attacking, the enemy might be caught flat-footed. The rules of war had changed from earlier epochs in the sense that neither honor nor international law required a warning before shots were fired.

When nations actually issued formal declarations of war, these documents invariably encompassed much more than a decision to wage war. A formal declaration contained propaganda justifying the war, provided notice to domestic populaces and other nations about the advent of war, specified the rights of enemy resident aliens, commanded the use of military force, and dictated the goals of the conflict and possible terms for peace.[17] Conditional declarations of war would promise conflict unless an enemy satisfied certain demands.[18]

When Congress drafted the Articles of Confederation, it did so against this backdrop. Under the Articles, the Continental Congress could "determin[e] on . . . war," meaning it could decide to wage it.[19] Moreover, this Congress also controlled the purse. This essentially was the British system, if not in theory then in practice. Recall that the Crown never declared war without parliamentary approval. Arguably, the American system made more sense. The power to decide to wage war rested with the entity that also could decide how best to wage and fund it.

In that era, a commander in chief was nothing more than an officer who commanded a particular unit.[20] Each company had a commander in chief, as did each regiment.[21] Britain literally had thousands of commanders in chief, because it had so many different armies (for example, the British Indian Army and the British Army of North America) and because each of these armies had many subunits.[22] For good reason, no one thought that commanders could start wars or that they were autonomous, free from the chain of command or the direction of the reigning monarch or Parliament.[23]

Just as it adopted much else from Great Britain, America adopted this prevailing understanding of "commander in chief." During the Revolutionary War, America had multiple commanders in chief, one of whom was George Washington. Washington and all the other commanders in chief were subordinate to Congress. The Continental Congress's "sole and exclusive right and power of determining on . . . war" precluded any claim that mere commanders could declare war.[24] Moreover, Congress's sweeping power to create rules for the military made clear that it could direct its commanders. George Washington never claimed power to disobey Congress and carefully hewed to its grants of authority and their constraints. He was the servant of Congress in every way.

The delegates at the Philadelphia Convention largely recreated the system under the Articles. Rather than "determining on . . . war," Congress had the power to "declare war." But the two phrases were synonymous, with people at the time describing the Continental Congress as likewise having the power to "declare war" and claiming that there had been no alteration of the system.[25] As under the Articles, Congress enjoyed the authority "To make Rules for the Government and Regulation" of the armed forces, a clause that expressly granted a comprehensive power.[26] Finally, the Constitution granted Congress the power to raise, equip, and fund the army and the navy.[27]

There were two notable changes, however. First, the Constitution created a separate executive—the president—and made that person the "Commander in Chief."[28] Congress could no longer appoint the topmost commander and was stuck with the president, for good or ill. If Congress disapproved of the commander in chief's conduct, it could attempt to impeach and remove him, a difficult, if not impossible, task.

Second, the Constitution granted presidents a host of other powers. To begin with, they could veto legislation, meaning that if a commander in chief disapproved of Congress's military bills, whether they related to declaring war or otherwise, he could try to block their passage.[29] Congress might have to consider a president's preferences, if only to avoid a veto, which in many (if not most) cases it might be unable to override. In the right hands, the veto could yield the commander in chief leverage over Congress and the substance of federal law. Moreover, presidents could appoint individuals to military offices and could, using their executive power, remove incumbent officers.[30] This was far greater authority than commanders in chief had during the Revolutionary War, when Washington had been forced to serve with generals who actively sought his office. Given a president's other constitutional powers, the commander in chief was no longer merely a servant of Congress. Nor was he merely the "first General and admiral," despite what Hamilton said.[31] By virtue of the rest of Article II, the commander in chief was more.

The allocations to Congress were understood to be exclusive, despite the absence of any language indicating as much. The Constitution never says that presidents cannot declare war or raise and support the armed forces. Yet to grant Congress the powers to declare war and to raise and support the armed forces was to signal that no one else, including the commander in chief, could do the same.[32]

Lest you doubt my claims, consider what the founding generation said and did. They understood that Congress was supreme and that the commander in chief, though the leader of the armed forces, was in many ways subordinate to Congress. "It will not be in the power of a single man, or a single body of men, to involve us in [war], for the important power of declaring war is vested in the legislature at large," said James Wilson.[33] So neither the president nor a chamber of Congress could plunge us into war. Moreover, as others noticed, the process was tricameral: "The [Constitution] requires the joint consent of both branches of Congress together with [the] Concurrence of the [President] to declare war . . . and as war is not to be desired and always a great calamity, by increasing the Checks, the measure will be difficult."[34] Thomas Jefferson was absolutely right that vesting authority in Congress was an "effectual check to the Dog of war."[35] The war dog could neither bark nor bite without Congress (and likely the president) deciding on the matter.

These readings of the Constitution did not change with the advent of the new government and its first commander in chief. Alexander Hamilton, the foremost apostle of executive power, said, "the Legislature can alone declare war, can alone actually transfer the nation from a state of peace to a state of hostility."[36] The first secretary of state, Thomas Jefferson, noted to James Madison that the "Executive cannot decide the question of war."[37] Finally, consider the words of the Constitution's first commander in chief. Writing to a governor about a possible war with the Creek Nation, President

Washington said, "The Constitution vests the power of declaring War with Congress, therefore no offensive expedition of importance can be undertaken until after they shall have deliberated upon the subject, and authorized such a measure."[38] The three highest executive officers made an argument against interest—admitting that only Congress could "decide the question of war."

To some modern readers, these perspectives may seem astonishing. Didn't the first president (and his topmost advisers) want more power because of the innate "love of power" in the breast of all men?[39] Don't modern presidents routinely "decide the question of war" on their own? But we must remember that the modern reading of the Constitution was nowhere on the horizon. Absolutely no one from the founding generation said that presidents had the constitutional power to start a war. We also must bear in mind that everyone who spoke on the subject thought that Congress had a monopoly. Deciding to wage war was Congress's decision, to be made via the ordinary lawmaking process.

Some final clarifications about the declare-war power are necessary. First, the power to "declare war" has confounded far too many Americans. Congress exercises that power whenever it authorizes warfare of any sort. When Congress approves a minor land war or a large naval war, that is an exercise of the declare-war power just as much as a general declaration of war. Congress can exercise that awesome power whether or not it uses "declare," "war," or "declare war" in its law. There are no magic words that Congress must use to declare war.

When modern Americans discuss how many times Congress has declared war and respond either five (the War of 1812, the Mexican-American War, the Spanish-American War, World War I, and World War II) or eleven (the number of declared enemies in those wars), they fundamentally misunderstand what it means to "declare war," at least as the Constitution uses the phrase. Congress has declared war in far more than five wars and against dozens of countries. Over our nation's history Congress has authorized wars, large and small, against a host of American Indian and foreign nations. The famous Marines' Hymn, with its mention of "the shores of Tripoli," refers to a limited war that Congress declared in 1802, without using the phrase "declare war."[40]

Second, all Americans wars are necessarily declared. There is no such thing as undeclared war, at least if we use the constitutional definition. Every American war, from the eighteenth century onward, was declared either by Congress using a document or by the executive using the jarring informality of guns, cannons, and bombers.[41] Under the Constitution's functional reading of "declare war," the category of an undeclared war simply does not exist. A war started by the executive would be unconstitutional, precisely because the executive would have thereby declared it.

What about regulation of the military, during peace or war? Here too there was remarkable consensus. Congress could and did micromanage. It regulated army encampments, marches, and even drills.[42] Congress created a criminal code for the army—articles of war—regulating the conduct of soldiers in minute ways.[43] Finally, Congress controlled the conduct of war itself. It established the strategic objectives of warfare—regime change, protection of commerce, and independence.[44] It dictated the type of war—on land, on the sea, or both.[45] It decided where the battles could be fought—on the high seas or in American waters.[46] It specified the targets—every enemy asset, only vessels, or only armed vessels.[47] During the naval war with France at the end of the eighteenth century, we find all these limitations on the conduct of war. Congress defined the goals—a limited war with France. It defined the targets—French armed vessels. And it defined where they could be attacked—in American waters and the high seas, but not in French waters.[48] In short, Congress regulated the military and warfare, from A to Z.

No early commander in chief uttered a peep against this micromanagement. They understood that Congress had been given sweeping authority under the Declare War Clause and its related power to make "Rules for the Government and Regulation" of the military. In other words, presidents did not raise objections because there were none to raise. The idea that Congress could not dictate military matters simply did not occur to George Washington, a man who had served as commander in chief under the Articles of Confederation. Though Washington did veto a non-military bill on constitutional grounds, he did not object to any bills on the grounds that Congress was unconstitutionally meddling in military matters.[49]

The claim that Congress cannot micromanage also did not occur to his successor, John Adams. Adams signed the laws that controlled the naval war against France. Though Adams appointed Washington commander in chief of the army, the general never intimated that Congress had infringed on Adams's authority by directing the war.[50]

A commander in chief's ability to limit Congress's micromanagement of military matters arises not from the military office but from the veto pen wielded as president. When President Washington vetoed a military bill on policy grounds (one of only two vetoes during his two terms), he confirmed what was implicit in the Constitution, that presidents could act on their policy preferences, including on military matters.[51]

Transitions

The passage of time often blurs and distorts prevailing legal understandings. That is no less true for constitutions. So as years and decades passed after the Constitution's creation, its meaning gradually morphed and warped.

Early wars, for example, were invariably authorized by Congress; presidents never started any of them. Congress obliquely authorized the American Indian expeditions during the Washington years.[52] The Quasi-War with France was emphatically Congress's war, with Congress enacting many laws that authorized limited uses of force.[53]

When Thomas Jefferson wanted a war against Tripoli, he secured a war declaration from Congress.[54] In seeking to go to war against Great Britain and Algiers, James Madison procured two declarations of war from Congress, one with the magic words "declaring war" (albeit in the title) and one without any such phrase or an equivalent.[55]

The first substantial deviation from this pattern occurred during the Monroe administration, when General Andrew Jackson conducted a war in Spanish Florida against Seminole Indians and seized forts from the Spanish. The administration believed that it had congressional authority from Congress to fight the Seminoles but did not imagine that it had either congressional or constitutional authority to seize Spanish forts.[56] Contrary to express orders, Jackson seized two forts, and Monroe ordered Jackson to return them. The reason: the president (and therefore his general) lacked the authority to seize Spanish territory.[57] As Monroe put it, "By ordering the restitution of the posts [amiable relations between the United States and Spain] were preserved. To a change of [that amity] the power of the Executive is deemed incompetent; it is vested in Congress only."[58] This was a case of a general usurping Congress's power to war against Spain.

The next major constitutional misstep led to the Mexican-American War. President James K. Polk wanted America to stretch from sea to shining sea because that was her manifest destiny. Acquiring that vast expanse required a war with Mexico, and Polk precipitated one. The United States had absorbed the once independent Republic of Texas, but there remained a festering dispute about where Texas ended and Mexico began. Congress never took a stance on the Texas border, but Polk deployed American troops to disputed soil in order to trigger a Mexican attack.[59] He assumed that such an attack would lead to war, in the course of which the United States might seize what is now the Southwest. Polk got his war when a skirmish broke out between American and Mexican soldiers. At that point, Congress declared that a state of war existed "by the act" of Mexico.[60] Essentially, by provoking Mexico into a tussle, President Polk started a war that Congress did not want. Some legislators denounced Polk for violating the Constitution.[61] Congressman Abraham Lincoln introduced his "Spot Resolution," insisting that Congress had the right to know the exact spot where Polk had inserted troops, so as to determine whether the Mexican attack had occurred on American soil.[62]

The congressional vote to recognize a state of war was lopsided. Though Polk had his defenders, none claimed that he had the constitutional authority to march American troops onto Mexican soil. Likewise, while Polk had sparked a war, and in the minds of many had thereby acted unconstitutionally, he never actually claimed that he had the constitutional authority to wage war on his own whim. Rather, Polk set in motion events designed to suggest that he had merely defended American soil from Mexican incursions.

As discussed earlier, during the Civil War Lincoln began to invoke his authority as commander in chief in unprecedented ways. With the Southern states seceding and Washington, DC, sandwiched between two slave states, Lincoln faced the possibility that Southern forces might quickly envelop the nation's capital. Congress was not in session and Lincoln decided to act alone. He raised armies, expended funds, seized enemy property, and suspended the writ of habeas corpus, thereby authorizing indefinite detention without trial.[63] When Congress returned, he tried to justify his acts. He made two different arguments. First, he all but conceded that he had acted unconstitutionally insofar as he had usurped Congress's authority over the size of the army. Second, he argued that the president could suspend habeas corpus.[64] Congress ratified the army-related acts but for more than two years refrained from responding directly to the habeas corpus issue.[65] In 1863, it enacted a detailed habeas statute that the president and his administration ignored insofar as it required the release of detainees who were not indicted by a grand jury.[66] The Great Emancipator was focused on reuniting the nation and was unwilling to let constitutional scruples get in his way. He never justified his administration's failure to honor this law and others, presumably concluding that the less said the better. Regarding civil liberties, his essential position was that it was far better to violate them than to leave the nation permanently divided. Lincoln ranks among our greatest presidents because he kept the nation together. But no one should doubt that to do so, Honest Abe violated the Constitution's separation of powers.

Between the Founding and the Korean War, there were a number of transgressions involving extremely limited uses of force overseas. Many of these involved American commanders, typically naval officers.[67] In these incidents, the naval commanders acted alone, without authority either from Congress or the president, typically in order to rescue Americans, protect American property, or punish aggressors. As discussed later, these actions have served as a foundation for the modern argument that presidents may use military force against foreign nations. In fact, they are entirely irrelevant to that claim.

The Living Commander in Chief

On June 24, 1950, North Korea invaded South Korea with a massive force of one hundred thousand fighters. Caught totally unprepared, the South Koreans and a small US force reeled under the onslaught, abandoning the capital, Seoul, within days.[68] The United Nations weighed in, with a Security Council resolution demanding that the North withdraw.[69] When that proved insufficient, the Security Council issued another resolution asking member states to aid the South in repelling the North's attack.[70]

Harry S. Truman quickly decided to fight. At the time, Truman had the distinction of being the only person to serve as president during two major wars.[71] He served at the tail end of World War II, after the death of Franklin Roosevelt, and witnessed the surrender of all the enemies of the United States. In that war, Congress had declared war against six nations—Germany, Japan, Italy, Bulgaria, Hungary, and Romania. Each declaration occurred after the other nation had first declared war against the United States.[72] During World War II, then, the original scheme was functioning fairly well.

Less than ten years later, Truman concluded that he did not need Congress's approval for the Korean War. Congress would be informed, but nothing more. After authorizing the bombing of North Korea, the president declared, "We are not at war."[73] America had responded to a "bandit raid," and the use of force was a "police action."[74] He thereafter deployed two army divisions to counter the North's attack.[75] America would be in a land war in Asia, just five years after defeating the Japanese.

Some in Congress, including Senator Robert Taft of Ohio, denied that the president had the constitutional authority to wage war in Korea. Taft said the nation was "engaged in a de facto war" and if the president could wage war in Korea, he might equally wage war in "Malaya, or Indonesia, or Iran, or South America."[76] The president's actions were a "complete usurpation" of congressional power.[77] If Congress did nothing, it would thereby "terminat[e] for all time the right of Congress to declare war."[78] Taft was prophetic. But while a few others criticized Truman, most favored war and chose not to press constitutional objections. With Neville Chamberlain's Munich moment a recent memory and the nation gripped by anti-communism, few wished to do or say anything that intimated weakness or division. That would only embolden Kim Il Sung and his allies, Joseph Stalin and Mao Zedong.

Truman's grasp of the law seemed nonexistent. The former county judge appeared unfamiliar with the Constitution and its traditions. He easily could have received congressional approval and should have sought it. Yet he said approval was unnecessary. After all, he was commander in chief and "just had to act."[79] On another occasion, he said he "had not been acting as President, but as Commander-in-Chief."[80] Besides, he had intervened "for the United Nations."[81] Still, Truman must have been somewhat aware of the constitutional questions because he said he did not want to appear as if he had tried "to get around Congress and use extra-Constitutional powers."[82] Sometimes the guilty betray their culpability; he inadvertently described exactly what he was doing.

Truman's advisers took a similar, and similarly unfounded, approach. The State Department prepared a memo that argued that presidents could use force "without a declaration of war."[83] Although the document provided a list of examples, the State Department's assertion was a gigantic red herring, for the legal question is whether the president can wage war without congressional authorization, not whether presidents have waged war without Congress using the phrase "declare war." As discussed, Congress can exercise the declare-war power without using either word or the phrase. The State Department's very first example in its list supporting Truman, the military seizure of Amelia Island off Florida's coast during the Madison administration, was expressly authorized by Congress.[84] How this episode helped establish that presidents can use force unilaterally is a mystery. The second example was the 1814 incursion into Spanish Florida to "expel the British." But recall that Monroe regarded Andrew Jackson's seizure of Spanish forts as unconstitutional because the president saw it as an act of war that only Congress could have ordered.

Since Truman, the list has more than doubled, as executive branch advisers have tried to expand it by filling in conflicts missing from prior lists and as subsequent presidents have used force overseas without congressional authorization. In 1967, executive lawyers added the naval wars against France, Tripoli, and Algiers. But Congress *expressly authorized all three*. None of those congressional wars can possibly establish that presidents enjoy constitutional authority to wage war. Yet the 1967 report citing these examples claims that the president, acting "[o]n his own authority," has "full control over the use" of the armed forces and may commit them "to armed action to protect the national interest beyond the borders of the United States."[85]

Next time you see one of these lists, run away, for they are totally misbegotten, as Francis Wormuth and Edwin Firmage proved long ago.[86] Different versions were compiled for different reasons and concatenated as if they all related to the same question, thereby ignoring the caveats that their original authors had built into them. They are like some sort of bad, commander-in-chief chain novel. Moreover, as Arthur Schlesinger Jr. pointed out, many of these executive adventures were undertaken on the sole authority and responsibility of American naval officers on the scene, with no presidential involvement.[87] Absolutely no one believes that every ship captain should be able to wage war without congressional authorization; hence these examples have no place on any list arguing for greater executive leeway in waging war. Presidents and their legal advisers certainly do not defend the proposition that every military officer has some sort of constitutional right, ex officio, to bombard Canada or China.

Nonetheless, based on the strength of such episodes (and others), the Office of Legal Counsel (OLC) has opined repeatedly that the president may use extensive military force overseas, ranging from peacekeeping deployments in areas of conflict to actual ground hostilities. Some administrations have gone so far as to suggest that there are no limits to the president's powers to wage war. OLC opinions from the two Bush presidencies have this flavor. After all, the president has used force multiple times without congressional authorization. In contrast, other OLC opinions—those typically issued during Democratic administrations—hint at limits to what the president may do overseas. But these opinions never impose any hard limits. The OLC opinions naturally invite the question—what limits remain to the president's power to wage war?

Modern Tests for the Constitutionality of Presidential Wars

Very few limits, if any, remain, it would seem. Today, the OLC uses a two-part test to discern whether the president can order the use of force. First, the president must "reasonably determine" that force would serve "sufficiently important national interests."[88] Second, the "nature, scope, and duration" of the military operations must not constitute war, for only Congress can declare *war*.[89] This framework is so absurd that one hardly knows where to begin.

The first part poses no genuine limits. No president will ever use force overseas and admit that the interests served are personal (to, say, garner glory, bolster popularity, or distract from a scandal). No president will ever use force overseas and concede that the national interests are mere trifles. Every time presidents use military force they can plausibly claim that they are acting in the vital national interests of the United States. After all, the category of "important national interests" is extremely broad. According to the OLC, it includes protecting Americans and their property, stabilizing a region of the world, supporting the United Nations, assisting an ally, mitigating humanitarian disasters, and protecting American military forces.[90] Moreover, the test is not whether the deployment of forces actually serves "important national interests" but whether the president can "reasonably believe" that it does. When will mere lawyers ever tell a president that his or her beliefs regarding the needfulness of military action are unreasonable? One wonders why the OLC bothers with the first part of the test. A cynic might conclude that it is meant to offer the illusion of constraint.

The second part seems to constrain—the president cannot exercise Congress's power to declare war. Or, in other words, only Congress may authorize true war, with the president able to authorize those uses of force less than war. But like the first part, this second part is all bark and no bite.

To begin with, what is "war"? War is not what the Founders regarded as war. In the eighteenth century, even limited uses of force constituted war. Nor is war under the OLC's test what ordinary people today regard as war. President Obama's military adventure in Libya was a war in the conventional sense, involving as it did a massive naval and aerial campaign. America repeatedly bombed Libya, with thousands of sorties. There were also CIA forces on the ground, assisting the rebels and targeting Libyan forces. But apparently the Libyan war was not "war" under the Constitution.[91]

Instead, "war" in the OLC's reading of the Declare War Clause is defined in an incredibly abnormal way. In OLC opinions, "war" encompasses those uses of force that presidents have not yet acquired by practice. To use a mathematical term, "war" is the "remainder." Whatever uses of military force that presidents have not yet employed are left to Congress under the Declare War Clause. Concretely, this means that when considering "nature, scope, and duration," the OLC assumes that whatever presidents have done in the past is not "war." Because President Reagan invaded Grenada and took control of the island, that cannot be war. Because George H. W. Bush invaded Panama to oust Manuel Noriega, that cannot be war. Because President Clinton bombed Kosovo and stationed thousands of troops in Bosnia, neither of those uses of force are war. And because President Obama bombed Libya, that cannot be war.

The OLC takes great pains to insist that the deployment of ground troops may be different. And it might seem so, at least at first glance. When troops are on the ground, casualties may seem inevitable, withdrawal may prove more difficult, and escalation may seem more likely. And yet the OLC approved President Clinton's Bosnia deployment of twenty thousand ground troops in hostile circumstances, where combat had already occurred and was thought likely to continue.[92]

It is difficult to take the OLC's discussion of ground troops seriously. If practice is the yardstick, then the presence of ground troops actually seems irrelevant. The OLC apparently has never encountered a deployment of ground troops that it regarded as unconstitutional. It has never told a president, at least not in a public opinion, not to conduct a ground war because doing so would usurp Congress's power to declare war. Indeed, there are OLC opinions that rather clearly suggest there are no limits to the use of ground forces. For instance, in 2001 the OLC opined that George W. Bush could use military force without any congressional authorization.[93]

More importantly, the OLC evidently believes that the Korean War was constitutional. After all, it has cited the Korean War as helping to demonstrate that presidents can use force without congressional authorization.[94] If Truman's war was unconstitutionally initiated under the OLC's framework because it involved ground troops, then the OLC should say as much and stop citing it. But in fact, there is little or no chance that the OLC could regard that war as unconstitutionally commenced. If practice amends the Constitution, as the OLC insists, then the very fact of America's participation in the Korean War makes presidential initiation of a similar war constitutional. The OLC would be hard-pressed to simultaneously insist on the utility of practice and then renounce or denounce the most famous presidential practice of unilateral war-making.

If the Korean War is constitutional, as the OLC supposes, what war wouldn't be? Korea was a brutal and massive land war; no one calls it a "police action" anymore, except with a snort. It was a world war, at least if we look at the combatants. More than two and a half million troops participated, with massive contingents from the United States, South Korea, North Korea, and China, and sizable ones from Australia, New Zealand, Canada, and Turkey.[95] Millions died.[96] More than thirty-six thousand Americans died and over ninety-two thousand were wounded.[97]

Is there a constitutionally significant difference between the actual Korean War Truman fought and a hypothetical second Korean War, one where a president uses three million troops and nuclear weapons? While there likely would be a difference in sorts of weapons and total casualties, one wonders why these differences are relevant for deciding how practice has amended the Constitution. Why can't the relevant category be the "use of force overseas" by the president? If so, it would seem that modern presidents can insert troops anywhere they desire because earlier presidents have waged war dozens of times. Further, we might well say that because presidents have used all sorts of weapons in a host of wars, presidents can use any kind of force, including nuclear weapons.

This discussion merely reveals how the practice of looking at practice and drawing lessons is extremely artificial and subjective. When we decide what the president can do by reference to practice in the war powers area, what are we supposed to be counting? Is it any use of force? Is it only uses of force overseas? The use of massive force overseas? The use of massive force overseas without a declaration of war? The use of massive force overseas without congressional authorization? The use of massive force overseas with few expected casualties? The use of massive force overseas for short periods of time? There is no neutral way of describing practice. Nor is there a disinterested means of gathering and categorizing prior incidents and deciding which ones matter. Because of the inescapable subjectivity of the inquiry, the answers generated often reflect the desires of those asking the question.

Counterfactually, even if the OLC belatedly and unexpectedly condemned the Korean War as unconstitutional, its analyses are built on dynamic categories whose contents shift over time. Hence whatever remains of the Declare War Clause—whatever little bit remains exclusively with Congress—may still yet be acquired by presidents over time. If presidents routinely fight large ground wars on their own initiative, eventually a president's use of five million troops to wage war will not be war. Likewise, the repeated use of nuclear weapons by presidents would amend the Declare War Clause.

One last point about the misbegotten practice of relying on practice. Recall that Justice Felix Frankfurter's opinion declared that practice could add a gloss to the Constitution if there was a "systematical practice . . . never before questioned." Though many of the commonly cited executive uses of force triggered significant congressional and public dissent, those voices are wholly neglected in OLC opinions. This OLC approach reveals what should be obvious by now: attempts to lay down rules about when and how practice matters are hopeless. After all, subsequent practice has wholly superseded Frankfurter's argument that opposition matters. This evolution should not be surprising. Any test that specifies when and how practice amends the Constitution contains its own seeds of destruction as the practice departs from the initial test.

In sum, the OLC's opinions and its two-part test for presidential war powers are alarming. The first part seems designed to provide the illusion of restraint. And the second part never seems to limit what presidents actually do. While the use of ground troops might generate hand wringing, the Korean War demonstrates that the deployment of hundreds of thousands of ground troops is now constitutional. Essentially, executive branch lawyers know where the presidential war power begins—the president can order all sorts of warfare. But to borrow from Justice Robert Jackson, they will not "say where it . . . ends."[98] Moreover, even if the OLC regards certain presidential wars as unconstitutional, that conclusion has to be regarded as potentially ephemeral. Since the OLC opinions do not erect any enduring limit on presidential war powers, they make it possible to wholly sidestep the Declare War Clause. The conceivable glosses on the executive's power to wage war—the potential embellishments to a power never given in the Constitution but only acquired by presidential transgressions—are truly limitless.

So-Called Undeclared Wars

After the Korean War, there was some movement back to the original scheme of Congress being in charge of war. For instance, President Dwight D. Eisenhower declared that "there is going to be no involvement of America in war [in Southeast Asia] unless it is a result of the constitutional process that is placed upon Congress to declare it."[99] Yet he sent hundreds of American advisers to train South Vietnamese troops, a tactic that his successors would sharply escalate.[100] John F. Kennedy inserted thousands, and Lyndon B. Johnson, eager to use military force against North Vietnam, sent more.[101] After the North Vietnamese supposedly fired upon two American vessels, Congress passed the Gulf of Tonkin Resolution, which neither "declared war" nor commanded the use of force. It merely authorized an attack on North Vietnam and a defense of Southeast Asia.[102]

Later, many condemned Congress for not "declaring war" against North Vietnam. The absence of a formal declaration supposedly made the conflict unconstitutional. Anti-war candidate Eugene McCarthy lamented, "We don't declare war anymore, we declare national defense."[103] Decades later, similar complaints were lodged against the 2001 and 2002 Authorizations for Use of Military Force (AUMF). Congress should have "declared war" against the Taliban, al-Qaeda, and Iraq, and its failure to do so signaled a constitutional failing. For many, the system was malfunctioning. Though the United States had fought many wars since World War II, it had not formally declared war since that war.

These particular critiques were (and are) without merit. First, as noted earlier, because of the way the Constitution uses "declare war," an undeclared war is, by definition, impossible. All "wars" between nation-states are declared wars. Sometimes Congress declares them according to the constitutional process, via a bill presented to the president that eventually becomes law. Alternatively, presidents sometimes unilaterally, and unconstitutionally, declare war by attacking another nation. So, for example, the Korean War was declared by President Truman rather than Congress. Second, as noted earlier, Congress can exercise its declare-war power whether or not it uses any particular phrase. The fixation on certain words is not only pointless but also counterproductive because it draws attention away from real issues. Finally, the two Iraq Wars, and the war against al-Qaeda, were constitutional successes. In each case, Congress decided to authorize military force. Many disagree with some of these decisions and many regard these wars as failures. But at least in each case, Congress flexed its authority. For this observance of the original scheme, those Congresses should be praised, not panned.

Authorizing Existing Wars

Sometimes the president wages war and then seeks congressional authorization after the fact. Take, for example, the Mexican-American War, when Polk marched American troops into disputed territory in order to precipitate a war. He got his war and then got his declaration from Congress. Kosovo is a more modern example. After President Clinton bombed Kosovo for three weeks, he received from Congress billions of dollars for "ongoing contingency operations" there.[104]

In the Mexican-American War, Congress was quite explicit in its after-the-fact approval—it issued a declaration acknowledging that a state of war existed. For Kosovo, Congress's appropriation was the sanction. This was a tad ambiguous, to be sure. But if you grant billions for "contingency operations" in an ongoing war, you have approved it, at least for the duration of the appropriation. As far back as the Founding, it was understood that if you appropriated money for a war, you had exercised the power to declare war.

These after-the-fact approvals are far from ideal. According to the original constitutional scheme, presidents are supposed to go to

Congress first and ask for authority rather than making congressional leaders react to the president's military moves. When placed in this awkward situation, Congress often will find it impossible to say "no" to the president because the nation is already at war and short-term political considerations may demand unwavering support for our fighting troops. This "rally around the flag" effect is often very strong, for no one wants to be accused of callous or unpatriotic indifference to soldiers on a battlefield.

When modern presidents start a war and quickly seek congressional approval, they are often attempting to exploit Congress's temporary weakness to further executive goals. As Jide Nzelibe notes, recent presidents have sometimes gone to Congress in order to share the political risk. If the war goes poorly, Congress will share some of the blame because, after all, its members sanctioned it. This may be ideal for the president because he creates the war and then offloads some of the fallout on his rival.[105]

The most recent example of a president starting a (newish) war and then seeking congressional approval is the intermittent war against the Islamic State of Iraq and Syria (ISIS). In 2014, the Obama administration attacked ISIS. Initially, executive officials seemed confused about the source of authority for this attack. Some cited the Constitution, presumably relying on practice. After all, in 2011 the president had commanded the military to wage war on Libya, a conflict that Congress did not sanction at the outset. Others cited the 2001 AUMF, on the theory that ISIS was but a branch of al-Qaeda. And still others pointed to the 2002 Iraqi AUMF, on the notion that since ISIS was in Iraq, the Iraqi AUMF authorized attacks against ISIS.[106]

Despite these numerous sources of legal authority, any one of which was sufficient, Obama asked Congress for a new authorization to cover ISIS. The new authorization would empower the executive to wage war, with two important caveats. First, there could be no "enduring offensive ground combat operations." And second, the proposed AUMF for ISIS came with an expiration date of three years.[107]

Years later, the war against ISIS endures and Congress has done nothing with this or any other proposed "ISIS AUMF." Presumably some legislators want to duck the issue. But more than a few must have been utterly perplexed and dismayed by the Obama administration's proposal. President Obama sought new legal authority to fight ISIS at a time when his lawyers were insisting that he already had legal authority to fight ISIS. Moreover, the proposal's limits were meaningless because they did not constrain the president's preexisting legal authority, the authority he already was relying on to fight ISIS. Even if the proposed AUMF did not itself authorize "enduring offensive ground combat operations," it also did not bar using prior AUMFs and the Constitution itself to order such operations. In other words, even if Congress had enacted the proposed ISIS AUMF, either Obama or a future president could have ordered the military to engage in enduring offensive ground operations. The same point is true for the three-year limit. The administration claimed authority to wage war against ISIS under other authorities that had no time limit, making this three-year cap absolutely meaningless. Had the ISIS AUMF passed, future presidents could fight ISIS for centuries using their other constitutional and statutory powers.

The Obama administration's attempt to secure a redundant and meaningless ISIS AUMF marked a low point. If presidents believe they lack legal authority, they should go to Congress *before* they start a war. But if they believe they already have the legal authority to wage war, they should not draft an empty war resolution, full of faux constraints, whose only effect is to have Congress opine on the wisdom of the fight. People are cynical enough about war powers without presidents pushing pointless, nonbinding resolutions masquerading as binding laws.

Regulating the Commander in Chief

If practice can put a gloss on executive power and grant the president a concurrent power to declare war, it can put a gloss on the Commander-in-Chief Clause as well. And it has, at least if we look at modern conceptions of the commander in chief. As noted earlier, early Congresses micromanaged the military and its topmost commander. They regulated the military's march, its camps, and its stationing. They regulated whom the armed forces could attack and where they could attack. They created a series of rules and regulations to discipline the armed forces and provided punishments for their violation.

Where we once had original clarity, we now have an unstable muddle. Congress continues to regulate the armed forces in a whole host of ways, likely because the Constitution expressly states that Congress can make "rules for the[ir] government and regulation." Nonetheless there are many legislators who deny, in particular circumstances, Congress's ability to regulate military operations. Typically, these denials tend to dovetail with policy objections to the congressional regulation at issue.

Not surprisingly, presidents and their advisers tend to agree with these congressional dissenters. Their theory, stated in its broadest terms, is that the president is not commander in chief if someone else can tell the armed forces what they can and cannot do. Or, put another way, if Congress can direct the military, we have 535 commanders in chief instead of one. But as we have seen, this theory is radically inconsistent with early understandings and practice. Furthermore, presidents and their advisers don't really believe the modern theory. In particular they are rather unwilling to say that any congressional regulation is an unconstitutional encroachment on the commander in chief because such a claim would sweep away too much standing law.

Instead, the modern theory typically relies on a seemingly narrower formulation: the president has the exclusive authority to direct military operations. Describing the commander in chief's authority in this way may make it seem more plausible, sound, and practical. No one wants Congress to decide whether to capture a hill or fire a warning shot across a vessel's bow. But this narrow formulation lacks a limiting principle and cannot separate permissible congressional regulation from impermissible intrusion. A law that makes it a crime to desert a post *is* a rule directing military operations. A law about consorting with the enemy likewise regulates military operations. Almost every congressional law relating to the military is a rule regulating military operations, either directly or indirectly.

This muddle plays out in OLC opinions. During the Clinton administration, Congress tried to bar the use of federal funds if American troops were placed under the command of UN personnel. The OLC claimed it was "for the President alone, as Commander-in-Chief, to make the choice of the particular personnel who are to exercise operational and tactical command functions over the U.S. Armed Forces."[108] Hence the proposal was unconstitutional because it tried to wrest that choice away from the president. This was a stunning claim. The original Constitution most certainly does not provide that the president decides who will assume operational and tactical command of segments of the military. Congress, not the president, creates military offices, and the Senate has a check, in the form of the Appointments Clause, over who occupies these offices. Moreover, the phrase "commander in chief" certainly does not imply anything about choosing personnel. During the Revolutionary War, the army's commander in chief, George Washington, had to serve with many whom Congress had appointed.

These sorts of disputes about the Commander-in-Chief Clause were on a very low simmer for decades. During George W. Bush's presidency, they flared spectacularly. After the 9/11 attacks, officials thought that coercive interrogation might be necessary to prevent future attacks. Critics cried "torture" and insisted that such suffering was not only unnecessary and immoral, but illegal to boot. After all, Congress had banned the use of torture, via a law implementing international law obligations against torture.

My friend John Yoo wrote an opinion for the Office of Legal Counsel claiming that Congress could not regulate the executive's treatment of enemy prisoners.[109] In part he relied on the Clinton OLC legal opinion that denied that Congress could regulate the commander in chief's placement of troops under foreign command. If Congress could regulate the treatment of prisoners, it could regulate whether the president could order a battlefield retreat or advance, the opinion argued. Because the latter must surely be unconstitutional, it followed that Congress could not regulate the treatment of prisoners.

When the memo was made public, legal scholars savaged Yoo. Many despised the Bush detention and interrogation policies and claimed that of course Congress could regulate the treatment of prisoners. Yoo's claims to the contrary, they argued, were utterly wrong. In fact, they were downright scandalous. According to these academics, the opinions constituted a form of malpractice that should result in disbarment.[110]

When running for president, Senator Obama also said that the president had to abide by statutes regulating the military.[111] But when he reached the Oval Office, he too found it convenient to deny that Congress could regulate certain aspects of the military. Acting contrary to several laws, his administration released five Afghani members of the Taliban from Guantanamo Bay in return for the American deserter Bowe Bergdahl. One of the reasons given for failing to abide by the laws was that Congress could not tell the commander in chief that he had to wait thirty days before releasing prisoners from Guantanamo.[112] Neither the president nor his lawyers explained why Congress could bar torture but could not make presidents wait thirty days before releasing enemy prisoners. Republicans disparaged the executive's argument, saying that the president had violated the law and paying no heed to the claim that the commander in chief couldn't be told how to detain prisoners.[113]

These legal disputes were heavily influenced by politics. Democrats and liberals would have lionized Yoo had he written a memo insisting that Congress could not force presidents to mistreat, torture, or execute prisoners. In that world, Yoo would have made the exact same argument but in service of a progressive agenda. And Republicans and conservatives might have defended a Democratic president's steadfast refusal to release dangerous prisoners of war in defiance of a congressional law mandating their release.

But muddled partisan disputes are about all we can expect under the living presidency approach to the Commander-in-Chief Clause. We've seen how such arguments played out in the past two administrations. It was hardly edifying. When presidents disliked certain military restraints, they (and their lawyers) trotted out the Commander-in-Chief Clause, an argument that rests, at bottom, on the idea that the import of the clause can change with the times. Each time the argument did nothing but serve the president's immediate policy ends. Neither administration took its claims to their logical stopping point, namely that Congress simply cannot regulate the armed forces because if it could, the president would not really be the commander in chief.

From an originalist perspective, one not influenced by modern politics or ethical considerations, the answers are clear. Congress has long regulated the treatment of enemy prisoners. During the Revolutionary War, though Congress generally required that prisoners be well treated, it also demanded that its commander in chief mistreat them as a way of deterring British abuses. In particular, it commanded George Washington to abuse British prisoners whenever the British victimized American prisoners, going so far as requiring executions.[114] This system was reinstated under the Constitution. Congress wanted to ensure that foreign prisoners were mistreated if Americans were abused. It was *lex talionis* (the law of retaliation) and Congress "required" retaliation against prisoners of war, notwithstanding any tender feelings that the commander in chief might have.[115]

If Congress can require torture and execution, it can require that neither occur. And if Congress can require torture and execution, it can require that the president provide thirty days' notice prior to releasing foreign prisoners. As a matter of domestic constitutional law, Congress could force the president to release—or keep—all prisoners of war. Other than the Bill of Rights and implicit constraints on legislative power, there are no restrictions on how Congress can decide to treat foreign prisoners of war.

Are there any separation-of-power limits on Congress's authority over the military? Absolutely. Congress could not create an independent general or admiral because the Commander-in-Chief Clause implicitly forbids a command structure in which some members of the military are not subordinate to the president. Similarly, Congress cannot replace the Constitution's commander in chief with someone of its own choosing. Beyond these important constitutional constraints, however, the limits on congressional power over the military are grounded solely in process and politics.

First, to regulate the military, both chambers have to pass the exact same bill. Then their bill goes to the president, who may veto it for any reason. To override the veto, Congress has to intensely disagree with the president, because two-thirds of both chambers must vote to override it. This degree of disagreement is quite rare. The long and short of it is that if presidents do not like a new congressional regulation of the military, they can thwart it. A second constraint is political and practical. Legislators are smart enough to appreciate that inflexible standing laws may be too constraining. Congress is never going to regulate the taking of a hill or whether a particular port should be bombarded, because it recognizes that this level of direction is foolish.

War Powers Act: Partial Failure or Partial Success?

We've seen that the Constitution was meant to vest Congress with the power to start wars. In 1973, Congress thought so too. That year, Congress enacted the War Powers Act, over Richard Nixon's veto.[116] The act announced Congress's determination that the president could use force in only two situations: when Congress authorized force (via a declaration or otherwise), and in the event of an attack on the United States, its territories, or its armed forces. The act also provided that unless Congress authorized the use of force, presidents had to withdraw troops from hostilities within ninety days.

Has the War Powers Act solved the problem of presidential wars? Many think not. They note that since its passage almost fifty years ago, presidents have repeatedly—more than a dozen times—used force and introduced troops into hostile situations.[117]

Even when presidents admit that the act applies, they have dodged its restrictions. For instance, in 2011 President Obama claimed that despite the massive bombing of Libya and the killing of thousands, the US armed forces were not involved in hostilities because our forces faced little risk of death or capture.[118] (In other words, our troops were not involved in hostilities but were merely committing them.) This meant that there was no need to withdraw American forces from Libya after sixty or ninety days. This strained argument was pressed into service because while President Obama wanted the Libyan war to continue, Congress would not sanction the conflict. Since Obama did not wish to claim that the War Powers Act was unconstitutional, the only option left was to make the risible claim that while US armed forces were destroying Libya's forces, they were not engaged "in hostilities."

We must not allow the quest for perfection to be the enemy of the good. One question, to which there can be no precise answer, is whether the War Powers Act has tempered the willingness of presidents to use force. Would there have many more presidential uses of force without it? And did the act shorten military adventures because presidents are reluctant to exceed its ninety-day limit?

In my view, the War Powers Act has been somewhat effective. For instance, some presidents have sought congressional authority to stay beyond the ninety-day limit because they wished to remain within the act's strictures.[119] That counts as a success. In the case of Libya, I believe that President Obama fully expected that the war would be a quick affair. He resorted to legal legerdemain only when the war dragged on and he realized that he would not receive congressional approval for his war.

This is all to say that the War Powers Act has not worked perfectly—few laws do. But we do not judge laws prohibiting murder by whether they deter all murders. Likewise, we shouldn't judge the War Powers Act by reference to an unrealistic standard of complete deterrence of executive wars.

The Power to Defund War

In the original system, Congress controls the war on the front end through its power to declare war. It also may direct the war as it progresses, deciding the targets and the theaters, as Congress did during the naval war with France. But Congress has yet another lever: like the British Parliament, it can cut off funds. The Constitution implicitly recognized this option when it limited army appropriations to two years.

The original scheme for funding and defunding wars, however, like so much else, is in some disarray. Hand-in-hand with the growth of presidential war powers has arisen a willingness to concoct restraints on Congress's ability to defund wars. Some advocates of broad executive authority claim that Congress cannot merely reduce funding. Instead, Congress must either fund the entire war or defund it entirely.[120]

This assertion rests on the belief that presidents have a constitutional right to start and fight wars and that an ability to partially defund a war would conflict with this right. But as we have seen, the original scheme did not grant the president exclusive authority over operations, in times of war or otherwise. Congress directed military operations quite often and in great detail. Moreover, this hairsplitting about the penumbras of the modern version of the commander in chief further diminishes the power of Congress. If, as a matter of constitutional law, Congress simply must fund executive wars, then Congress no longer has the purse. The president has it, at least in part.

If this claim ultimately succeeds and becomes a regular feature of conventional constitutional thinking, a portion of Congress's authority over public funds will be destroyed, a casualty of the president's ever-burgeoning authority as commander in chief.

Implied Authority to Wage War

Presidents derive their legal authority from two sources: the Constitution, and the laws of Congress. When Congress (re)created an army in 1789, it did not specify every use of it. For instance, it never claimed that the army could be used for only five purposes. Even if it had, there might have been implied authority to use the army. For instance, the creation of any army certainly includes authorization for using it to defend against invasion. Just as firefighters do not need a specific text instructing them to fight fires, soldiers don't need precise authorization to defend their nation.

Of course, one can take the implied authority argument too far. I don't believe that the creation and maintenance of an army, without more, implicitly authorizes the president to wage war against other nations. Even a mammoth standing army, one superbly equipped, does not imply an authority to wage war at will. There are too many indications that members of Congress do not regard military laws and the massive funding of the military as an implicit license to wage war.

The more general point is that in questioning whether some presidential military action is legal, we must consider the possible constitutional and statutory bases for that action. Even if presidents lack constitutional authority to start wars, when statutes cede the authority to use the military against foreign nations, presidential wars are legal. In thinking about what it is authorizing (and not authorizing) by way of military force, Congress must bear in mind the web of laws that exists and how presidents are likely to construe them. Given the current context, where presidents declare war on their own say-so, it might be wise for Congress to make crystal clear that neither standing laws nor its annual (and massive) military appropriations constitute implied authority to wage war.

* * *

Modern presidents have more raw war power than George III ever had. The executive's asserted constitutional power to start wars fully equals that monarch's legal power to declare them. Moreover, modern executives have a colossal standing military force and an iron-clad expectation of receiving annual appropriations to pay and outfit it. The weapons at the disposal of every modern president make the military might of the eighteenth-century British monarchy seem paltry by comparison.

The president's military power comes from two informal amendments to the War Constitution. The first is what we might call the Declare War Amendment. Before this informal amendment became part of our Constitution, the nation could wage war only after Congress, by law, authorized it. By contrast, modern presidents enjoy a concurrent power to declare war, one acquired through practice. To be sure, presidents may go to Congress when approval is certain and they wish to share the credit or blame. But often they will not request approval because they don't suppose they need it to wage war.

Second is what we might call the Commander-in-Chief Amendment. Whereas early commanders in chief were legally subordinate to the laws of Congress, as they had been under the Articles of Confederation, modern commanders in chief occasionally assert that Congress cannot limit the president's command of the armed forces. The argument is beguilingly simple. "I cannot be commander in chief if you can command my armed forces, or me." This informal amendment is a work in progress, in the sense that even as presidents and their advisers cite it to ignore certain congressional laws, they have not fully internalized the argument or taken it to its logical extreme. If this argument ultimately prevails, hundreds of existing laws will become unconstitutional. No president has yet been willing to say this.

Further informal amendments may be in the offing. For instance, when Congress attempts to curb wartime spending, presidents sometimes choose to ignore the restraint and expend funds without an appropriation. President Obama did this with the prisoner swap for American prisoner Bowe Bergdahl. Though Congress had barred the use of funds to transfer Guantanamo prisoners without thirty days' notice, the military ignored the separate spending restriction. This tactic of disregarding spending restraints is particularly easy whenever war funding is phrased as a limit—no money shall be spent on some act or acts. More troublesome will be situations where Congress funds a war with $100 billion but the president believes that $150 billion is absolutely necessary to wage it successfully. Will presidents withdraw the extra funds despite the absence of an appropriation for the extra $50 billion? This may seem a bridge too far given that the Constitution expressly bars withdrawing money from the Treasury without a law authorizing the drawdown. But if presidents can amend the parts of the Constitution concerning war powers, there is no reason to suppose that the parts related to appropriations must be left undisturbed.

Though President Truman succeeded in starting a war on his own say-so and thereby helped transform the War Constitution, he was rather disturbed by what his acts portended for the future. He admitted, "I sit and shiver . . . at the thought of what could happen with some demagogue in this office I hold."[121] And now, so do the rest of us.

CHAPTER SEVEN

From CHIEF DIPLOMAT *to* SOLE MASTER *of* FOREIGN AFFAIRS

The Constitution appears to say surprisingly little about presidents and foreign affairs. Presidents must receive foreign diplomats, may appoint America's overseas envoys, and may make treaties. In appointing diplomats and making treaties, presidents must first secure the Senate's consent. In the case of treaties—major contracts with other nations—the president must secure the concurrence of two-thirds of the senators present, a high hurdle. That's all the Constitution specifically says about the president's role. In contrast, the Founders assigned Congress a number of roles: it can regulate foreign and American Indian commerce, define and punish violations of the "law of nations," and, of course, declare war. Further, they granted Congress a number of lesser powers that bear on foreign relations, such as the power to regulate wartime captures. If we regard the relative strength of the branches as roughly proportional to their seeming prominence in the Constitution, we might well conclude that presidents were meant to be feeble in foreign affairs, while Congress was supposed to dominate.

But at the Founding, no one read the Constitution this way. From the beginning, the first president and Congress read Article II's

Vesting Clause, which grants "executive power," as conferring additional foreign affairs powers. Specifically, the "executive power" encompassed all those foreign affairs powers not otherwise granted to Congress or constrained by the Senate. Among other things, presidents would serve as an organ of communication with foreign nations. They could direct and remove America's diplomats. They could dismiss foreign diplomats stationed in the United States. They could make minor international agreements (those less significant than treaties).[1]

The Founders basically split the executive power over foreign affairs. They left questions of war and foreign commerce to a plural body, Congress. On these matters, Congress would continue to act as a plural executive, subject to the president's veto. Further, the Founders checked the ability to pledge the honor of the United States internationally by requiring that presidents secure a supermajority in the Senate before making treaties. Additionally, presidents would need Senate support for the long-term appointment of ambassadors. The rest of the executive power over foreign affairs—the least significant parts—was left to the president to exercise alone.

In the twentieth century, presidents began to unravel the allocations to Congress and circumvent the Senate's checks. The biggest transformation in foreign affairs, discussed earlier, is the informal Declare War Amendment, whereby the president went from being an important player in discussions about war to the sole decider, a unilateral war declarer. But there have been other informal amendments as well. This chapter focuses on three sorts of amendments. First is the modern presidency's power to make treaties without securing the consent of two-thirds of the Senate. Today's Treaty Clause is but a shell of its former self, with only marginal relevance. Second is the executive's proclivity to ignore laws that constrain its ability to conduct diplomacy as it sees fit. In particular, presidents trumpet a sweeping, nebulous foreign-affairs power in order to ignore inconvenient or undesirable laws. Third is the presidency's encroachment on congressional prerogatives, where presidents have seized legislative authority that properly rests with Congress. The executive justifies these actions by asserting an ill-defined power over international matters; by exploiting a widespread sense that presidents are (and ought to be) in charge of foreign affairs; and by leveraging a common conviction that a parochial Congress is unfit to play a major role in this arena.

Origins

Before adoption of the Constitution, the Continental Congress wielded the executive power over foreign affairs.[2] This meant that the job of conducting foreign affairs—war powers, treaty-making, diplomacy—was entrusted to one institution, albeit one with many members and, therefore, many voices. The situation was far from ideal because delegates to that Congress served short terms, were absent for months, and were distracted by other duties. The result was foreign relations by a distracted and absent horde of amateurs.

Attempting to ameliorate this problem, Congress in 1781 created a full-time minister, the secretary of foreign affairs, who would handle day-to-day matters as a devoted agent of Congress.[3] Even with a dutiful secretary, however, Congress was still inattentive and incompetent, and suffered all the drawbacks of plural leadership. The second secretary, John Jay, complained that Congress was not fit to steward foreign affairs. "The executive Business of Sovereignty depending on so many Wills, and those wills moved by such a Variety of Contradictory motives and Enducements, will in general be but feebly done."[4]

The Constitution adopted a more complicated structure, essentially constructing three executives. The new Congress would be a plural executive with respect to war, just as its predecessor was. Similarly, Congress was charged with regulating foreign commerce. On these two matters, the president would be the agent of Congress, in much the way that John Jay had been. There was, however, one major difference. The president who was an agent when it came to executing wars and foreign commerce laws also would serve as a check on Congress's exercise of both powers. With the veto, presidents could either prevent the passage of bills in these areas or influence their final contours. This was a curious juxtaposition of independent will and compliant agent. After presidents exercised independent judgment in helping to make laws, they were to be the dutiful agent of Congress's will, as expressed in its laws.

With respect to treaties and appointments, the Senate and the president would serve as the executive. The president could negotiate treaties and would make them on behalf of the United States. The president would nominate individuals to serve in the diplomatic corps and would actually appoint them. But before making treaties or long-term appointments, the president would need the consent of the executive council, the Senate. This mimicked some state systems, where the executive was a council, at least on certain matters. New York had an appointment council, composed of the governor and senators.[5]

In the case of appointments, the constitutional process was less rigorous than the one for making ordinary laws. The views of representatives in the House might be ignored, for all the president needed was a Senate majority. In the case of treaties, however, the constitutional procedure would generally be more demanding than the one for making laws. For many treaties, it would be easier to secure a simple majority in both chambers than it would be to secure a two-thirds Senate majority. But the Constitution never authorized the president to make treaties after majority votes in both chambers. The only way to make a treaty was to secure a two-thirds Senate supermajority.

The president would wield the remaining foreign affairs authorities unilaterally, via the "executive power." Congress would need to supply funds and create offices, but the president would decide which countries to recognize, what to say to them, and how to steward the day-to-day foreign affairs of the United States. Hence, although nothing in the Constitution specifically provided that the president would serve as the nation's organ of communication, presidents have always served in that capacity. Early on, letters addressed to Congress from foreign nations were left unopened and sent to the president. Legislators judged that they could not open and respond to these messages because Congress was no longer the principal organ of communication: the president was.[6] Moreover, the president directed, and could oust, America's diplomatic corps. For instance, without any statutory warrant, Washington fired ambassador James Monroe (who later recovered to serve as the fifth president).[7] Indeed, the entire State Department, including Secretary Thomas Jefferson, served under Washington's direction.[8]

At the Founding, the general contours of this complicated allocation of "executive power" were well known. In an opinion for George Washington, Secretary of State Thomas Jefferson observed that the "transaction of business with foreign nations is Executive altogether. It belongs then to the head of that department, *except* as to such portions of it as are specially submitted to the Senate. *Exceptions* are to be construed strictly."[9] Jefferson should have added that Congress also benefited from some major exceptions, like the war power. Alexander Hamilton said the presidency was "the organ of intercourse" with foreign nations, deriving that conclusion from the grant of "executive power."[10] He also observed that because Washington had the executive power, he could declare America's neutrality between France and England.[11] To the emperor of Morocco, Washington himself noted that he had the honor of receiving the emperor's letter and replying to it because he now enjoyed the "supreme executive authority" under the Constitution.[12] This was Washington asserting that his executive power included the authority to serve as the principal organ of communication. While many criticized certain aspects of Washington's tenure, rather few claimed he had usurped foreign affairs that properly rested elsewhere. Moreover, absolutely no one claimed that presidents were limited to receiving ambassadors, appointing them, and making treaties. Everyone understood that presidents had more foreign affairs authority than a shallow, uninformed reading of the Constitution might suggest.

EARLY ERRORS

As an abstract matter, saying that "the transaction of business with foreign nations is Executive altogether," as Jefferson did, was entirely true. Foreign affairs was an executive power because it had long been regarded as such, both in Europe and, importantly, in America. The more difficult question is what Jefferson's maxim meant for particular foreign affairs questions given the Constitution's complicated allocation of executive power across the House, the Senate, and the presidency. Unfortunately, at least two early slipups were traceable to executive overreach: the creation of diplomatic offices and the prosecution of American Francophiles. They are worth recounting, for they foreshadow the constitutional errors that have multiplied since.

The Washington administration had concluded that the president could, acting on his own constitutional authority, create overseas postings. He decided where America would send diplomats (which nations) and their rank (ambassador or some lesser office such as "minister plenipotentiary").[13] The Senate could reject any nominee, thereby signaling its disagreement with the president's decisions on destination, rank, or both. If senators thought that an ambassador to France was unnecessary, they could simply reject any and all nominees for an ambassadorial posting in France.

Yet under our constitutional scheme, Congress has complete authority to create offices. Congress has created every other non-elected federal office, including district attorneys, judgeships (including on the Supreme Court), tax collectors, generals, and departmental secretaries.[14] Though presidents undoubtedly were granted broad authority to conduct foreign affairs, it was not unlimited, and there is no reason to suppose that it extended to the creation of foreign postings. Just as presidents lacked constitutional authority to create an office of secretary of foreign affairs (Congress created this office in 1789), they likewise could not create overseas offices. Washington ought to have asked Congress to create these diplomatic postings.

The second slipup involved prosecuting Americans for joining France's fight against Britain. From President Washington's vantage point, Americans fighting for France had violated peace treaties that the United States had struck with Britain.[15] Maybe so. But no treaty or written law actually made it a crime for American citizens to wage war against Britain. Moreover, no one thought that the president could invent a crime. After juries acquitted an American accused of fighting for France, Washington did the right thing and sought a legislative solution.[16] This came close to admitting that the initial prosecutions were a blunder. Congress obliged by creating the Neutrality Act of 1794, which made it a crime to wage war against a nation with whom we are at peace.[17]

Compounding the Early Errors

These two missteps reflected a misunderstanding that stubbornly persists—that because foreign affairs have always been the purview of the executive, international affairs are for the president to manage alone. This simplistic mindset has encouraged presidents (and their lawyers) to eschew rigor and overlook distinctions. The predicate is absolutely true—foreign affairs was and is an executive power. But the conclusion—that stewardship of foreign affairs rests with the president alone—does not follow from the predicate. As discussed earlier, the Constitution slices and dices executive authority in multiple ways, with the president enjoying unilateral authority over only those foreign affairs matters not assigned to Congress and not checked by the Senate. Hence no one should suppose that presidents were supposed to reign supreme in foreign affairs. In modern times, however, this un-nuanced perspective has warped too many minds.

The Supreme Court has not helped. In fact, it has encouraged presidential power grabs, likely because the justices generally share the intuition that presidents should steward foreign affairs. In *United States v. Curtiss-Wright Export Corporation,* a case involving the constitutionality of delegated authority to the president, the Supreme Court approvingly quoted a congressional committee report: "The President is the constitutional representative of the United States with regard to foreign nations. He manages our concerns with foreign nations."[18] As Harold Koh has noted, the executive loves to cite *Curtiss-Wright* in its legal filings. The executive branch arguments often have the flavor of "*Curtiss-Wright,* so I am right"—meaning the president prevails in foreign affairs.[19] Though the recent case of *Zivotofsky v. Kerry* gratuitously undercut the pro-executive features of *Curtiss-Wright,* the Supreme Court did not overturn *Curtiss-Wright* and in fact echoed much of its pro-executive rhetoric. The Court praised the benefits of "one [executive] voice," unity, decisiveness, and the executive's ability to engage in "delicate and often secret diplomatic contacts."[20] Why the Supreme Court went out of its way both to bury executive authority in foreign affairs and, in the same breath, to praise it, is a mystery. Whether executive branch lawyers cite *Curtiss-Wright* or *Zivotofsky,* the result is the same: they will claim that the president prevails in foreign matters. Perhaps the pro-executive adage will be changed to "*Zivotofsky,* so I must prevail over thee."

Four Ways to Bypass the Treaty Clause

The Treaty Clause is straightforward. If a president wishes to make a treaty, he or she must secure the Senate's sanction. In fact, presidents must garner the consent of two-thirds of senators present, a rather high hurdle. This structure harnessed presidential leadership with a substantial check on treaties. Why were senators involved, as opposed to representatives? Because under the original Constitution the state legislatures chose senators, and many supposed that state legislators would take care to select senators who would vote, in all matters including treaties, to preserve state autonomy and influence.[21]

At the Founding, treaties were significant contracts between nations, typically concerning subjects like commerce, alliances, and peace. Hence every American treaty would be an international agreement, either bilateral or multilateral. Our Constitution added another feature, one that made treaties potentially more than just contracts. Under the Supremacy Clause, treaties also can serve as "supreme Law," meaning that they can create legal rights and duties that supersede state law.[22] Thus, while treaties invariably constitute international contracts, some subset of them also make or change domestic law.

While the Senate performed a vital role in whether presidents could ratify treaties, Congress as a whole had a more limited part to play. It might be called on to enact new federal law to implement treaties, either to provide funds or conform existing federal laws to new treaty obligations. Via its legislative powers, Congress also could supersede treaties, thereby displacing their status as domestic law. For instance, Congress might declare war against a foreign nation, thereby supplanting (or violating) a peace treaty.

Despite Congress's powers to implement, supersede, and violate treaties, it could not *make* treaties. It lost that power in the move from the Articles of Confederation. As Michael Ramsey notes, the Founders were clear that Congress could not make treaties.[23] In fact, they repeatedly said the House of Representatives had no role in making them, meaning that Congress, as a whole, had no role.[24] While some complained of the House's exclusion from the treaty process, others defended its marginalization. For instance, Alexander Hamilton said that the House, because it was a numerous, fluctuating body, properly had no role in the "formation of treaties."[25] Hence despite its power over foreign commerce and the military, Congress could not make commercial or military treaties.

Nor could presidents, at least not unilaterally. While presidents, as noted earlier, had some limited authority to make lesser compacts on their own, they could not make the significant international agreements—treaties—without the Senate's consent. In James Wilson's words, "Neither the President nor the Senate solely can complete a treaty."[26] Had presidents enjoyed a separate power to make treaties unilaterally, the Treaty Clause's requirement of Senate consent would have been superfluous.

What Congress and the president could not do separately, they could not do jointly. Nothing in the Constitution grants Congress and the president the power to make treaties in concert. Indeed, *there is not a single constitutional power that requires the concurrence of Congress and the president before it may be exercised.* Lawmaking does not, for Congress can override a veto and thereby ignore the president's objections.[27] And the constitutional amendment process does not, because Congress can send amendments directly to the states for ratification, bypassing the president.[28]

To be sure, the Treaty Clause did not expressly declare that it was the only means of making treaties. But it didn't need to state the obvious. It was understood that if the nation was to make a treaty, the president would need the consent of a Senate supermajority. A constitutional allocation can be the exclusive means of obtaining a result either because it declares as much or because no other institution has the power to secure the result. In the case of treaties, the Treaty Clause is exclusive because no other institution or institutions have a plausible case for making treaties in another manner.

The end result was a simple scheme, one consistent with the best reading of the Constitution. Only a treaty could pledge the good faith of the United States on matters of major international importance. Presidents could not make treaties unilaterally because the Constitution had expressly constrained their treaty-making power. Congress could not make treaties because it lacked a concurrent grant of the treaty power. Hence the only way to make a treaty was the means plainly specified in the Constitution: presidents could make treaties only after securing the consent of two-thirds of the Senate.

In early practice, there was not even a hint that there was another way to make a treaty. For instance, treaties that failed to secure the Senate's consent were not rerouted to the House to be enacted as ordinary laws. In fact, no one seems to have even mentioned the possibility that presidents might, with the advice and consent of simple majorities of both chambers, make treaties. It bears noting that when in 1796 the House demanded John Jay's treaty instructions in order to judge whether it should appropriate funds to implement the Jay Treaty (made with Britain), Washington refused on the ground that the House had absolutely no role in treaty-making.[29] While the House claimed a right to the Jay Papers because it believed they were relevant to the question of whether it ought to grant funds to implement the treaty, neither the House nor anyone else refuted President Washington's obviously correct assertion that the House had no role in making treaties.

The first time that something like a Treaty Clause bypass occurred was with the accession of the Republic of Texas. In 1844, President John Tyler negotiated a treaty with the republic, but it failed in the Senate.[30] During Tyler's waning days in office, Congress passed a law offering Texas admission upon the satisfaction of certain conditions.[31] Months later, Tyler's successor, James Polk, signed a federal law that actually annexed Texas.[32] America later annexed Hawaii the same way, via federal law.[33]

Did these annexations of foreign nations by law rather than treaty violate the Constitution? Perhaps not. The actual question is whether Congress could acquire territory by ordinary law. Maybe Congress could not enact a law to acquire territory from a sovereign nation when that nation would continue to exist as an independent sovereign, albeit with less territory. That might need to be done by treaty alone, as was done many, many times with both American Indian tribes and foreign nations. But what about a nation that was disappearing entirely because it was joining the United States? Maybe that could be done by ordinary law, rather than by treaty alone.

In the years that followed, neither the president nor Congress sought to use a congressional bypass for treaties. In particular, during the latter half of the nineteenth century, when treaties failed in the Senate, presidents did not cite the Polk example as precedent to circumvent the Treaty Clause and seek congressional approval. For instance, in 1860, the Senate rejected a treaty with Spain to settle claims. Although a supermajority of senators actually favored it (the vote was 26 to 17, or just over 60 percent), the numbers fell short of the required two-thirds supermajority.[34] It apparently never occurred to anyone that President James Buchanan could redirect the treaty to the House to pass it as a simple law. Other nineteenth-century treaties that enjoyed majority (but not two-thirds) support in the Senate were also not rerouted to the House for approval.[35]

In the early part of the twentieth century, the nation enacted the Seventeenth Amendment, which changed the rules for electing senators; instead of being selected by state legislators, senators are chosen by the people of each state.[36] This change, however, did nothing to transform, much less alter, the Senate's constitutional powers. More specifically, it neither diminished the Senate's preexisting treaty role nor granted the House any treaty authority. It would take informal amendments—grounded on constitutional violations—to bypass the Treaty Clause.

1. Congress Consents to Treaties by Simple Majorities

During the twentieth century, presidents started turning to Congress to make treaties, as Bruce Ackerman and David Golove have shown.

This practice took two forms. Sometimes Congress sanctioned a treaty after it was negotiated, essentially granting its advice and consent. Other times Congress authorized presidents to make significant international agreements. This was sanction given in advance, a delegation to make treaties. When either situation occurred, presidents could make the treaty on behalf of the United States without securing the Senate's super-majoritarian consent under the Treaty Clause.[37]

For now, let's focus on the first innovation, congressional advice and consent to proposed treaties. Some supposed that the Senate supermajority requirement was too stringent and had thwarted useful international pacts, including the Treaty of Versailles (the peace treaty ending World War I). Relatedly, some in the House resented the Senate and wanted to curb its larger role in foreign affairs. If the House could participate in the making of treaties, via after-the-fact consent, it would be the Senate's equal, at least in terms of making significant international agreements.[38]

Seeking Congress's consent to a treaty's ratification via ordinary lawmaking soon became an option whenever it was clear that the treaty could not clear the two-thirds threshold in the Senate. Indeed, when Congress belatedly sanctioned a Saint Lawrence Seaway treaty that the Senate had rejected decades earlier, it became clear that audacious presidents might pursue *both* options for a single treaty.[39]

Perhaps to paper over the embarrassment of circumventing the Treaty Clause, these international accords came to be called "congressional-executive agreements." They are congressional-executive because both Congress and the president want these international agreements to be made. But the underlying agreements are still treaties. In modern times, then, presidents enjoy at least two ways of making treaties—the textual method of securing the consent of two-thirds of the Senate, and the living presidency scheme of obtaining a simple majority in both chambers of Congress.

Essentially, majorities in Congress have conspired with the president to circumvent the Treaty Clause. Constitutional doubts are brushed aside because there is a record of hundreds of treaties (congressional-executive agreements) made without the required Senate consent.[40] If a senator or representative endorses a treaty and is told that there is an established, alternative route for making it, he or she will feel little or no compunction about bypassing the Treaty Clause.

Many laud the modern bypass of the Treaty Clause. Some suppose that it is more democratically legitimate because of the House's participation.[41] Others criticize the two-thirds Senate requirement as too demanding and therefore favor the less-onerous bypass.[42] As a policy matter, these opinions have undoubted virtues.

My point is that the bypass has no constitutional warrant, at least from the perspective of the original Constitution. Congress does not have the authority to amend the Constitution via simple majority vote and abet the president's unconstitutional treaty-making. Presidents can no more make treaties with the connivance of Congress than they can make treaties with the sanction of the Supreme Court. If the Supreme Court, by a 9–0 majority, gave its consent to the making of a treaty and the president thereafter ratified the treaty, the president would have violated the Constitution. And that would be no less true even if it happened dozens, even hundreds, of times.

2. Congress Delegates Authority to Make Treaties

Having experienced the benefits of Congress serving as a substitute for the Senate, it was natural that the president would welcome a further innovation, namely congressional delegation of authority to conclude treaties. In advance of any negotiation, Congress by law would authorize the executive to conclude a treaty, eliminating the need for any after-the-fact consent by either the Senate or Congress. Indeed, numerous federal laws explicitly authorize the executive to conclude international agreements.[43]

Whether the Senate could, by two-thirds majority, wholly eliminate its consent function by authorizing the president to make treaties is a difficult enough question. I rather doubt that the Senate could delegate away its advice and consent role. But the notion that *Congress* can delegate power to make treaties is extremely dubious. After all, if Congress can delegate powers, the only powers it can possibly assign away are those that it may itself rightfully exercise under the Constitution. Because Congress lacks a treaty power, it has no constitutional authority to delegate treaty-making authority.

A related aggrandizement, one more dubious still, comes from the practice of executive branch lawyers reading generic statutes, many of which say nothing about international agreements, as if they implicitly delegated power to make treaties.[44] In other words, executive lawyers have occasionally read language about what a federal agency might do domestically as if the law silently authorized the making of international agreements on those subjects. But the president's power to make international agreements does not increase merely because Congress has passed laws on a certain subject. For instance, a congressional law on domestic mercury pollution is not a covert invitation for presidents to make an international treaty on mercury emissions. Likewise, no one has thought that because Congress has created a criminal code, the president, acting alone, can make a treaty about crimes. This recent practice of discovering hidden delegations counts as a massive aggrandizement because, as the Supreme Court once said, one does not ordinarily hide "elephants in mouseholes."[45] Statutes that do not expressly convey an authority to make international agreements should not be misconstrued as authorizing unilateral presidential treaty-making.

3. Presidents Misuse Sole Executive Agreements

The Constitution itself provided one bypass to the Treaty Clause. As noted earlier, the Constitution distinguishes treaties from a lesser species of international contracts, called compacts. While the Constitution explicitly bars states from making any treaties, it also plainly declares that states may make compacts with Congress's consent.[46] This distinction between treaties and compacts suggests that while the Treaty Clause regulates the making of treaties, it does not constrain the making of minor compacts.

Given the president's authority over foreign affairs, arising out of the grant of "executive power," the president may make such minor compacts without securing the Senate's consent. This reading coheres with early practice. Some early presidents (including John Adams and James Madison) drew on their executive power over foreign affairs to make minor international agreements without the Senate's consent.[47] About fifty such "sole executive agreements" were made prior to the Civil War.[48]

The number of sole executive agreements ballooned in the twentieth century, with one author claiming that from 1946 to 2006, almost fifteen thousand such agreements were struck.[49] As the United States became more deeply engaged in world affairs, there was a greater perceived need for international agreements, minor and major. But one also has to suppose that another reason for the sharp uptick in sole executive agreements has to do with the presidential perception that for certain agreements, neither Senate nor congressional consent would be forthcoming. If there was a need for an agreement, but no prospect of congressional or senatorial sanction, then the category of what could be done via sole executive agreement had to be enlarged to meet the perceived need.

Franklin D. Roosevelt's bases-for-destroyers deal, reached with Great Britain in 1940, was the sort of significant international agreement that in earlier times would not have been struck unilaterally.[50]

Arming a belligerent with significant weaponry is no small matter, particularly when the nation is already tilting toward that belligerent in a whole host of ways. Such behavior comes close to an act of war, something presidents are not constitutionally authorized to do. But Churchill could not wait for the destroyers, and Roosevelt could not stomach a possible Senate or congressional rejection. This pattern has been repeated, with major military agreements being struck without the consent of the Senate under the Treaty Clause and without the approval of Congress.

Another innovation in practice has been the use of sole executive agreements to alter the legal rights and duties of Americans. One can see how this might be useful in adjusting disputes with foreign nations, particularly when Americans have claims against foreign nationals and governments. Yet as Michael Ramsey points out, this is also problematic, because presidents now have some unilateral authority to alter the rights and duties of citizens, something traditionally left to legislatures via democratic lawmaking or to presidents acting in conjunction with the Senate via the Treaty Clause.[51]

4. Presidents Make "Nonbinding" Commitments

Though the power to make sole executive agreements has expanded over time, such agreements are not yet perfect substitutes for treaties. Sometimes executive branch lawyers will tell presidents that they cannot make an international agreement without securing the consent of either the Senate or Congress. In these situations, presidents sometimes switch instruments. In particular, they move from a binding contract to a nonbinding "political commitment." A political commitment, whether memorialized or not, is not supposed to be an international contract at all but is rather nothing more than an expression of policies and plans. The failure to honor a political commitment has no implications under international law because the United States has not made any legal promise in making a political commitment. Think of it as a commitment to have lunch. While there may be political repercussions from the breach of political commitments, there are no consequences in terms of international law.[52]

Political commitments are constitutional precisely because they are nonbinding and therefore are not international agreements. The Treaty Clause does not apply because they are not contracts, much less treaties. Likewise, they are not sole executive agreements because, again, they are not agreements. Nonbinding political commitments have a long history: they were used to resolve the Cuban Missile Crisis, limit emigration from Japan to the United States, and set up a post–World War II order.[53]

The most famous modern political commitment is the so-called Joint Comprehensive Plan of Action (JCPOA), a document meant to curb Iran's nuclear program. Executive branch lawyers carefully wordsmithed it to ensure that the United States did not make any promises. Instead the JCPOA merely outlined what each of several nations (it was multilateral) would commit to do, without including any legal obligation to fulfill such commitments. The Iranians were to halt their nuclear ambitions and other nations were to end sanctions and unfreeze Iranian assets. But no nation was obliged to do (or not do) anything.[54]

If you haven't heard of the JCPOA, perhaps you've heard of its other names, the "Iranian nuclear agreement," or sometimes the "Iran deal." But to call it an "agreement" or a "deal" is to misunderstand its supposed nature. Again, the lawyers consciously tried to avoid making a contract or agreement. For that reason, the JCPOA never uses the words "treaty," "compact," "agreement," or any synonym. In a briefing, a State Department official signaled that there was no actual "agreement." She confided that "lawyers don't like us to call it an agreement," presumably because doing so generates confusion.[55] In a letter to Congress, a State Department official declared that the JCPOA "is not a treaty or an executive agreement, and is not a signed document."[56]

But perhaps the lawyers are wrong about what the JCPOA is. Again, every non-lawyer calls it the "Iranian nuclear agreement" or the "Iranian nuclear deal." Presidents Obama and Trump both called it an agreement or a deal, repeatedly. Senators and representatives did the same. So did three secretaries of state—John Kerry, Rex Tillerson, and Mike Pompeo.[57] When President Donald Trump discarded the JCPOA, he announced that he was "withdraw[ing]" from the Iranian "Agreement."[58] Others, both in Congress and outside, criticized him for damaging the credibility of the United States. John Kerry said that the president had broken "America's word."[59] For his part, former President Obama wrote that "the consistent flouting of agreements that our country is a party to risks eroding America's credibility, and puts us at odds with the world's major powers."[60] The Iranians themselves criticized the United States for breaking its word.[61]

Each of these comments, and hundreds more, suggest that the JCPOA, despite its artful language and the underlying lawyering, was, in fact, an international agreement. The United States and Iran treated it as such, both at its inception and thereafter. If the relevant actors—the foreign-policy leaders of both nations—treat a formal document as if it created a legal obligation, that document is in fact binding and is an agreement.[62] This was a situation where the lawyers tried to honor the living Constitution as they understood it— presidents could not unilaterally make an actual compact given the JCPOA's particular features. But their attempt to do so was unsuccessful because the principals—those making the "commitment"— understood the JCPOA rather differently. We handed over a billion dollars to Iran in return for an obligation to delay and decommission Iran's nuclear weapons program. Fashioning this as a non-agreement was an attempt to paper over reality. It was an effort to have form control the substance. The effort failed.

Anyone reading this discussion can be forgiven for being a little confused. But the problem lies not in the exposition. Scholars steeped in the field often find the distinctions elusive. What is the difference between a political commitment and an actual agreement? Can a commitment involve promises, or are promises the hallmarks of an agreement? Can a nation "violate" a nonbinding commitment? What are the consequences of violating an agreement as opposed to a political commitment? There are no easy answers to such questions, because while scholars speak of agreements as being fundamentally different from mere commitments, the categories are closer than they appear. There often are few real-world consequences to violating a treaty. There are reputational consequences, but those also flow from breach of political commitments.

So while learned lawyers may distinguish between political commitments and binding agreements, it will be hard for ordinary Americans to appreciate what may appear to be a metaphysical distinction. No president will be arrested or prosecuted for violating either a treaty or a political commitment. And foreign nations can retaliate just as much for the violation of political commitment as they can for a treaty transgression.

Nonetheless, if we are to limit the president's ability to make treaties, we must be able to more neatly separate binding agreements from truly voluntary commitments. It may be that executive officials are attempting to blur this distinction precisely because they are trying to create yet another bypass to the Treaty Clause.

Power over Cables, Pipelines, and Aerial Railways

The executive's expansion of its foreign-affairs powers goes beyond bypassing the Declare War Clause and circumventing the Treaty Clause. In particular, anything with a foreign angle can be seen as under the executive's sway. In 1875, President Ulysses S. Grant notified Congress that he opposed the laying of a transatlantic telegraph cable by a French company until certain conditions were met. When these stipulations were met, his opposition ceased. Whether he was making a constitutional claim is a bit uncertain, for he did not assert that he had legal authority to bar the cable. Yet he did promise to "prevent the landing of" future cables that failed to meet his announced criteria.[63] Whatever the case, his successors have laid claim to a legal power over cross-border cables, primarily by citing Grant. Later presidents extended the cross-border cable power to cover pipelines and electric lines, as well as aerial railways and trams.[64]

Today, presidents claim *constitutional* authority to bar trans-border cables and pipelines. That is why President Obama believed he could halt the construction of the Keystone Pipeline meant to traverse the Canadian border.[65] No law of Congress and no constitutional provision gave him authority over pipelines. But he had such authority, courtesy of Grant and subsequent presidents.

This executive aggrandizement both trespassed on private rights and intruded on congressional power. The private right related to the free enjoyment of private property. In the absence of any federal law, the executive now claims an ability to infringe on the rights of property holders. The congressional power in question was the authority to regulate foreign commerce, a power that is widely understood to grant Congress authority to regulate channels of commerce like pipelines and wire communications.[66] Generally speaking, presidents are not thought to have *any* authority over foreign or domestic commerce. Nonetheless, the presidency's assumption of authority over cross-border cables and pipelines is now utterly accepted by courts and commentators. This expansion fairly proves, yet again, that if presidents do something long enough, it becomes woven into expectations and will be said to be part of our law.[67]

FLOUTING CONGRESS'S LAWS

If presidents can bypass a vital provision of the Constitution, the Treaty Clause, sidestepping congressional restrictions on the executive's conduct of foreign policy is easier still. In his admirable book *Power Wars,* Charlie Savage considers the modern executive's claim that Congress cannot interfere with the president's ability to send whomever he pleases to meet with foreign envoys.[68] According to the OLC, the president has the "exclusive power to conduct diplomacy." This power encompasses the rights to discuss "any subject that has bearing on the national interest," send representatives to conduct such parleys, and determine the particular officials who will manage these discussions and negotiations.[69]

Savage notes that prior to 1990, executive branch legal opinions claimed that Congress cannot tell the executive what to say to foreign nations. So far, so good, for it seems true that nothing in the Constitution empowers Congress to regulate what the president might say in foreign discussions and negotiations. But in 1990, this sensible assertion was insensibly stretched by the OLC to encompass the notion that Congress cannot constrain whom the president might send on diplomatic missions. In this way a narrow principle about what the executive might *say* to a foreign nation was enlarged to cover a power to select the *instruments* of conveying messages. As Savage points out, however, the Appointments Clause clearly constrains the president's ability to select diplomats. With the Senate's consent, he may appoint "ambassadors, other public ministers, and consuls." This clause always has been read to signal that presidents cannot make enduring appointments to high offices without the Senate's consent. Unlike the Treaty Clause, no one reads the Appointments Clause as optional when it comes to appointments of high officers.[70]

The problem with these OLC opinions runs even deeper. The claims that modern executive lawyers make in this area are actually broader than the one that Savage rightly savaged. In most instances, Congress does not actually declare that the president may not send this or that diplomat. More often than not, Congress instead decrees that the executive may not use congressionally granted funds to pay for the diplomacy in question.[71] Hence when executive lawyers objected to these laws, they were not merely saying that the president could choose whom to send on diplomatic missions. Rather, the lawyers were actually asserting that presidents had a constitutional right to funds to carry on these diplomatic missions.[72] For instance, if Congress provided that no funds were to be spent on a mission to Iran, the constitutional claim was that the president had a right to use funds to conduct such a mission. Taken to its logical conclusion, the executive branch's position is that Congress must supply sufficient funds to implement the president's diplomatic agenda, whatever its scope. Failing to do so is unconstitutional because it improperly limits the president's conduct of diplomacy.

This argument does not hold up. Even if Congress cannot dictate what the executive may (or may not) say to other nations, that by no means proves that Congress must fund the diplomatic corps that the president believes is necessary. If Congress never subsidizes this book, its failure would not be an attempt to muzzle me, even though I might be much more effective at spreading my message about the living presidency if I received congressional funding. Congress's failure to subsidize me certainly would not violate the First Amendment. Similarly, a federal law that fails to fund diplomacy in no way impinges on the president's constitutional right to conduct diplomacy. He can parley with whomever he wants, whether or not Congress chooses to subsidize that speech.

In fact, because it is in charge of the purse strings, Congress may decide what presidential initiatives to fund, either domestically or overseas. If Congress doesn't wish to fund resource-intensive international summits, a massive embassy staff, or a small mission to an international entity or some far-flung country, it need not do so.

That is why the modern OLC opinions decrying congressional restrictions on spending are doubly dubious. They assume that presidents have an absolute right to appoint anyone they wish to conduct diplomacy. That's never been true. They also assume that restrictions on funding impinge on that right. But a restriction on funding an activity is hardly the same as enacting a legal restriction on the activity itself.

The Supreme Court recently said as much. In *Zivotofsky v. Kerry*, discussed earlier, the Court held that presidents may decide which nations and governments to recognize. The Court further held that Congress could not interfere with those recognition decisions. Yet the Court also clearly said that presidents had no right to choose their own diplomats or to funding to further their recognitions policies. The president "cannot . . . appoint an ambassador without the approval of the Senate. . . . The President, furthermore, could not build an American Embassy abroad without congressional appropriation of the necessary funds." The Court's point was that legislators who disagreed with the president's underlying foreign policies might neither consent to an ambassador nor fund an embassy.[73] In other words, the Constitution does not require Congress to legislate in aid of the president's preferred foreign policies.

The Court was surely right. Congress has long provided a massive multibillion-dollar diplomatic budget. That is wise policy. But presidents have no constitutional right to millions for the construction of an embassy in Jerusalem. Nor do presidents have a constitutional right to the funds necessary to maintain the American embassy in Tel Aviv.

If presidents cannot appoint an ambassador without the Senate's approval, as the Court noted, it is hard to see why they have an unyielding right to send emissaries overseas. And if they cannot construct an embassy without congressional assistance, presidents surely have no right to the funds necessary to cover the expenses of their emissaries. Just as presidents have no right to an army of their choosing, they likewise have no right to their ideal diplomatic corps. Congress could slash the State Department budget in half and there would be no constitutional problem. In fact, it could eliminate that department altogether. Doing so would be an utter disaster. But as everyone familiar with government surely intuits, policy disasters are not invariably unconstitutional.

Delegations of Authority, Real and Imagined

One of the principal sources of presidential power in foreign affairs is not constitutional at all but instead arises from the laws of Congress. In order to maximize flexibility in foreign affairs, Congress often delegates broad authority in foreign affairs to the president. Where Congress has subject-matter authority over a matter—for example, funding and commerce—such delegations may be quite useful and fitting. For instance, Congress has ceded broad authority to the president to impose tariff and non-tariff barriers on foreign commerce. Due to the breadth of such delegations, it often seems that presidents regulate foreign commerce, not Congress.

Should Congress ever seek to retract these delegated powers, it would face a Sisyphean task. For though most presidents eagerly embrace delegations, they seldom (if ever) welcome congressional retractions. To thwart such attempts, presidents can deploy—or even just threaten—their veto power. After all, why would legislators begin a process that seems doomed to fail? Even if majorities in both chambers were to pass a bill to retract Congress's constitutional authority over foreign commerce, the president's expected veto of the bill means that supermajorities in both chambers would be required. Overriding a veto has been close to impossible in the modern era, when legislators sharing a party affiliation with the president are typically unwilling to publicly criticize, much less actually resist, presidential actions.

Besides conveying broad authority, these congressional delegations of power have a secondary, pernicious effect on the executive mindset. If you convey a good deal of authority in a particular area, the recipients may come to regard themselves as having a general sway over a larger area, even when there is no express delegation of power. The Supreme Court has endorsed this very approach in a case involving foreign affairs: the existence of a law granting broad discretion, one "closely related" to some disputed executive authority, "may be considered to 'invite' 'measures on independent presidential responsibility'" over the disputed area.[74] To make this concrete, consider the following: if Congress delegates broad authority over import tariffs and the president acts on a related subject, say inspection of imports, the tariff delegation may be read to "invite" presidential regulation of inspections. This Supreme Court pronouncement is nothing short of bizarre. A tariff delegation is not an implicit invitation to regulate inspections. It is akin to construing an invitation to afternoon tea as if it were a standing offer to raid the home's refrigerator. But whatever I think, the point is that when Congress grants authority over some subject, the executive and the courts sometimes will understand Congress as also delegating authority over related subjects.

Beyond the tendency to broadly construe actual delegations and find delegations where there are none, executives are tempted to infer a general aura of deference to the executive branch. To executive officials, it may seem obvious that Congress wants to "get out of the way" and not tie the president's hands, or, for that matter, render the president impotent in some vital area of foreign affairs.

Hence a heady mix of factors suggests presidential supremacy, at least to executive branch lawyers. Presidents have constitutional authorities traceable to the Vesting Clause. On top of that, Congress generously grants still greater authority in order to give flexibility to the branch that is always on duty and has greater knowledge in foreign affairs. And finally, executive branch officials are quick to read congressional silence as if it were an implicit delegation of authority, or as the Court put it, an implicit invitation for the executive to act as it deems necessary.

The executive's penchant for using actual delegations as a springboard for further acquisitions brings to mind an adage: give an inch and they'll take a mile. When Congress grants the executive an inch or two in foreign affairs, often for the soundest of reasons, the executive branch is apt to take that mile.

THE PRESIDENCY'S CHEERLEADERS

Why is the executive branch apt to take a mile? One reason is that modern presidents believe that they have more freedom of action in foreign affairs than they actually do, and this attitude encourages them to find (or manufacture) the latitude needed to take the actions they deem necessary. If you tell presidents they have broad discretion in order to safeguard the interests of the United States, they will, unsurprisingly, often find such foreign affairs discretion even where none was granted or intended.

Who whispers in the ears of presidents, telling them they enjoy broad latitude in foreign affairs? Two groups help foster presidential unilateralism in foreign affairs, in part because they favor America's continued deep engagement with all parts of the globe and see presidents as far more apt to foster foreign ties. First, State Department personnel thrive on increases in presidential power because most executive discretion is exercised not by transitory presidents but by the permanent establishment. As noted earlier, surges in presidential power often serve to empower the bureaucracy, the thick layer of personnel that remains entrenched in Washington as presidents come and go. Put another way, the authority of Foggy Bottom is directly proportional to the scope of powers, constitutional and statutory, said to rest with the president.

Second, scholars of international law often favor presidential power. To be sure, many such scholars criticize the vast expansion of presidential war powers. But that is because they (in line with international law) frown on warfare as an instrument of state policy, and they recognize that the original scheme better upholds modern international-law values than does the modern regime of presidential war-making. After all, it is far more difficult to wage war if presidents cannot do so unilaterally but must instead wait for Congress to declare war.

Outside the important war realm, however, presidents (and the executive branch) are generally more apt to honor international law. Generally speaking, presidents, and their diplomats, care more about international law and practices than does the average member of Congress. And if one wants more international cooperation and American leadership in the international realm, one generally will favor unilateral presidential authority in foreign affairs. It is easier to make international agreements if only one person, the president, must approve them. For internationalists, sometimes the Founders were right (war) and sometimes they were wrong (treaties and perhaps foreign commerce). Where the Founders were wrong, internationalists often imagine that presidents are right to wrest away congressional and senatorial authority.

✳ ✳ ✳

Shifts in understandings and erosions of constraints can occur with remarkable little appreciation of what is happening. At one time, presidents made nonbinding commercial commitments with other nations, often with the approval of Congress. This was consistent with the Treaty Clause precisely because these commitments were *not* agreements. Over time, however, those commitments became reconceptualized as binding agreements. Some even considered them treaties. Later, presidents and their allies cited these commercial "agreements" to demonstrate that presidents could make all manner of agreements without having to satisfy the Treaty Clause. Presidents could go to Congress instead and forge congressional-executive agreements.

Nothing about existing practices signals an end to such shifts. We have not arrived at some stable equilibrium. Given the incentives and motives of presidents, and their aides, today's conceptions will not be the same as tomorrow's. Those who seek more international law and greater engagement with the world will naturally look to the institution best suited to gratify their desires, the presidency.

The muddle and lack of clarity in modern conceptions greatly favors the continued expansion of executive power. The proliferation of multiple and bewildering categories of international agreements, the tendency to cite minor factors to justify the choice of one instrument over others, the perceived need for quick action in foreign affairs, and the grant of "executive power"—these factors and others will lead to the further erosion of limits on presidential power. In this area, as in others, the past is likely prologue.

Going forward, expect presidents to continue to push the boundaries of their office. For instance, with the Iranian nuclear deal as a model, there might come a day when documents formerly seen as political commitments are recharacterized as sole executive agreements. If a president can transfer a billion dollars to an avowed enemy of the United States (Iran) in return for assurances about nuclear weapons, in a context where everyone refers to this arrangement as a "deal" or "agreement," there are many things that might be done by sole executive agreement that in other ages would have been done by treaty. One can even imagine a president unilaterally making an agreement that the United States will come to the defense of another nation on the grounds that because presidents can make executive agreements, they can make alliance agreements.

Likewise, expect presidents to continue to denounce and ignore congressional "micromanagement" of foreign relations. The claims that the chambers of Congress have no say in who may serve as a diplomat and that Congress cannot use its power of the purse to constrain what the executive may do in foreign affairs may prove a potent weapon against Congress, deployed to nullify and neuter congressional laws.

Lurking in the background of such presidential poaching on congressional turf will be the widely shared intuition that executives are absolutely right to expand their sway over foreign affairs. On many matters, the public prefers one person with a national, cosmopolitan perspective. Presidents and their aides know more about foreign affairs, certainly as compared to the relatively insular members of Congress. Presidents attend summits, have access to top-secret information, and are somewhat focused on foreign matters. Compared to a plural, parochial Congress, a single executive generally will be seen as a more attentive, skillful, and wise steward of foreign affairs.

Some might be tempted to argue that presidential growth makes the most sense in foreign affairs and hence we ought to tolerate it here, even if we eschew it elsewhere. But one cannot contain the contagion of executive expansionism and limit it, via jawboning, to the realm of foreign affairs. To borrow from the Supreme Court, one might say that praise for executive expansionism in foreign affairs will be regarded by the executive as an open invitation to expand elsewhere, including in the domestic realm. In fact, that expansion project is already well under way.

CHAPTER EIGHT

From DUTIFUL SERVANT *of the* LAWS *to* SECONDARY LAWMAKER

More than fifty years ago, the political scientist Aaron Wildavsky wrote that although America had one president, it nonetheless had "two presidencies." One—the domestic presidency—was constrained by law and Congress. The other—the defense and foreign policy presidency—had a freer hand, able to advance the incumbent's perception of our foreign interests.[1] Wildavsky perceived that in foreign affairs, Congress and the courts were reluctant to second-guess assertive presidents. Where domestic law was concerned, however, those two branches were more confident, while the presidency was more timid.

The Constitution's text appears to endorse such timidity. The Faithful Execution Clause of Article II imposes on presidents a duty to "take Care that the Laws be faithfully executed," a phrase that might suggest little discretion.[2] In the famous 1952 *Youngstown* case discussed in Chapter 4, Justice Hugo Black insisted that the president's duty to faithfully execute the law refutes the idea that "he is to be a lawmaker."[3] Indeed, it may seem that faithful execution presupposes that someone else is authoring the laws and that the agent—the president—must implement those laws. To be sure, though presidents have a hand in making all congressional laws (because of presentment and the veto), they are not the sole authors of them, and nothing in the Constitution suggests that they enjoy an outsized role in divining their meaning. As one eighteenth-century expert on executive power observed, executives have a solemn duty to perform what the legislative power has decreed in the same way an Athenian slave had to honor the orders of his master.[4] At some level, presidents were to be the servants of the law, and of its creator, Congress.

Today, there is something quaint about the notion that presidents must faithfully carry out the law. Justice Black's understanding of the executive is as antiquated as a rotary dial telephone, at least if we use modern practice as the benchmark. We are in a radically different context, one suffused with discretion, evasions, and excuses. Modern presidents regularly use their authority to advance their policy agendas at the expense of the legislative policies of Congress. Moreover, no one should doubt that presidents, and the executive branch they steward, transgress the laws they are meant to execute. Finally, modern presidents are very much lawmakers who are, in many ways, more significant legislators than Congress. They can make laws at the stroke of a pen, relying either on legislative authority that Congress has clearly delegated or on a dubious claim that Congress implicitly conveyed such power. Either way, the executive's laws—whether they are styled as rules, regulations, or orders—are America's laws and the public violates them at its peril. To borrow a concept from Justice Antonin Scalia, the modern executive branch is something of a junior varsity Congress.[5]

The transformations are all around us, and every institution—Congress, the courts, the executive, and the public—has helped usher in those changes. It is fair to say that practically everyone, at one time or another, has been an enabler of presidential lawmaking and lawbreaking. To be sure, such lawmaking or lawbreaking often sparks a hue and cry that the executive has acted illegally. Detractors may add what seems too obvious to say: the president cannot make law. But such critics are typically fair-weather friends of the original Constitution's separation of powers. In other contexts, such critics are apt to praise and defend executive lawmaking and law-breaking, especially when it serves their agendas.

Origins

We might have had a rather different executive, an at-will employee of Congress. At the Philadelphia Convention, Connecticut's Roger Sherman suggested as much, likely because he regarded the executive as nothing but an entity for "carrying the will of the Legislature into effect."[6] His proposal did not fly, because enough delegates wanted the executive to check Congress. Delegates eventually concluded that a president who was guaranteed a salary, selected in the states by elite electors, and removable only via impeachment would be more apt to stand up to, and constrain, Congress.

But many delegates regarded mere independence as insufficient. In their view, the president needed some authority over Congress, to spur it forward and to check its worst impulses. The spurs took the form of authority to make recommendations and summon Congress. The president could make legislative suggestions to Congress and hope that the chambers took them up. The president also could call Congress back from a recess in order to place something on its agenda. Both of these legislative prods were feeble because while presidents clearly can summon Congress into session, nothing in the Constitution compels the chambers to consider their legislative recommendations, much less vote on them. The president can lead the congressional horses to water, but can't make them drink.

The check came from the president's power to raise objections to bills, the "veto." Use of a presidential veto prevents a bill from becoming a law unless, after receiving those objections, both congressional chambers reapprove the bill by a two-thirds supermajority.

Though this scheme did not replicate the British Crown's absolute veto, it mirrored the system in the Massachusetts Constitution and granted the federal executive considerable authority over the content of federal legislation.

The veto led some commentators to regard the presidency as a "third branch in the legislature."[7] They believed that because overrides require a supermajority in both houses, a qualified veto often would amount to an absolute veto. Further, many knew that vetoes could be issued for any reason.[8] The president might raise constitutional, policy, or, for that matter, even petty objections. For these reasons, some critics complained that the veto gave the president far too much authority over legislation.[9] Others praised the veto as helping to ensure, first, that presidents could shield their institution from congressional encroachment, and second, that those who executed Congress's laws (presidents) would have a salutary influence in their creation and content.

Once a bill became law, the clear rule was that presidents had to enforce that law (there was an exception for unconstitutional "laws"—more on this later). In fact, the Faithful Execution Clause expressly enjoined that presidents "shall take Care that the laws be faithfully executed."[10] The duty to faithfully execute coupled with the negative implications of the veto left no doubt that presidents *had* to execute the laws of Congress. There was no need for a veto power if presidents had a general power to refuse to enforce any law. This rule was in keeping with express features of the British system. The Crown could not suspend parliamentary law, meaning that it could not merely waive the constraints that laws imposed on the executive or the populace.[11] Presidents inherited this disability. They too could not suspend laws on the grounds that they were inconvenient, troublesome, or undesirable.

If presidents could not waive laws, there was no reason to suppose that they could make them unilaterally. After the Crown claimed the power to raise taxes in the seventeenth century, the English Bill of Rights denounced this power as "illegal."[12] The presidency inherited this incapacity as well. Per the Constitution, the "legislative powers herein granted" were given to Congress, to be exercised via bicameral passage and presentment to the president. Hence while presidents had a check on Congress's making of laws, they had no power to make laws on their own. For instance, presidents could not make criminal laws. Nor could they tax or spend on their own authority.

If we stopped here, we'd have a fairly accurate assessment of the Constitution, the expectations of the Founders, and early presidents. The faithful execution duty plus the lack of lawmaking power made the president a servant of the laws, and therefore of Congress. He might check bills before they became law. But once those bills became law, he generally had to execute them. Further, while presidents could pardon offenses against the law, they could neither suspend the operation of a law nor authorize individuals to violate them. They could not decree that some law would not apply for a year or a decade. They could not grant individuals a legal right to disregard a federal law.

At the Founding, there was one man who was prescient about what might become of the duty of faithful execution—about how future readers might misread it. William Symmes Jr., who opposed ratification, penned an interesting critique of the Faithful Execution Clause. He complained that faithful execution was a vague standard. He also pointed out that if a federal law was as unclear as the Faithful Execution Clause, "must not [the president] interpret [the] act? For in many cases he must execute laws independently of any judicial decision." Symmes recognized that the courts are involved in only a fraction of all legal questions because most are resolved by the executive with absolutely no judicial involvement. When that is true, the executive (and not the courts) declares what the law is. Symmes also understood that when laws are imprecise, the president would mold them via interpretation. Finally, he foresaw that presidents might ignore laws that they believe are unconstitutional. Congress might enact laws "that destroy his independence, & in this case to supersede [the] very Constitution. Is there no instance in which he may reject [the] sense of [the] Legislature & establish his own? And so far would he not be to all intents & purposes absolute!"[13] In other words, if a president could reject the sense of Congress, the president, and not Congress, would be the lawmaker. Presidents would be especially tempted to do this when they could plausibly claim that Congress had trespassed on presidential power, thereby violating the executive's constitutional powers.

Symmes uncannily anticipated what bedevils us today. Presidents are "absolute" in all those cases where there is no judicial review or where Congress expressly authorizes executive lawmaking. Moreover, modern presidents are lawmakers not only when they fill in the details of vague laws but also when they "reject [the] sense of" Congress. Finally, modern presidents are increasingly willing to conclude that Congress's laws are unconstitutional and therefore that the faithful execution duty does not apply.

A BEGUILING CONTINUITY

The vast majority of federal laws are executed without much ado, by subordinate executives who more or less act as faithful agents of the law. Executive officers and employees, sometimes with the assistance of lawyers, discern a law's meaning, and administrators, investigators, and prosecutors help implement that law. Administrators execute the numerous social welfare laws that Congress has passed. Investigators try to discern whether individuals and firms have violated congressional laws that regulate private conduct and hand off this information to prosecutors so they may collect fines and put criminals in jail. While difficult legal questions invariably arise, the eventual answers are not typically influenced by a desire to advance a goal dear to the incumbent president. One could say more about all this, but the nuances of this routine are unimportant. The point is that presidents do not attempt to systematically influence, much less skew or undermine, the execution of most federal laws.

But side by side with this relative continuity with the Founding are discordant features that run counter to the original scheme. While presidents (and their administrations) faithfully execute most laws, that is not the uniform practice across all laws. Rather, presidents deprioritize, evade, or void some subset of federal law when they believe policy or necessity demands it. Moreover, presidents may shrink or expand laws in order to accomplish their policies. Finally, Congress sometimes delegates legislative power to the executive branch, thereby allowing the president to serve as a rival legislative authority.

RISE AND FALL OF THE VETO

Despite the worry that presidents would constitute a third chamber of Congress, in practice early presidents were reluctant to exercise their veto authority. Early presidents did not object to many bills. Washington vetoed two. Neither John Adams nor Thomas Jefferson vetoed any. James Madison vetoed five bills, with James Monroe finding only one objectionable. John Quincy Adams followed his father's example, vetoing nothing. Andrew Jackson vetoed five bills and was denounced as a tyrant.[14]

The perceived increase in the frequency of policy vetoes aggravated nineteenth-century politicians opposed to executive power—the Whigs. This party claimed that while vetoes grounded on constitutional objections were legitimate, policy vetoes were constitutionally suspect because they intruded on congressional policies and prerogatives.[15] The Whig assertion that the veto was for constitutional objections alone was never true to the text or the Founders' expectations.[16] Indeed, one of Washington's two vetoes rather clearly rested on policy considerations.[17] But the Whig complaint seemed plausible to many because our earliest presidents appeared uncertain and hesitant on matters of domestic policy. In the initial years and decades after ratification, presidents did not seem like a third chamber, much less like lawmakers of any sort.

After the Civil War, policy vetoes became increasingly common as the Whig theory lost its allure. The rise of such vetoes coincided with the notions that presidents ran for office with a policy platform and should wield their constitutional powers to fulfill their campaign promises. Moreover, Andrew Jackson's view of presidents as tribunes of the people made it palatable for presidents to issue policy vetoes. According to this view, presidents should have no compunction about acting to curb a wayward Congress. Both Andrew Johnson and Ulysses Grant would issue many policy vetoes, with Grover Cleveland issuing hundreds and earning the moniker "the Veto President."[18] Extremely vigorous use of the policy veto resurfaced during the administrations of Franklin Roosevelt and Harry Truman, who both followed Cleveland's example.[19]

In the twenty-first century, we are witnessing the twilight of both constitutional and policy vetoes. Vetoes are rarities because presidents exert influence in other ways.[20] Presidents have gotten smarter and more strategic. They now adopt what is best described as a lifecycle approach to voicing and acting on their objections. Throughout the legislative process for bills, presidents take advantage of multiple opportunities to voice and advance their preferences. They no longer regard presentment as the sole window for furthering their policy and constitutional agendas.

When Andrew Jackson vetoed a bill and said that Congress might have consulted with him prior to passing it, his critics castigated him for making such an absurd and presumptuous suggestion. He had no more power to opine on bills before they were presented to him than the Supreme Court had power to rule on the constitutionality of bills before Congress. Today, however, this once controversial strategy is now routine. Presidents regularly signal their stance regarding bills pending within the chambers. Typically, this is expressed by a formal "statement of administration policy." Through an interagency process, the executive decides and announces whether it will sign a bill as is, sign if changes are made, oppose a bill, or veto a bill. There are nuances in expression—for instance, sometimes advisers merely tell Congress that they will recommend that the president veto a bill. Other times the president himself commits to vetoing a bill if it is presented to him. The point is that if the chambers know in advance that the president might veto, they can decide either to modify the bill and hopefully avoid a veto, or to test the president's mettle and see if he will follow through on the threat. The more often Congress modifies bills in response to executive opposition, the less often presidents will veto a bill. So while we may see fewer vetoes, the decline may signal that presidents are exercising influence at earlier stages.

There is another explanation for the decline of the veto. As explained later, presentment is clearly not the final stage for voicing and acting on constitutional objections and policy preferences. If newly enacted laws seek to limit the executive's latitude, post-enactment minimization and nullification are now options for pushing back. Likewise, if Congress's new laws do not supply the additional authority that presidents often seek, executives might find that other laws can be twisted into supplying the needed power or discretion. In other words, when Congress chooses not to oblige a president's desire for greater authority or for an appropriation, sometimes a president belatedly discovers that existing laws can advance the executive's agenda after all.

A Lawmaker Extraordinaire

The possibility of a usurping Congress greatly troubled the Founders, who had witnessed state legislatures repeatedly encroaching on the constitutional powers of state executives and judges. In their experience, legislative authority was an "impetuous vortex" misappropriating the powers of the other branches.[21] But while Congress certainly has acquired more legislative powers at the expense of the states and thus has fulfilled the dismal expectations of certain Founding-era opponents of the Constitution, it generally has not usurped the powers of its rival branches. Rather, what is striking is how much authority Congress has bestowed on its most potent rival, the presidency.

Though many, including the Supreme Court, assert that the "the legislative power of Congress cannot be delegated," Congress has repeatedly done so, both to the president and to executive agencies under the president's sway.[22] Of course, it almost never declares that it is conveying "legislative power"—the curious exceptions are when it authorizes territorial legislatures to exercise legislative power or authority.[23] Instead, Congress camouflages its delegations by authorizing federal agencies to make "rules." But many such rules are just laws by another name.

Despite the Supreme Court's declaration that legislative power cannot be delegated, the courts have upheld acts that have delegated the authority to combat "inequitable distributions of voting power" among investors, to fix "fair and equitable" commodities prices, and to regulate broadcast licensing as the "public interest, convenience, or necessity" require.[24] These nebulous generalities impose no real limits on the delegations to agencies. They certainly do not establish an intelligible and limiting principle and really are more of a fig leaf—they perhaps supply the illusion of a constraint on the lawmaking discretion conveyed. The substance of the law—the answers to the most difficult questions—is left to the unfettered discretion of the agencies. Indeed, someone reading congressional law would in many cases be misled, for executive law supplements and, in some cases, actually supersedes congressional law. It may seem unbelievable, but Congress occasionally has authorized agencies to create rules that supplant Congress's own statutes.[25]

Moreover, if we judge laws by sheer volume, many more laws are created by agencies via delegated authority than by Congress. This imbalance makes sense, for it is far easier for agencies, via delegated authority, to make laws than it is for Congress to do so. Congressional laws require bicameralism and presentment and must take into account the wishes of hundreds of legislators across two chambers. In contrast, agencies can make law with just a handful of people acting in concert. In fact, sometimes one person, acting alone, can make agency law.

The Supreme Court has not only turned a blind eye to undeniable delegations of legislative power, it has itself delegated legislative power, albeit in a limited and obscure way. Rather than discerning and then implementing the best interpretation of a law—the reading that, all things considered, makes the most sense given the law's text, context, and intent—the courts often will defer to an agency's merely reasonable interpretation of that law. In other words, when a law is susceptible to multiple readings, agencies get to choose among them, regardless of that law's best reading. If an agency openly declared that "we choose to adopt this reasonable reading and reject the best interpretation of the law," it should prevail so long as its interpretation is reasonable.

This so-called *Chevron* deference—named after the 1984 Supreme Court case *Chevron U.S.A., Inc. v. Natural Resources Defense Council*—amounts to a judicial delegation of legislative power.[26] After all, when *Chevron* deference applies, Congress typically has not actually signaled that it wishes to delegate such interpretive questions to agencies, or declared that an agency's "reasonable" reading of one of its laws can supersede the best interpretation. Yet the courts often conclude that the agency can choose among the reasonable readings. In such cases, the *courts* are delegating *Congress's* powers to the executive.

All in all, our federal government is suffused with executive lawmaking, courtesy of delegations from Congress and the courts. When Congress or the courts delegate lawmaking authority directly to the president, the point is obvious, for in such cases the president is no longer a servant but rather a legislator. Likewise, when executive agencies receive delegations of power from Congress, the president's hand in these agency laws is more obscure but nonetheless significant, for in practice and in law, the president wields tremendous authority over these agencies. Significant agency rules are essentially the president's rules since, as then Professor (now Justice) Elena Kagan noted in 2001, presidents order executive agencies to craft them, superintend these rulemakings, and publicly claim credit for them.[27] Given these delegations to the executive, it no longer makes sense to envision the president as a servant of Congress.

An Amender of Congress's Laws

Because the executive believes in the practice-makes-perfect argument for the Constitution—that repeated practices can change the Constitution's meaning—it should surprise no one that the executive has the same view about ordinary laws. The Supreme Court endorsed this notion in the 1915 case *United States v. Midwest Oil Company.* By law, Congress allowed individuals to purchase federal land after paying nominal fees. The problem was that the federal government was selling oil-rich land for a pittance, then purchasing oil at high market rates. President William Howard Taft, contrary to the text of federal law, withdrew certain public lands from sale on the grounds that the government should not be selling these lands at a fraction of their value. Individuals sued, claiming that the federal law gave them the right to purchase public lands. The Supreme Court concluded that though the federal law contained nothing signaling a presidential power to withdraw public lands from sale, the president could do so anyway.[28] By repeatedly withdrawing tracts of federal land over the course of decades, the justices argued, presidents had essentially acquired the power with the implied approval of Congress. The idea is that if presidents do something repeatedly and Congress never objects, then Congress implicitly endorses the presidency's power to act.

Taft's withdrawals undoubtedly were the best policy. But the legal wisdom of inferring congressional approval is doubtful. The idea that Congress implicitly approved an executive power to withdraw lands because it never passed legislation condemning or barring withdrawals places too much weight on legislative inaction. The bicameral Congress is like an unwieldy aircraft carrier that cannot be expected to continuously react to the executive with either speed or decision. In contrast, the unitary executive is like a fighter plane that can quickly and repeatedly attempt to expand its legal authority and build on its prior legal claims. Moreover, members of Congress know that a president may veto bills that seek to either curb executive action or reject dubious readings of existing law, a prospect that tends to diminish their willingness to monitor and police executive assertions of authority. In this context, Congress's failure to conspicuously reject certain executive acts should not be read as an endorsement of them, much less as evidence that Congress regards the executive as having acted lawfully.

Nonetheless, the *Midwest Oil* mindset continues to have remarkable staying power. It exerts a powerful grip on executive thinking probably because it provides a roadmap for the expansion of executive authority. Consider the executive's mischief with respect to the Affordable Care Act (ACA), also known as Obamacare. Among other things, the 2010 law required employers to supply health insurance to employees. As with many laws, Congress specified the effective date of this "employer mandate." In this case, Congress provided that the employer mandate would not be effective until 2014. The idea was to provide transition relief by separating the enactment of the law in 2010 from when employers would have to comply. The greater the delay in the provision's "effective date," the greater the congressionally sanctioned transition relief.

Yet in 2013, the Obama administration decided to further delay the employer mandate and its accompanying penalties. In a letter to a member of Congress, a Treasury official claimed that because the department had long granted its own "transition relief" to taxpayers, it could grant additional transition relief relating to the employer mandate. The letter cited about a dozen instances when the executive had offered temporary relief to taxpayers, often immediately after the passage of an act and often for a few months.[29] Hence although the ACA decreed that the employer mandate would commence in 2014, the executive would turn a blind eye toward employers who failed to supply health care to their employees. This meant that employers would not have to supply health insurance in 2014, despite the act's clear imposition of that requirement.

This was a practice-makes-perfect argument. Because the executive had given transition relief in the past, it could do so again. But as with all such arguments, the argument raised thorny questions. The ACA itself provided a three-and-half-year period of transition relief. It also allowed for narrow exemptions from the employer mandate in limited circumstances. Because Congress had supplied rather generous transition relief and had conveyed administrative authority to grant some exceptions to the employer mandate, there was rather little reason to suppose that Congress meant for the executive to enjoy an implied authority to grant still further relief, transitional or otherwise. In fact, it seems extremely unlikely that Congress granted significant transition relief knowing that the executive might grant more relief at its whim, relying on obscure practices.

In any event, prior executive grants of transition relief tended to be for extremely short periods, almost always granted when the underlying law itself did not delay the effective date at all, and invariably granted in the immediate wake of a new law's enactment. In contrast, the Obama administration's transition relief extended for an entire year, came years after the statute's enactment, and would take effect after more than three years of congressionally bestowed transition relief. The Obama administration had taken the concept of "transition relief" and stretched it beyond recognition.

Moreover, one has to wonder what, precisely, prior practice had established. Taking one view, practice had established that in the tax context in particular, the executive had acquired a narrow authority to grant extremely short-term transition relief when Congress provides that a law will take effect almost immediately. Almost all of the past practices fit that narrow description. Call this "genuine transition relief for tax statutes." Or maybe these practices established a broader power to provide "tax relief" beyond what a new tax law itself provides. For instance, Congress might enact a new tax law and delay the effective date for seven years. Yet the executive may add two or three more years of delay. That seems to be how the Obama administration read prior practice. Call this "relief from tax statutes." It is not really *transition relief*, because in our hypothetical scenario, Congress had already provided a seven-year delay in the law's effectiveness. In the extreme, someone might argue that such practices had generated a generic power to provide relief from any law, new or old, tax or otherwise. Someone so inclined might say that executives have acquired broad authority to relieve people from the burdens of laws, akin to a power to suspend the law. Call this a "relief power."

The point is that there is no natural or obvious way of extracting a principle or rule from the handful of examples that the Treasury Department cited. Just as uses of military force can be characterized narrowly or broadly for purposes of establishing war-powers precedents, so too can "relief" be categorized restrictively or expansively.

In my view, there is little doubt that the Obama administration used an aggressive reading of those prior examples in order to dispense extended relief many years after passage. And there should be no doubt that the next several administrations may cite the employer-mandate delay to grant even longer-term relief years after passage.

Indeed, as noted, someone easily could extract a "relief power" from prior practice, whereby the executive claims that Congress has acquiesced to a presidential power to grant relief from all regulatory and taxation statutes. Because they tend to favor deregulation, Republican administrations might be particularly eager to cite the Obamacare example in order to grant all sorts of relief to regulated parties. They also might say that Congress has acquiesced because it never objected to this "relief power."

Enlarging, Contracting, and Breaking the Law

But what if a president is doing something for the first time, and so cannot invoke past practices? Sometimes the next best option is to take a relatively narrow law and read it expansively. During the Great Recession, President George W. Bush used a law appropriating funds for the bailout of "financial institutions" to rescue auto manufacturers, namely General Motors and Chrysler.[30] No plausible reading of the law permitted treating automobile companies as if they were financial institutions. Recognizing this, the House had passed a bill to fund an auto rescue. But the Senate did not pass this bailout.[31] After admitting that Congress had not enacted an auto bailout bill, President Bush announced that the "executive branch [would] step in" and dole out funds anyway.[32] The car companies were to be subsidized without regard to legal niceties.

The next administration was no better. President Obama continued the auto bailout, likely because he too could not bear to be blamed for doing nothing while General Motors and Chrysler failed. The intense desire to prop up the auto companies led two administrations to violate, directly and brazenly, the constitutional rule that no funds can be withdrawn from the Treasury except by virtue of a law.

Similar concerns—blame and disaster avoidance—motivated a parallel Obama scheme to shore up Obamacare. The ACA authorized federal payments to insurers but did not provide money to actually pay those companies.[33] The appropriation of funds was to come later. This scheme was in keeping with the norm that granting legal authority to a governmental entity to take an act does not automatically supply the funds necessary to take an act. For instance, legal authority to build a dam does not come with authority to expend funds to build it. A separate appropriation is needed.

In recognition that the ACA supplied no appropriation, the Obama administration repeatedly approached Congress for a new appropriation so that it could make the payments to the insurance companies. But the Republican House balked. Realizing that no genuine appropriation would be forthcoming, the administration repudiated its earlier stances and asserted that the ACA itself appropriated the necessary funds.[34] As a district court judge noted, the administration's argument that it had the legal authority to expend federal funds to subsidize the insurance companies was "a most curious and convoluted argument whose mother was undoubtedly necessity."[35] In other words, because the executive thought subsidies were essential, it relied on a bad reading of existing law.

Both bailouts involved taking narrow language and implausibly expanding it. But sometimes the executive does the opposite, choosing to diminish existing law in order to evade it. In particular, when Congress attempts to restrict executive action, the executive sometimes minimizes the congressional restriction. Recall that a federal law required a thirty-day waiting period before the release of any prisoners from Guantanamo. The period was meant to give Congress time to respond to the proposed release of dangerous prisoners and possibly bar their discharge. There were no stated exceptions to the thirty-day period.[36] Prior law had absolutely barred releases of Guantanamo prisoners, and the thirty-day period was a compromise designed to grant the executive some flexibility. The Obama administration, however, read into the law an implied exception to the thirty-day requirement: if the life of an American was at risk, then advance notice was unnecessary.[37] Because Private Bowe Bergdahl's life was said to be in jeopardy (he was being held by the Afghani Taliban), the administration invoked this life-in-jeopardy exception. But there was no exception, implied or expressed, in the law. The administration read into the law a faux exception because that served its policies of securing Bergdahl and releasing Taliban prisoners. In essence, after Congress belatedly and reluctantly granted some flexibility to the executive (the thirty-day rule), the executive misread that compromise to grant itself even greater latitude.

In another case, the Obama administration settled on "paralysis by analysis" as a strategy to avoid honoring a law, or less politely, to break it. By law, Congress had required the termination of aid to any nation that had experienced a military coup.[38] The law was meant to disincentivize military coups. If foreign military officers knew that American assistance might cease, they would be less likely to conduct a coup because their nation (and military) would lose foreign assistance.

Yet when the Egyptian military conducted a coup in 2013, the administration said that it was not obliged to cut off Egypt's $1.5 billion in US aid. In the face of much speculation about how this could be possible, a State Department spokesperson laid bare the rationale: "The law does not require us to make a formal determination as to whether a coup took place, and it is not in our national interest to make such a determination."[39] In other words, though federal law requires an aid cutoff whenever there is a military coup, if the administration never came to a conclusion about whether there had been such a coup, it would not have to cut off assistance to Egypt.

This was an uncommonly silly argument, one that would not have been made absent a compelling sense that America ought to continue its aid to Egypt. If the executive need not honor a law merely because its lawyers and policymakers choose to suspend their mental faculties indefinitely, then the executive has a practical power to evade *any* law. After all, lawyers and officials can always choose to study some legal issue indefinitely, thereby evading the law's obligations during their endless evaluation.

Imagine a taxpayer saying that she was not going to pay her taxes until she had first decided whether she had income, then further declaring that she was going to study the matter indefinitely because no law required her to conclude whether she had income. She might even add that "it is not in my personal interest to make such a determination." Taxpayers could never evade tax laws so easily. We would laugh at the sheer presumption. But apparently the executive believes it enjoys the power to procrastinate.

I would like to suppose that this argument is so embarrassing we will probably never see it again. But because repetition—practice makes perfect—eventually legitimizes claims of new authority, there seems to be at least a chance that paralysis by analysis might become a generic means of bypassing any inconvenient constraint on executive authority. We might again hear an executive essentially say, "We are very slowly gathering the facts and deliberating over the meaning of the laws. Because it's not in our policy interests to reach a conclusion, we don't envision ever doing so." Which of the Founders could have predicted that the executive might circumvent the law so easily?

Nullifying the Law on Grounds of Unconstitutionality

The original Constitution granted the president a veto to be used for policy and constitutional reasons. Left somewhat unclear was whether a president could refuse to enforce an existing federal law on the grounds that it was unconstitutional. For instance, if Congress declared that the president could no longer pardon anyone, could the president ignore this supposed law on the grounds that it was unconstitutional and therefore void? We know laws can be treated as nullities and therefore ignored because we are familiar with judicial review, a power nowhere specifically mentioned in the Constitution but discussed extensively at the Founding and exercised by judges ever since.[40] Courts routinely refuse to enforce or honor laws they believe are unconstitutional. Does executive review have the same grounding? Is it also implicit within the Constitution?

As noted earlier, Thomas Jefferson was the first to exercise executive review. During the presidency of John Adams, Congress had passed a Sedition Act that made it a crime to print "scandalous and malicious" writings with the intent to defame Congress or the president.[41] When Jefferson became president in 1801, some sedition prosecutions were ongoing. Jefferson terminated them, concluding that his "faithful execution" duty did not extend to laws he regarded as unconstitutional. In fact, he said he could no more enforce the Sedition Act than he could implement a law that required Americans to bow down before a golden image.[42] I believe that Jefferson was right to refuse to enforce the Sedition Act. Because he believed it to be unconstitutional, he simply could not enforce it, given his oath to preserve, protect, and defend the Constitution.

The modern executive embraces the notion that it need not enforce laws that it believes are unconstitutional. While the executive's refusal to honor congressional laws is most pronounced when the laws in question attempt to constrain presidential power, the executive also exercises the power over other subjects.

Modern presidents exercise executive review of existing law in three contexts. First, immediately after signing a bill, modern presidents often issue the now notorious signing statement, which, among other things, often spells out whether the executive regards certain provisions as unconstitutional. In these signing statements, presidents may signal that they will not honor or enforce the unconstitutional provisions. Second, when it comes time to actually implement a law, which may have been passed before or after the current president took office, the executive has yet another chance to opine that the law is unconstitutional and will not be enforced. That is, the president may adopt the route first taken by Thomas Jefferson with respect to the Sedition Act, when he declared the act unenforceable years after it was signed by President Adams. Third, when someone challenges the constitutionality of a law in court, the executive may, instead of defending the law, publicly endorse the claim and denounce the law that it currently enforces. This tactic is essentially a request that the courts likewise condemn the law as unconstitutional and bar executive enforcement of it.

Within these settings, the executive can adopt strategies of nullification, avoidance, and minimization. First is what we might call the direct strategy. Here the executive declares its belief that some federal law is unconstitutional and straightforwardly declares it will not implement it or defend it. Whatever the merits of the executive's constitutional claim, there is no obfuscation or misdirection. Everything is above board because the executive openly voices a belief that the law is unconstitutional.

Second is the avoidance game. In this scheme, the executive first observes that some federal law raises challenging constitutional questions. At this point, the executive does not claim that the law is actually unconstitutional, only that it *might* be. The president then sidesteps the thorny constitutional questions by adopting an alternative reading, one calculated to bypass the constitutional issues altogether. In this scenario, the executive dodges the best reading of the law in favor of some interpretation that is less plausible, but supposedly still plausible nonetheless. Such interpretational gymnastics can be problematic. Interpreters are not supposed to utilize this method of avoiding a constitutional question unless there actually is a *reasonable* alternative reading of the law. Yet the executive sometimes plays the avoidance card even when no plausible alternative is available.

Third is the somewhat disreputable suggestion game. Sometimes, in order to avoid saying that a law is unconstitutional, the executive will embrace what seems to be an artificial, wholly implausible reading of it. For example, imagine a law declaring that the executive "cannot negotiate a treaty with Russia." And suppose that the executive regards any such law as unconstitutional. Rather than forthrightly declaring the law unconstitutional and proceeding to ignore it, the executive will sometimes adopt a rather specious reading, or construe the law as not mandating anything at all but merely expressing some weak congressional preference against treaty negotiation. The executive might say that Congress is merely *suggesting* that the president not negotiate a treaty. If the law is construed as but a suggestion, it is constitutional. A congressional suggestion, of whatever sort, seems perfectly fine, because it imposes no actual constraints. It is more of a nonbinding resolution than an actual law. Moreover, the executive can heed congressional suggestions by quickly considering and rejecting them.

For several reasons, executive review of all sorts is more common than in Jefferson's era. In part, this rise reflects a growing confidence. Modern executive officials sometimes speak of deferring to the constitutional wisdom of the Supreme Court. But in practice, executives regularly act on views that are out of sync with that Court's pronouncements. Sometimes executives anticipate, or try to precipitate, changes in the Supreme Court's doctrine, and executive review may help generate those doctrinal changes.

Another factor that helps explain the president's greater willingness to engage in executive review is the broader range of contending and plausible constitutional interpretations. When Jefferson voiced his powerful objections to the Sedition Act, the realm of plausible interpretations of the Constitution was relatively narrow. While there were fierce disagreements, there was much less distance between the opposing sides in that dispute and other constitutional controversies. They were all originalists, after all.

Today, presidents (and their attorneys) operate in a world brimming with constitutional disputation and can draw on a smorgasbord of claims. They can focus on the Founders when that advances their policy agenda, and they can embrace living constitutional approaches when doing so seems most advantageous. They can cite prior presidential practices to expand their authority and, in another context, deny the relevance of modern congressional practices that run counter to broad executive authority. They can refer to judicial doctrine that favors the presidency and minimize those opinions that are less than helpful. In this way, presidents can advance novel and expansive readings of presidential power to satisfy an interest group, say, the gun lobby; articulate a contested theory of constitutional rights that appeals to a part of their electoral coalition, say, abortion-rights activists; and minimize congressional power in a bid to undermine congressional regulation of the executive, a move that can give them greater latitude to advance their policy agenda and the interests of allies.

In sum, a world where executives (1) have multiple opportunities to voice constitutional objections, (2) can employ any number of diverse interpretive techniques and theories to justify those objections, and (3) can flit between static and dynamic theories of constitutional change, presidents enjoy tremendous authority to deploy the Constitution either as a sword to seize new authority or as a shield to fend off congressional attempts to rein them in. Thomas Jefferson's narrow and laudable exercise of executive review of the Sedition Act—what he called a narrow *duty* to ignore unconstitutional laws—has, in today's context, become a powerful discretionary tool to advance the interests and policies of the incumbent president.

Going forward, it seems likely that presidents will grow increasingly willing and eager to engage in executive review. Gratifying a special interest group that wants a federal law to be nullified or left undefended before the courts comes with benefits. Presidents can curry favor, doling out nullification as a sop. Imagine a Republican president telling the business community that some hated regulatory law exceeds the scope of congressional power under the Constitution. Envision a Democratic president telling a reproductive rights group that a curb on doctor-patient speech violates the First Amendment. One day, discretionary executive review may even secure the vaunted status that judicial review currently enjoys.

LAYERING OF STATUTORY AND CONSTITUTIONAL ARGUMENTS

Given the growing ease with which the executive may craft statutory and constitutional claims to justify the implementation of its policy agendas, we can expect future presidents to regularly rely on another strategy: a two-step whereby doubtful statutory arguments are backstopped by aggressive constitutional claims.

The executive branch sometimes initially shuns constitutional arguments against a law, preferring to rely on the claim that Congress expressly or implicitly authorized the executive to take action. Want to wage war against a foreign nation? Don't immediately reach for the Constitution and cite past practice. Instead, argue that Congress either authorized the war or at least recognized a presidential power to start wars. That is what the Obama administration claimed with respect to Libya in 2011. It argued that the War Powers Act, a law clearly meant to constrain presidential authority, instead constituted an implicit congressional endorsement of a general presidential power to wage war for at least sixty days without any congressional authorization.

In fact, the Obama administration often eschewed constitutional arguments in favor of sometimes dubious statutory arguments. So rather than say that the Commander-in-Chief Clause authorized the president to ignore some law, administration attorneys would tend to say that a seemingly clear congressional law was not as clear as a reading of the text and context might suggest. In the end, the administration still obtained its principal goal—an ability to act as it wished—but it did so without relying on constitutional claims. If the goal is to take some action that seems contrary to law, the principals—the president and his highest aides—likely do not care much whether the executive's justification relies on constitutional claims as opposed to statutory ones. Either way the president gets to proceed as he wishes.

Statutory claims come with an added benefit: presidents and their lawyers can declare that if Congress believes the president is mistaken about the interpretation or the policy, it can always change its laws. This seems like a deep bow to the separation of powers. Yet everyone in the know realizes that changing statutes is no easy task, especially when the sitting president will oppose it. But the piece of gratuitous advice to Congress sounds far less imperious than informing Congress that the Constitution forbids that which Congress has attempted. The claim of statutory authority generates a welcome atmospheric difference with no real-world consequences for the pursuit of the president's policy agenda. Sitting presidents will get what they want—albeit by making a rather insincere point—and in the short term Congress will be unable to thwart them.

Finally, reliance on dubious statutory interpretations does nothing to eliminate the constitutional argument. If, by some miracle, Congress does change its laws and thereby eliminates the assertion that its laws authorize some presidential act, presidents can still sandbag Congress with a belated constitutional claim.

Going forward, executive lawyers who do not counsel a layering of claims should be scolded. In an age suffused with informal legal change and doubtful legal arguments, it is often possible to assert that a congressional law authorizes the very acts that it was designed to forbid. On the chance that the statutory interpretation argument fails to convince, executive lawyers can go on to argue in the same legal opinion, testimony, or brief that the Constitution forbids whatever manacles Congress has arguably imposed on the presidency.

DECIDING WHICH LAWS TO ENFORCE

Some imagine that the executive must mechanically execute the law, without fear or favor. But the Constitution makes clear that presidents enjoy some discretion. First, presidents may pardon offenses, a power that enables them to mitigate or partially nullify the law.[43] Presidents certainly may pardon a broad class of offenders when they believe the underlying law is unconstitutional. Likewise, presidents may pardon an entire cohort of offenders when they have policy disagreements with the underlying statute. For instance, a president who believes that a law imposes too strict a penalty can commute the sentences of all those found guilty. Armed with the pardon, there are no mandatory minimums that presidents have to respect. Further, presidents may grant amnesty to classes of offenders, either before or after conviction. A president who was moved by motives of mercy, or otherwise, could pardon *all* federal offenders. Such blanket pardons were common in Britain, and there were examples on this side of the Atlantic, as when the commander in chief of the Continental Army repeatedly granted broad amnesties to commemorate events like the issuance of the Declaration of Independence. The point is not merely that presidents have considerable pardon authority. It is also that the pardon power effectively gives them discretion over laws that create and define offenses and how they ought to be enforced.

The president also can influence which laws will be enforced through the allocation of scarce funds. Congress supplies the money and personnel that the executive deploys to enforce federal laws. Because Congress always limits those resources, the executive is typically under-resourced compared to the volume of transgressions. Moreover, Congress often grants a pool of enforcement funds to enforce a number of disparate laws. This effectively means that the executive can prioritize the enforcement of certain laws and deprioritize others. Put another way, by passing many laws and supplying insufficient resources to "fully" enforce them against violators, actual and alleged, Congress implicitly delegates the setting of enforcement priorities to the executive.

This prioritization power gives the president tremendous discretion. During the Obama administration, the president signaled that he wanted far fewer marijuana prosecutions brought, presumably because he thought that limited federal resources would be better expended deterring and punishing other offenses.[44] Likewise, in allowing certain nonviolent illegal immigrants to remain in the country, the Obama administration concentrated resources on higher-priority, violent illegal immigrants.[45]

While many Americans may have shared these enforcement priorities, there was nothing obvious about them. A president who can deprioritize marijuana enforcement can be followed by one who adopts a zero-tolerance approach to marijuana. A president can deprioritize the enforcement of a popular criminal law, perhaps one recently enacted by Congress, and instead prioritize the prosecution of some antediluvian offense dating back to the eighteenth century. A law on the books matters little if potential violators believe that the executive will not enforce it; other federal laws will loom quite large if people suppose that the executive will use every available resource to go after offenders.

As a general matter, the more enforcement discretion an officer has, the less tethered he or she will feel to any particular law. Where there is unbridled enforcement discretion, the officer's own sense of justice and sound policy may supersede any sense of duty when it comes to setting priorities and wielding power.

Executive Gamesmanship

In playing many of these executive games—law bending, law-breaking, law voiding, and law prioritizing—presidents and their aides are shrewd. They will tend to deploy these tactics when they imagine that their allies will cheer them on. That is, they will play fast and loose when they believe there is an electoral or policy payoff and when they can expect some level of partisan and popular support. When presidents decide to spend money without an appropriation or decline to enforce some law, they count on the beneficiaries to defend them. When presidents choose to fulfill a partisan pledge unilaterally, say, by trying to unilaterally dismantle Obamacare or by providing quasi-legal status to illegal immigrants, their co-partisans in Congress and the public often will applaud their boldness because they share the same agenda.

Executives are calculating in another way, for in playing these games, they also will weigh the possibility of judicial intervention. As noted, a judicial check may be unavailable because the courts believe that they lack a general commission to monitor the executive's alleged excesses. For instance, the courts have stated that "the decision whether or not to prosecute, and what charge to file or bring before a grand jury, generally rests entirely in [the prosecutor's] discretion."[46] Hence if the president chooses to cease marijuana prosecutions, the courts will not check that decision. Likewise, when the president illegally grants a subsidy, outraged citizens will be unable to secure judicial intervention. No taxpayer could seek judicial relief to halt the illegal subsidies that Presidents Bush and Obama doled out to American automakers.

CORRUPTING DISCRETION

The constitutional executor of our laws—the president—enjoys truly breathtaking amounts of discretion when it comes to laws and their enforcement. Presidents make laws because Congress has delegated its legislative powers; they amend Congress's law via persistent practice; they stretch, minimize, and occasionally break those laws; they declare them unconstitutional and hence unenforceable; and they set enforcement priorities, reinforcing the salience of some laws and suppressing others.

Massive discretion tends to corrupt, perverting the presidency's relationship to Congress and its laws. If you grant the executive remarkable lawmaking powers, express and implied, presidents will invariably come to see themselves as makers of the law rather than as the servants of it. In addition, when you bestow considerable lawmaking powers on an already powerful officer who ran for national office on a policy and constitutional agenda, you can expect that officer to wield lawmaking discretion to advance personal and policy goals. Finally, you can expect that the executive will, on occasion, simply usurp legislative power out of habit and self-interest. Presidents will create law to shore up pet programs, and they will dismantle those laws they detest. If absolute power corrupts absolutely, as Lord Acton warned, it seems fairly certain that sweeping discretion in the hands of the executive will likewise corrupt the executive in sweeping ways.

How long can chief executives continue to conceive of themselves as *executives* when they conspicuously run for office on a policy agenda and then, once in office, use their lawmaking authority to implement this agenda? The answer, I suspect, is not much longer. The ongoing transformation that Woodrow Wilson described in 1908—that "the President is becoming more and more a political and less and less an executive officer"—is almost complete.[47]

* * *

How did modern presidents become secondary lawmakers? Over centuries, the accumulation of various forms of discretion has corrupted the office. Starting out as an extremely timid third chamber of Congress, by the end of the nineteenth century the executive had become a confident co-equal chamber, with presidential candidates running for office on a policy platform and, once in office, vigorously wielding the veto to flex their policy muscles. By the twenty-first century, presidents have come to regard Congress almost as an option. If Congress supplies legal reforms, presidents are quite pleased. But when Congress proves recalcitrant, executives eagerly deploy interpretative and constitutional strategies to generate a form of inferior law—presidential law. Presidential law is inferior in the sense that it may lack the legitimacy and stability of congressional law. Nonetheless, modern presidents have come to realize that policy by presidential fiat is sometimes better than serving as Congress's servant and quietly acquiescing to Congress's obstinacy.

The transformation of the executive brings to mind a critical comment from Woodrow Wilson about the presidency's relationship to Congress:

> There are illegitimate means by which the President may influence the action of Congress. . . . He may also overbear Congress by arbitrary acts which ignore the laws or virtually override them. He may even substitute his own orders for acts of Congress which he wants but cannot get.[48]

Today it is still somewhat newsworthy when presidents "ignore the laws or virtually override them" or when an executive, in the face of a recalcitrant Congress, "substitute[s] his own orders" for Congress's laws. But the controversies, when they arise, are seen through a partisan prism. As one might expect, the president's opponents huff and puff about the president's duty of faithful execution. For their part, co-partisans often will not denounce such measures. Rather, many will cheer when presidential games advance the party's agendas. A president's allies will sense that much of the hand-wringing is insincere, since precious few dyed-in-the-wool partisans will complain when their party's standard-bearer is in the Oval Office and engages in the same sorts of trick plays. Faithful execution of Congress's laws is what many expect of presidents of the other party.

I will not claim that presidents are the full equivalent of Congress, in part because they have yet to fully see themselves as a complete, secondary lawmaker. They certainly do not believe that they have some generic right to make executive law. Instead, they typically attempt to somehow tie their lawmaking to Congress's handiwork. Moreover, as noted, presidents do not have agendas that extend to every federal law. Presidents are often indifferent to the vast corpus of congressional law, perfectly content to allow executive officials to execute most of Congress's laws without presidential involvement, much less interpretive or constitutional shenanigans.

It speaks volumes about the flexible nature of the modern presidency that an executive office, with an express duty to faithfully carry out the laws created by Congress, has been transformed into a parallel, junior varsity lawmaker. That the presidency is not yet the functional equivalent of Congress should not blind us to this remarkable revolution. Presidents, once mere boosters and dutiful supporters of the legislative team, are now off the bench, fully in the game, and leading their own legislative team.

CHAPTER NINE

How *to* Recage *the* Executive Lion

During Andrew Jackson's presidency, statesmen like Henry Clay and John Calhoun condemned what they saw as Old Hickory's overreaches. Although many of their criticisms were ill-conceived, we can learn a thing or two from the likes of such giants. One cutting critic, Daniel Webster, insisted that in the "contest for liberty, executive power has been regarded as a lion which must be caged. So far from being . . . considered the natural protector of popular right, it has been dreaded, uniformly, . . . as the great source of its danger."[1] In his view, only "watchfulness of executive power" could safeguard our liberties.[2]

On his last point, "Godlike Daniel," as he was known in his time, was right. We must not lose hope; rather, we must be vigilant and fight back. Those in favor of the limited presidency of the Founding must be counter-revolutionaries and struggle against the self-serving, creative energies of our presidents and their allies.

We can learn from the past, including our British American past. Our current predicament is best conceived of as replicating, in certain ways, the British constitution of old. The British constitution of the eighteenth century lacked our canonical text and was instead conceived of as the sum of disparate parts—laws, practices, and conventions. While certain features of the constitution might remain fixed for long periods, others fluctuated in the face of politics and changed circumstances. Nothing was permanent. Under that fluid system, there were periods when monarchs grasped for power and sought to upset the status quo. Sometimes they were successful, and other times they failed. The overall trend, though, was that the monarchy weakened and the legislature assumed the executive functions, so that now the Parliament practically has the entire legislative authority, and a portion of Parliament—the ministers—are the real executive. The reigning monarch of the United Kingdom is all pomp, circumstance, and tabloid fodder, with no real appetite to exercise whatever remaining powers rest formally in her hands.

Although the US Constitution was supposed to be fixed, and each of the three branches were to be legally bound to it, the reality is that we too have a British-style constitution, where new practices and understandings may supersede everything that is old. Though our Constitution's text has been relatively fixed, much of the unamended text has been reinterpreted and reimagined to yield wholly new meanings that would have been unfamiliar, even alien, to the Constitution's Founders. Because we do not see many formal changes to the Constitution, many of us suppose that we are ruled by the original version, albeit with some important amendments. But even if the most of the provisions in the Constitution were never formally amended, many of their meanings have changed in ways that have effectively amended the original document.

Since a British-style unwritten and flexible Constitution has largely supplanted the Founders' written and fixed Constitution, the British system provides helpful examples of how to handcuff a grasping executive. At various points in English and British history, institutions have pressed for reforms and fought to preserve and extend them through sheer doggedness. The Parliament, the courts, and others have labored to box in executive authority. Celebrated charters of liberty—the Magna Carta, the Petition of Rights, the English Bill of Rights, and the Act of Settlement—have curbed the Crown's propensity to usurp legislative authority, impose its will on the judiciary, and invade individual liberty.

American history is likewise littered with examples of Congress pushing back against executive overreach. Consider limitations on the president's power to fire officers. Whatever one thinks of their constitutionality (I am dubious), federal laws limiting the executive's power to remove federal officers ("for cause" laws) are ubiquitous and represent sustained efforts to curb presidential authority. These laws have been successful, for modern presidents respect these limitations and almost never even try to remove such officers.[3]

During Reconstruction, Congress sought to restrain President Andrew Johnson's authority over the military bureaucracy. Because legislators perceived him as too soft toward the South, they passed laws to weaken the presidency. For instance, Congress barred the president from directly ordering subordinate military officers; instead all his orders had to be routed through the general of the army, Ulysses Grant. This was clearly designed to weaken the president's ability to direct the military and supervise military reconstruction of the South. Again, whether constitutional or not, such laws represented a counterreaction. Furthermore, after the House impeached Johnson and the Senate came within a hair's breadth of convicting him, Congress found that he was more docile and agreeable. The draining and harrowing experience had curtailed Johnson's appetite for confrontation.

A third instance of congressional pushback can be found in the Nixon and Ford years, when Congress enacted a slew of reforms. With the bombing of Cambodia, the firing of Archibald Cox, the destruction of Oval Office tapes, and the Watergate burglary still fresh memories, Congress moved to rein in the executive. It passed the 1973 War Powers Act to curtail presidential war-making. In 1974, Congress by law required the president to notify certain legislators of covert action. That same year, it also approved the Congressional Budget and Impoundment Control Act to limit executive refusals to expend appropriated funds. It passed the 1978 Ethics in Government Act, which created independent prosecutors to investigate and prosecute high-ranking executive officials. For a moment at least, Arthur Schlesinger Jr.'s "imperial presidency" seemed to have abdicated. Or as Gerald Ford put it in 1980, the presidency had become "imperiled" instead of imperial.[4]

ACCOUNTABILITY OF THE UNITARY EXECUTIVE

The periodically fierce opposition to the presidency's burgeoning constitutional authority is perhaps natural. Alone among the Constitution's branches, the executive has a solitary, powerful, highly visible leader. It is easier to ascribe malevolence to a single person, and to galvanize opposition by decrying the president as a monarch or a rogue. In contrast, it is more difficult to be roused against a faceless multitude. Americans penned a Declaration of Independence that indicted George III even though most of their grievances were attributable to Parliament.[5]

The Founders knew this psychology. They understood that when there was a multitude, assigning responsibility might be difficult, if not impossible. Try to blame your representative for some decision of Congress, and he or she will deflect responsibility to the institution, its rules, customs, and, of course, the hundreds of other legislators. "They would not let me solve your problem," the congressperson will insist. Most of us are not in any position to know of the arcane rules and customs of Congress, much less the actual preferences of our representative's colleagues. We barely know our federal representatives, much less their true views.

The Founders knew that if you concentrated authority, you made it easier to pin responsibility. As James Wilson said, the president is not hidden behind councilors.[6] A president cannot say that advisers would not allow this action or that decision. Nor can a president blame them for decisions personally made and actions independently ordered. The buck stops with the president. The president is responsible for, among other things, nominations, pardons, and decisions on how the laws should be executed. Or as Wilson put it, constitutional "[p]ower is communicated to him with liberality, though with ascertained limitations. To him the provident or improvident use of it is to be ascribed."[7]

Executive unity is thus a double-edged sword. It not only serves to energize the executive; it also facilitates greater monitoring and accountability. As presidents pursue their interests—as they seek power, fame, sound policy—and thereby continually expand their constitutional office, Americans will find it easier to oppose them as compared to the diffuse, unaccountable multitude in Congress and the courts. We must seize this advantage, a legacy from the Founders, and make the possibility of a responsible executive a modern reality.

A Baker's Dozen for Congress

What can Congress do to restrain the presidency? Quite a bit, as it turns out. Congress has tremendous untapped power—it holds the purse and enjoys express constitutional power to carry into execution the powers of the presidency. Below I offer thirteen suggestions, some modest, some bold. I rather doubt that there are any constitutional difficulties with any of these suggested reforms, at least from the perspective of the original Constitution.

Later I offer a handful of solutions that a craftier, hard-edged Congress might enact: reforms that adopt a dynamic approach to the separation of powers. The basic idea behind those proposed reforms is that if presidents do not honor the original Constitution, they have no cause for complaint when Congress diminishes their office in a way inconsistent with the original presidency. Presidents cannot renovate and expand their constitutional office and simultaneously insist that Congress alone must honor the Founders' Constitution. Or more colloquially, a living presidency that can expand well beyond its original confines can also be forced to contract far within the boundaries of its original footprint.

1. Check the President's Principal Advisers

As things stand, Congress permits presidents to appoint many high-ranking officers in the White House (and its immediate environs) without Senate approval. This is a mistake. Congress, by law, should make all high-ranking White House officials subject to Senate advice and consent. It should take this step because such officials wield the most influence over presidents and their administration. They control the information flow to presidents and spend the most time with them, and thus are the voices that presidents hear and heed the most. Moreover, on the assumption that what senior White House officials say represents the president's will, these officials direct the vital work of other significant officers, including cabinet secretaries. Such White House officials are too important to lack the benefits of Senate vetting. A Senate check ensures a second assessment of character and qualifications.

Of course, Congress already has imposed advice-and-consent requirements on certain White House personnel. For instance, the director of the Office of Management and Budget and the US trade representative are advice-and-consent positions.[8] But there are far too many omissions. When it comes to the foreign policy of the United States, the national security adviser is one of the most consequential people in Washington, DC. Think of Henry Kissinger, who helped establish diplomatic relations with China. As Nixon's national security adviser, he surely was more powerful than Secretary of State William P. Rogers. Controversial figures like Susan Rice and Michael Flynn should be subject to Senate advice and consent.

The same is true of the White House counsel. Those supplying legal advice to cabinet secretaries—lawyers typically known as general counsels—are already subject to advice and consent. Given that practice, surely the Senate ought to vet an officer who supplies legal advice to the foremost executive, the president. I am not suggesting that any recent White House counsel has done anything amiss or that they would not have received Senate consent. Rather, my point is that senators should have a say over who heads this crucial legal office.

The White House chief of staff is one of a handful of the most powerful people in Washington. Typically, the chief of staff sets the president's schedule, controls what documents come across the president's desk, decides which high-ranking officials have the privilege of meeting the president in a confined setting (face time), and is a principal adviser. Officials in this position, which is far more important than hundreds of other positions that are subject to advice and consent, ought to be subject to Senate review.

I do not mean to be exhaustive here. There are more White House positions that ought to be subject to Senate consent. My limited point is that several of the undeniably most powerful executive officers are not subject to the advice-and-consent process, and they certainly ought to be. By comparison, many offices within the departments are subject to the Senate's check and yet their power, status, and influence do not hold a candle to White House advisers who never receive Senate consent. In the course of expanding advice-and-consent review to more White House offices, Congress might conclude that eliminating Senate consent requirements for dozens (or hundreds) of departmental officers will be necessary and appropriate. The Senate's bandwidth is necessarily limited, and it may need to focus on fewer officers, that is, only the most significant ones.

The Senate's role in consenting to appointments is vital, not only because senators vet a candidate's fitness for office, but also because senators often convince nominees to supply various assurances, including, among other things, their future use of delegated powers, the advice these nominees will give the president, and the nominees' willingness to resign should presidents abuse their powers. In a sense, nominees are stumping for the office, and like all politicians, they make promises. These guarantees are not always kept, but at least some nominees will not want to go back on their word. Many will recognize that if they break their vows to senators, they may not secure Senate consent for their next appointed office.

The extraction of promises might even be formalized. Senators could produce a list of standard promises expected of all nominees and a separate list specially tailored for the office in question. Senators have tremendous leverage and should better exploit it.

2. Augment Congressional Staff

When it comes to oversight investigations and institutional contests, size matters. Yet the size of congressional staff has declined precipitously since 1985, with the biggest decline a result of Republican efforts to economize during the Clinton era.[9] According to one study, the size of the personal staff for representatives in the House has declined by 20 percent.[10] The House's institutional staff (for example, staff for the sergeant at arms) has declined by 83 percent.[11] House committee staff has been cut in half. The declines in the Senate are less drastic, but still significant. The two biggest congressional agencies, the Governmental Accountability Office (GAO) and the Congressional Research Service (CRS), have likewise faced extreme cuts, the GAO by 41 percent and the CRS by 29 percent.[12]

To give itself a fighting chance, Congress must dramatically expand its staff. This surge ought to occur at every level. Agency staff at the GAO and CRS should be massively boosted. Personal staff of members should be vastly increased to enable members to better carry out their legislative and oversight functions. Committee staff, particularly personnel tasked with oversight functions, should likewise be augmented. And committee staff for the minority should be enlarged, because legislators in the minority also assist with oversight, and there is no reason for committee staff to be disproportionately apportioned to the majority as has long been the practice. In many ways, the current system of committee staff turnover, where hundreds of experienced personnel are tossed out with a change in the chamber majority, greatly discourages individuals from serving on committee staff because of uncertain tenure. To be sure, some turnover is inevitable because committee chairs control most of a committee's staff and those chairs may change even if party control does not. Nonetheless, legislators should be encouraging smart and eager citizens to join the cohort of committee staff, by creating more stable tenures.

Additionally, Congress ought to boost staff pay. Congressional staff are undercompensated for the work they do, which predictably leads many to seek greener pastures. The resulting loss of expertise makes it more difficult for legislators to legislate and conduct oversight. More generous compensation will reduce unwanted turnover and make it easier for legislators to retain prized staff whose opinions, knowledge, and work ethic they esteem.

Moreover, Congress ought to consider creating new agencies, including an Office of Legal Counsel for each chamber, each staffed with personnel roughly proportional to the Office of Legal Counsel in the Justice Department. Each Office of Legal Counsel should provide written and oral advice about the scope of Congress's constitutional authority, the constitutionality and meaning of bills and existing laws, and the constitutionality and legality of executive action. The chambers might conclude that the best structure consists of permanent staff supervised by political officers occupying the highest rungs, a structure that mimics the Department of Justice's Office of Legal Counsel.

The creation of two Offices of Legal Counsel, one for each chamber, might seem odd. But there are legal shops in every major executive bureaucracy, and many of these offer differing views on the meaning of laws. There is no reason why Congress cannot afford to receive occasionally divergent views. If the potential for discordant opinions is too troubling for some, then Congress can create a joint Office of Legal Counsel to serve both chambers, in much the same way that the GAO and CRS do.

3. Shrink the Apparatus of Expansion

As noted earlier, Congress funds the executive, including the very officers who help presidents expand their authority. Perhaps Congress ought to identify the handful of executive offices that it believes are most responsible for the expansion of presidential powers and carefully weigh whether to shrink the number of positions in those offices.

The obvious candidates are the Office of Legal Counsel in the Department of Justice and the White House Counsel. But one might also include the Office of the Legal Adviser at the State Department and other legal offices that have been at the forefront of expanding executive authority. Relatedly, Congress should at least study whether the Executive Office of the President has become too large and possibly constrain the number of full-time employees within it. Are personnel or offices within the Executive Office of the President helping chief executives exercise their constitutional and statutory powers, or are they instead nurturing the living presidency? Congress ought to wrestle with such questions.

If Congress reduces personnel in any of these offices, it also must preclude the use of detailees from other offices. If agencies can liberally detail (lend) their personnel to the Executive Office of the President or other entities that Congress wishes to shrink, then constraints on staffing are far less meaningful. What matters is how many staff work in an office, not which pot of money pays their expenses and salaries.

In considering such possibilities, Congress must be circumspect. Curbing the size of such offices might completely backfire. In particular, cutting the number of lawyers might diminish the impact of existing constraints on the executive because without sufficient lawyers, the principals, including the president, might be wholly ignorant of legal limitations on their statutory and constitutional authority. A legal constraint does nothing to constrain if high-level executive officials are ignorant of it. While ignorance of the law may not be an excuse, ignorance of the law often defeats the purpose of having the law in the first instance.

This complicated balance is for Congress to strike. After looking into the matter, Congress may well conclude that, all things considered, executive branch lawyers in some offices are far more of an accelerant than a retardant—that is, more apt to generate constitutional and legal change that expands the executive than to keep the executive in check.

4. *Shutter the* Chevron *Station*

Recall that under the *Chevron* doctrine, courts regularly construe laws as requiring judges to defer to an agency's reasonable construction of those statutes. The doctrine empowers the executive and likely serves to distort statutory interpretation. Congress should adopt a rather different approach. By statute, Congress should declare that the courts must decide questions of law without fear, favor, or deference to the executive. In those instances where Congress actually wants the *Chevron* doctrine to apply—where it wants the courts to defer to the executive's reasonable interpretations of the law—Congress will make that desire plain.

Indeed, the idea that federal legislators actually prefer *Chevron* deference seems unlikely. Why would legislators implicitly and repeatedly seek to empower their most powerful rival by allowing it to eschew the best reading of a law and instead substitute a merely reasonable one? Among other things, the hunger for greater authority already propels the executive to adopt dubious readings of laws. *Chevron* deference only fuels that desire and makes it more likely that the executive's preferences, rather than the choices reflected in Congress's laws, will be gratified. One might suppose that Congress actually prefers judicial resolution of legal disputes because it does not invariably trust the executive to decide matters unilaterally. Given the executive's propensity to further its various agendas, federal judges may seem like neutral third-party arbiters of the meaning of Congress's laws.

5. Stop Delegating Legislative Power to the President

Another reform, one related to ending *Chevron* deference, would be to curtail excessive delegations of legislative authority. There are some who doubt the constitutionality of the countless delegations of legislative power that litter the US Code. I share those misgivings. But put these qualms to one side for now. There are policy reasons for doubting the wisdom of allowing executive and independent agencies to write laws under the guise of writing rules. The proliferation of these agencies makes it rather difficult for the public to gauge the legislative outputs of Washington. More importantly for our purposes, the delegations of authority to executive branch institutions make the president rather powerful. Montesquieu predicted that if legislative and executive powers were to combine, tyranny would result, for then tyrannical laws might be executed tyrannically.[13] As things currently stand, I do not think that such tyranny is a regular occurrence. But our system would benefit from more separation of the legislative and executive functions. We ignore the practical wisdom of Montesquieu's maxim at our peril.

The best way to curtail these delegations to the executive would be to provide that the executive's rules will not be law unless Congress approves them. This would preserve the executive's traditional authority—making "recommendations" as the Constitution authorizes. And it would leave Congress wholly in charge of legislation, as the Constitution requires. If the executive's measures are wise or beneficial, Congress could adopt them. If not, the nation would not be saddled with executive lawmaking.

Further, in those limited cases where Congress chooses to continue to delegate its legislative authority, it should sunset that authority. In other words, delegations of lawmaking authority should expire after a fixed number of years, say three or four, with Congress forced to reconsider the wisdom of the delegation if legislators wish to renew it. As things stand now, most delegations have no expiration date and can be retracted only with new legislation. The difficulty is that the executive may veto attempts to retract delegated authority because the executive may wish to preserve its legislative power. Sunsets radically alter the bargaining position. A time limit on delegations obviates the need to overcome a presidential veto because delegations that Congress dislikes would eventually expire without the need to pass a new law.

Finally, Congress should decree that any agency rules generated via delegations automatically sunset after a set period. It is bad enough that many of Congress's laws do not come with an expiration date, thereby allowing laws from centuries ago to remain on the books with little reconsideration. It is far worse that executive laws may last for decades or centuries without any reconsideration by Congress, much less the agency that first enacted them. Periodically wiping the slate clean would be a sound reform. If Congress approves of the rules, it may codify them, on a permanent or temporary basis.

6. Add Sunset Clauses to Emergency Powers

There is a particular sort of delegation that seems especially pernicious: authorizing the president to take momentous actions in the wake of his or her declaration of a national emergency.[14] Embarrassingly, dozens of these emergency declarations have lasted for decades.[15] In the wake of such declarations, Congress is helpless because presidents wish to retain any crisis authority previously delegated and generally will veto laws that curb particular emergency delegations.

By law, Congress ought to provide that every such emergency, national security, or national interest declaration lasts no longer than six weeks after Congress next meets. This would ensure that if so-called emergency measures are to endure, Congress must make the choice. Further, any congressional extensions of presidential emergency measures ought likewise to have sunsets, ones that ensure regular legislative reassessment and revision. Any legal regime that authorizes a permanent state of emergency is far too lax, in the sense that the regime fails to recognize that real emergencies are truly exceptional.

7. End Signing Statements

Congress could effectively end the practice of presidential signing statements. Recall that presidents often issue signing statements that declare that one or more provisions in a newly signed law are, in fact, unconstitutional. Presidents do this to avoid having to veto the bill and to give voice to their constitutional views. This practice has proven controversial in recent times, because presidents have been increasingly aggressive in issuing such statements and in claiming that Congress's bills contain unconstitutional sections.

To counter this innovation, Congress could include a poison pill in its laws: a non-severability clause. Such clauses, when included in a federal law, essentially tell the world what is to become of the rest of the law when a portion of that law is deemed unconstitutional. As currently used, a non-severability clause typically provides that if a portion of the law is declared unconstitutional (presumably by the courts), the entire statute will no longer have any legal force.

Congress could extend the concept of a non-severability clause to executive declarations of unconstitutionality. If the president declares, in a signing statement or otherwise, that some portion of a statute is unconstitutional, Congress can provide that the entire statute would be null and void. This expedient would prevent presidents from exercising what many regard as a de facto line-item veto for provisions that the president deems to be unconstitutional. Instead, presidents would perhaps return to the earlier practice of vetoing bills that they regarded as unconstitutional. That was the early tradition because the Constitution expressly required presidents to defend the Constitution, including from legislative onslaughts.

Furthermore, such a poison pill would encourage Congress and the president to work out their constitutional differences before the bill gets presented to the president. As things stand now, there often seems to be little in the way of genuine constitutional dialogue. Congress takes its position as expressed in the statute, and the president takes his. There is no give and take because there does not need to be any. Presidents rarely bring matters to a head by vetoing bills on constitutional grounds. Why would they, when they can take what they want from a law and ignore the parts that they regard as unconstitutional? Moreover, the failure to have a cross-branch dialogue encourages constitutional "cheap talk" on the part of the executive. Presidents have no compunction about raising even the weakest of constitutional arguments because they pay little or no price, reputationally or otherwise, for doing so. In contrast, a non-severability poison pill might facilitate and encourage the serious deliberation needed to defend the Constitution.

In choosing to include poison pills, Congress would have to consider whether it would truly prefer that there be no law at all. Relatedly, members would have to carefully weigh the president's incentives and act to both preserve congressional authority and prevent presidential gamesmanship. In particular, Congress would not want non-severability clauses to serve as a means by which presidents could raise spurious constitutional objections in order to render the entire law null and void. Such presidential abuse of non-severability clauses might effectively grant presidents an absolute veto whenever they raised constitutional difficulties. Presidents could raise a constitutional problem, thereby triggering the non-severability clause and simultaneously eradicating the entire law. Because non-severability clauses are such powerful provisions, Congress would have to be selective regarding when to utilize them. For instance, Congress might tie non-severability clauses to items that presidents desperately want, thereby forcing the president to take the bitter with the sweet or, alternatively, veto the entire bill.

8. Rein in Executive Privilege

In the last three decades or so, we have seen an acceleration of the trend of the executive refusing to comply with congressional demands for information and testimony. This is sometimes called "executive privilege" and is said to be grounded on the principle that presidents have a right to frank advice. The idea is that no one will give a president candid advice if Congress (or the courts) can pry into the inner recesses of the presidency and reveal what was advised.

Presidents need advice, of course. Indeed, there is a constitutional clause—the Opinions Clause—that (redundantly) ensures that they may secure advice. But whether they have a right to *confidential* advice is doubtful. The Opinions Clause itself refers to "written opinions" perhaps because the public and Congress may hold the writer responsible for bad (or good) opinions. Moreover, despite the executive's claimed need for confidential advice, such briefings, opinions, and judgments often do not remain secret for long. Sometimes the *New York Times* or some other news purveyor reveals the "confidential advice" that a president received the day before. Other times, one or more "tell-all" books dish out juicy details about the terrible guidance that others gave and the sagacious advice of the author. Sometimes the president himself reveals the advice he receives in his memoirs, a practice that will, in the long run, decrease the tendency of officers to give frank and sometimes controversial counsel.

The general point is that as Washington currently operates, no advice given to the president has any true promise of confidentiality. Presidential advisers are incredibly naive if they suppose that what they tell the president, in writing or otherwise, will stay under a cone of silence. The only exception to this point relates to advice that is classified. Classified information is generally kept confidential, at least as compared to ordinary advice and information.

If executive privilege does a poor job of protecting confidences, why do we continue to have executive privilege? One reason is that it does a good job of stymieing congressional investigations of the executive. That is precisely how Dwight Eisenhower—the inventor of the phrase—used the privilege. He wanted to thwart congressional investigations of his administration. He had good reason for doing so. After all, he regarded Joseph McCarthy—the red-baiting Wisconsin senator—as a cancer on America.

Yet as a matter of constitutional law, Congress has a right to gather information, both to legislate and to oversee, and potentially impeach and remove, federal officers. This power of oversight and impeachment extends to the highest office of the land, the presidency, whose proper functioning is critical to the nation's health. Indeed, presidents have an express duty to provide Congress with information on the "state of the union," information that would include the operations and functioning of the executive branch. Congress cannot lose its constitutional right to access information needed for legislation and oversight merely because Senator Joseph McCarthy (and others) abused the congressional power of investigation, any more than presidents can lose their veto because some renegade president vetoed too many bills.

No early president ever denied Congress's power to conduct oversight. The episode from the Washington presidency often cited as the first invocation of executive privilege was nothing of the sort. When the House asked for certain papers related to a treaty negotiation, Washington made a qualified refusal. He began by declaring a general principle that modern presidents should heed: "I trust that no part of my conduct has ever indicated a disposition to withhold any information which the Constitution has enjoined upon the President as a duty to give, or which could be required of him by either House of Congress as a right."[16] Yet he would not hand over the papers in this instance because "[i]t does not occur that the inspection of the papers asked for can be relative to any purpose under the cognizance of the House of Representatives, except that of an impeachment, which the resolution has not expressed."[17] This was Washington saying that the only legitimate reason for the House to have these papers was impeachment, something the House never mentioned. But had the House suggested that impeachment was on the table, it seems rather certain that Washington would have supplied the papers because he would have a "duty to give" and the House would have "a right" to demand.[18] In other words, there is no executive right to withhold information from a chamber of Congress when it is conducting oversight that might lead to impeachment.

Congress should embrace Washington's fair-minded stance and openly declare that executive privilege does not apply to matters of congressional oversight. While keeping executive branch communications confidential may be desirable, the absolute need for congressional oversight of the executive rests on unassailable constitutional foundations. Our system of checks and balances requires a Congress able to check the executive, which is impossible if the executive can block inquiries by invoking executive privilege. Put another way, the clear-cut needs of impeachment investigations, something expressly authorized by the Constitution, wholly supersede any right to executive privilege.

9. Deputize Private Citizens to Whistleblow and Sue

Congress can draw on private citizens to check the executive. In particular, Congress can enact "informer" laws that incentivize citizens to help curb executive overreach. Such laws can impose fines payable to the Treasury for certain illegal or unconstitutional activities, such as starting wars or spending federal funds without an appropriation. Executive officials guilty of the underlying offenses would pay these fines out of their own pockets. Citizens who brought suit against the executive officers, prevailed in court, and helped to collect the fines would receive a portion of the fines, say, a third of the total amount. Essentially, Congress would pay a bounty to citizens who successfully proved that executive officials had violated federal law.

Such suits (and the underlying laws) are entirely constitutional. These informer statutes date back to before the Revolution, and early Congresses passed many such statutes, including ones that harnessed private avarice to ensure that executive officials complied with the law.[19] The courts have made clear that they will hear cases brought by private citizens seeking a share of fines because the individuals bringing suit have a concrete interest in the outcome. Moreover, presidents have little reason to complain because if the underlying acts are legal, the officials will prevail. If the acts are illegal, however, then presidents should be grateful that the system is calculated to prevent official misconduct. Finally, the subordinate officials have no cause for complaint. No executive official has a "right" to transgress Congress's constitutional laws, and none can complain that his or her office comes with the possibility of being sued for official wrongdoing. In a world where such suits and fines are possible, officials will take care to ensure that they are faithfully executing and honoring the Constitution and US laws.

10. Enact a Stronger War Powers Act

During the Nixon administration, Congress tried to reassert its control over war powers via the War Powers Act. Many judge its effort a failure, though as discussed earlier it is difficult to know whether in the absence of the War Powers Act, presidents would have started more or longer-lasting wars than they did with it in place.

Either way, Congress can add stronger teeth to the War Powers Act. Congress could provide that if a president attacks another nation without congressional authorization, the attack would immediately trigger a 75 percent reduction in the military budget. Pretty much everyone agrees that Congress controls the purse strings and can decide whether (and how much) to fund the armed forces and the wars they wage. Congress could flex its fiscal muscles to make clear that presidential adventures are extremely disfavored, if not forbidden.

A draconian cut in defense funding would incentivize presidents to secure congressional preapproval of wars, something the Constitution actually requires. Congress would have to weigh in and could refuse to authorize (or sanction) new presidential wars.

11. Take Constitutional Stands

It's politically smart to declare one's sense of the Constitution. The courts and the executive know this all too well, for each gains influence when they opine on constitutional matters. Courts could choose to merely declare who wins and loses cases, without supplying reasons. But supplying rationales makes their constitutional conclusions more persuasive and allows others to apply that reasoning to future cases. Similarly, executives issue constitutional declarations all the time, in vetoes, signing statements, court filings, legal opinions, and public speeches. These declarations give the executive a greater say in the shape and development of constitutional law, and that is one very good reason why the executive engages in this constitutional rhetoric. The more constitutional opinions a branch generates, the greater influence it can have on the future path of constitutional law.

In the past, the chambers of Congress have recognized that express constitutional declarations yield benefits. For instance, after George Washington refused to hand over the treaty instructions for the Jay Treaty, the House publicly insisted on its right to the information.[20] It essentially rebuffed Washington's claims about the House's authority vis-à-vis the implementation of America's treaties. A more recent pronouncement consisted of the Senate's conspicuous rejection of the idea that the meaning of treaties ought to vary over time. The Senate issued this rebuff in the wake of the Reagan administration's reinterpretation of the Anti-Ballistic Missile Treaty.[21] The Senate attached its rejection of the idea of living treaties to the Intermediate-Range Nuclear Forces (INF) Treaty of 1987 and, in the context of a later treaty, specified that the limit applied to all treaties.[22]

It seems clear, then, that Congress could issue constitutional opinions as a means of checking a grasping executive. For instance, the chambers of Congress could pass a generic resolution making it clear that each disapproves of executive amendments of statutes and the Constitution. More precisely, each chamber could declare that it does not believe that federal law, in its many forms, authorizes the president to act at variance with existing laws, either as a means of changing those laws or otherwise. The chambers also could reject the claim that consistent executive practice alone yields a change in constitutions and statutes. Finally, each chamber should go on the record and expressly reject the maxim "qui tacet consentit," to deny that its silence ever signals implicit acceptance of executive action.

Congress will enjoy greater influence in the resolution of constitutional controversies if the chambers articulate why Congress's laws are constitutional, why the executive has violated the Constitution in failing to enforce a law, and why it believes the president has transgressed some constitutional principle. In particular, expressly declaring that a president has violated the Constitution makes it more likely that outsiders will take congressional perspectives seriously. In contrast, no branch or institution will ever generate much influence by being unassuming, reticent, or relatively mute on matters of constitutional law.

12. Censure a Misbehaving President

Sometimes relatively tactful statements of constitutional principle are insufficient. On occasion, Congress may need to condemn presidential aggrandizement. In 1834, the Senate censured Andrew Jackson for assuming powers not conferred by the Constitution or laws. (A few years later, it expunged the censure.) In 1842, the House endorsed a report that condemned John Tyler for "gross abuse of constitutional power and bold assumption of powers never vested in him by any law." Apparently, representatives thought that Tyler had exercised his veto authority too energetically. And the Senate rebuked James Buchanan in 1860 for using party ties in awarding public contracts.[23]

Censures are easier to pass than impeachment motions because they carry fewer consequences; they enable Congress to respond, when appropriate, with indignation or outrage to circumstances that may not merit impeachment, trial, and removal. While mere words may seem cheap, they still can serve moral and constitutional purposes. They lay out markers regarding what Congress takes to be impermissible behavior, thereby putting the other two branches on notice. They also require members to engage with the Constitution and declare, for the record, their views on matters of public import. Rather than ducking the hard constitutional and legal questions, members should take stands on public controversies like the constitutionality of President Obama's Deferred Action for Childhood Arrivals (DACA) and the legality of President Trump's missile strikes in Syria.

13. Monitor the Executive Branch with a New Entity

A handful of the original states created a council—a "council of censors"—to monitor their governments' compliance with state constitutions and laws. These bodies kept an eye on all three branches of the state government and would generate periodic reports that would highlight missteps and violations. The public could read these reports and judge for themselves.

Congress could borrow from these examples and create a congressional entity whose sole mission would be to produce annual reports that highlight instances where executive officials have overstepped their legal authority. There might be an annual report on the official acts and omissions of the president, another on the Department of Defense, and still others focusing on other significant executive departments. Congress could both decide which executive entities were in need of annual reports and give the monitoring agency its marching orders. The point is that there would be one or more yearly reports on executive wrongdoing that members of Congress and citizens could read, discuss, and assess.

"UNCONSTITUTIONAL" REFORMS

The three reforms I propose next are, I believe, unconstitutional, at least under the Founders' Constitution. But Congress might sensibly conclude that if the presidency of today is not the presidency of the Founders and shows no sign of retreating to its more modest (but still quite powerful) beginnings, Congress likewise should play by the same, more loose and flexible rules. Congress cannot be limited to the Founders' conception of Congress when presidents do not act as if they are limited to the Founders' conception of the presidency.

1. Create More Plural, Independent Executives

According to the original design, the president has power to execute the laws. As Alexander Hamilton observed, he is the constitutional executor of federal law. But our practices radically depart from this design. Supreme Court doctrine makes it possible for Congress to vest independent executive authority in officers not answerable to the president. Agencies like the Federal Election Commission, the Securities and Exchange Commission, and the Federal Communications Commission execute federal laws (and their regulations) by bringing prosecutions. They are somewhat independent in that the president cannot fire the commissioners at will. Moreover, as noted earlier, presidents tend to pay less attention to what goes on in many of these commissions. Essentially, these so-called independent agencies are more apt to act somewhat independently of the executive.

Congress can use this template for new agencies and expand it to cover existing agencies. For instance, Congress could make the Department of the Interior or the Department of Energy independent agencies. It could expand the leadership, moving from single leaders to a plural commission, with each commissioner granted for-cause protections.

Congress even could grant independence to the Department of Justice. Jimmy Carter ran on a platform that included making the Justice Department an independent bureaucracy. After he entered office, he renounced the idea when the Justice Department told him that his plan was unconstitutional. But the department was wrong, at least under prevailing understandings. Given existing practices and Supreme Court doctrine, both of which clearly permit placing prosecutorial authority in the hands of independent officers and agencies, there is no reason why Congress could not create an independent Department of Justice.

2. Establish a New Impeachment Agency

In theory, the impeachment process is a powerful tool of congressional control. But everyone knows it is too difficult and time-consuming to present a real threat to a sitting president.

When faced with similar problems regarding legislation, Congress has adopted the tactic of delegating its legislative powers to an agency. It might likewise delegate its impeachment functions, both impeachment and trial, to an agency specially tasked with removing officers. The impeaching entity could be led by a commission composed of officers with for-cause protections and appointed by the president with the Senate's advice and consent.

The beauty of this structure, like all delegations from Congress, is that it bypasses the strictures of Article I. Impeachment would no longer have two stages and it would no longer require a supermajority. Impeachment would no longer occupy an inordinate amount of legislative time. Congress could harness impeachment expertise and allow an agency to decide what constitutes bribery, treason, and high crimes and misdemeanors. For that matter, the Impeachment Commission need not even be limited to those categories. Congress could give it authority to remove for other reasons, including actions that might be thought by some to be outside the category of impeachable offenses, like maladministration or neglect of duty.

If legislators are squeamish about appearances, they can impose a different nomenclature. Just as Congress does not call its junior-varsity legislators (the dozens of agencies that make rules) "junior Congresses" and just as Congress does not call the outputs of these agencies "laws," so too might Congress name the new entity the "Fitness Board of Review," rather than the Impeachment Commission, and call its actions "fitness discharges," rather than removals.

3. Delegate Budget and Regulatory Authority
to an Independent Agency

As things stand, if Congress wants to overturn an administrative action or signal its disapproval in a concrete way, it has to go through an arduous bicameral process and then present the reform to the president for veto or signature. This laborious process is often useless because presidents will oppose, with an insurmountable veto, attempts to shrink executive budgets or to nullify executive exercises of authority.

Yet Congress can cleverly bypass this process if it is willing to create a rival power center. Under existing doctrine, nothing prevents Congress from delegating its budgetary and legislative authority to an agency that would, in turn, supervise the executive. This Executive Review Agency could be vested with the authority to cut existing executive branch budgets and modify or rescind new rulemakings. The head (or heads) of the Executive Review Agency would be nominated by the president, but the Senate, via the confirmation process, could ensure that appointees are actually willing to police executive overreach and will not serve as the president's toadies. Moreover, for-cause protection, granted by statute, would encourage independence.

The Executive Review Agency would be charged with discovering violations of the law and the Constitution and sanctioning the relevant executive branch agency via budget reductions and rule rescissions and modifications. Because sanctions would be easier to impose than under the current system, agencies might be less likely to indulge wrong or illegal behavior.

THE IDEAL TIME FOR REFORMS

Because members of Congress are used to acting like party loyalists, the best time for adopting these reforms would be during the waning months of a presidential term but before a presidential election. Better yet is the same scenario coupled with widespread and deep uncertainty about who will prevail in the contest, especially if the two candidates are polarizing and members of both parties are willing to limit their potential benefits in return for drastically limiting their worst-case scenarios. Nothing would stir the reformist passions of Democrats more than a free-market, tax-cutting, religious-right Republican candidate, while nothing would spur Republicans more than a leftist, green, big-spending, "woke" Democrat.

Behind this useful veil of ignorance, federal legislators could be united by fear and more systematically devoted to protecting congressional prerogatives and checking presidential power. Something like this state of uncertainty arises every four years, and legislators should use it to temporarily unite and protect their institution from a grasping executive.

Our Reactive Courts

Though in our system of separated powers the courts are supposed to check the executive, our federal courts were clearly not meant to be the perpetual censors of presidents and their conduct. Even so, our federal courts can and should do more to curb the living presidency.

In some cases, existing doctrines of judicial restraint are unwarranted. For instance, nothing in the Constitution marks war powers questions off-limits for the courts. From the early years of the Republic on through the Civil War, judges repeatedly reviewed the legality of the executive's wartime actions, particularly seizures of property. Again and again, judges proved themselves willing to rule against the executive. Rather than reflexively shrinking from some categories of war powers cases, modern courts ought to re-evaluate doctrines that have the unintended consequence of empowering the executive. For instance, in a case with a proper plaintiff, courts should decide whether presidents have constitutional authority to wage war. As suggested earlier, executives will tend to be more aggressive when they know that judges will defer to the executive, or worse yet, refuse to judge the legality of executive action.

The courts also ought to abandon certain pernicious doctrines. In an era saturated with executive law, there seems little need for doctrines of deference, *Chevron* and otherwise, that grant the executive even greater law enforcement discretion. Such doctrines likely encourage more strained readings of the law, as lawyers strive to demonstrate that the law is unclear and that, given the statute's complexity, their reading is reasonable. Courts should unambiguously renounce doctrines that effectively permit executives to acquire constitutional and statutory authority via repeated practice. It is an inadmissibly capacious conception of the American Constitution to behold the modern practices and treat them as if they were the full equivalent of a formal constitutional amendment. None of our branches should be able to acquire new constitutional authority through serial violations of the existing Constitution.

Some judges are already responding in limited ways to the growth of executive authority and, in the process, reevaluating existing doctrine. Whenever there is a perception of executive overreach, as there is now, judges are more apt to respond in some way. That is, because they are only human, federal judges are more likely to intervene when they perceive that their interference would be useful or necessary in checking defiant or grasping presidents.

We have seen this judicial counterreaction from time to time. During the Roosevelt presidency, courts initially played a role in policing traditional limits on executive power and legislative power. During the War on Terror, many courts (including the Supreme Court) seemed eager to curb the supposed excesses of the George W.

Bush administration. During the Obama years, some conservative judges did the same. And most recently, progressive judges have arguably flouted longstanding constraints on the exercise of judicial power in order to thwart President Trump, on the grounds that he has transgressed limits, modern and historical, on the contemporary presidency.

Though judges cannot be the vanguard of the movement to rein in the executive, more than a few may elect to play some role in curbing executive overreach. Judges are not immune to the prevailing discontent about the presidency. Their black robes are perhaps meant to suggest impartiality, but underneath, some share the apprehensions that many of us feel.

We the People

In our republican form of government, the people are the ultimate guardians of the Constitution and of its presidency, which was designed to be powerful yet limited. Legislators in Congress are unlikely to reassert congressional power to check the executive as long as We the People are fair-weather friends of the Constitution's limited presidency. If we celebrate executive license and discretion when it suits our purposes and denounce it only when our party no longer occupies the Oval Office, our legislators will do the same. We cannot expect legislators to be more virtuous and consistent than their voters.

Virtue and consistency have surfaced in Congress from time to time, most recently in the 1970s. It can happen again, if we the voters choose to make ending the living presidency a true priority. Ending our long experiment with presidents who amend our laws by regularly transcending them will require ordinary citizens reacquainting themselves with a limited Constitution and a limited presidency. There is no substitute for steady adherence to enduring constitutional principles. And there is no alternative to informed, watchful voters.

$$* * *$$

None of these reforms are panaceas. They will not quickly rid our nation of the difficulties associated with an imperial, living presidency. Nor do they speak to the institutional torpidity, sclerosis, and cowardice that Congress evinces from time to time. Congress must act to thwart an aggrandizing executive. But the forces, fears, and motives that have so far prevented such a reaction will not disappear because of a book that catalogs a list of earnest proposals. To tweak a saying of Justice Robert Jackson's, by replacing his phrase "any decision of the Court," we can "have no illusion that [any book] can keep power in the hands of Congress if it is not wise and timely in meeting its problems. . . . [O]nly Congress itself can prevent power from slipping through its fingers."[24] For any serious reform to materialize, members of Congress must, from time to time, adopt the institutional perspective even as they regularly cling to the party perspective. This is certainly possible. After all, legislators regularly rise above party. Farm-state legislators exhibit a remarkable degree of unity across party lines when it comes to subsidies and price supports, for instance. In that case, they insist on prioritizing regional, local interests at the expense of party interests.

Despite what their hangers-on may whisper in their ears, members of Congress must never forget that most of them will spend their remaining political careers on Capitol Hill, not in the White House, since most lack even a remote shot at the Oval Office. And they must be made to see that their more realistic ambitions are at least sometimes best advanced by consistently insisting on the institutional prerogatives of the legislature.

For their part, voters ought to demand a renaissance of constitutional first principles. Our politicians are only as reliably virtuous as their voters. If voters remain fickle supporters of the original, limited presidency, we cannot expect our legislators to exhibit the firmness and constancy needed to recage the executive lion. So long as We the People are divided and inconsistent, with half of us attempting to push the lion into the cage and the other half straining to keep it out—and with these roles flipped every four or eight years—the lion will remain ever on the prowl, posing a clear and present danger to what remains of our original constitutional order.

Conclusion

Decades ago, while in a grocery store with my parents, I filched a candy bar, slipping it into my jeans pocket. My parents did not know of my dastardly deed. But because I chose to eat it in the car on the way home, they soon figured out that something was amiss. They had not bought a candy bar, and yet I was enjoying one. Because I was only four or five years old, they knew that I had not purchased it.

My father drove back to the grocery store and had me confess my sins to a store employee. I don't recall what the employee said, but thankfully there were no major repercussions. I was not even banned from the store. I was frightened and, one might say, scared straight.

When we got home my father told me a story about a "banana boy." It was meant to impart a lesson. It succeeded: the story has stuck with me all these years. Perhaps we can profit from it:

There was a boy who lived with his family in India. The family was extremely poor. One day the boy brought home a banana for his "ajji" (grandmother), who lived with the family. She quickly ate it, not pausing to consider how the boy came to have it. After all, bananas are a delight and the family rarely enjoyed them.

Seeing her happiness, the boy made a ritual of bringing a banana home every evening. His ajji eagerly ate the bananas and derived sustenance from them.

One evening, the police came to the house and told the family that they had the boy in custody. The boy had been stealing the bananas and would be punished. The ajji made her way to the police station to see her grandson and find out why he would do such a thing.

When the ajji drew close to the boy, he lashed out, slapping her cheek. The boy blamed her because she had not told him that stealing bananas was wrong. It was her duty to teach him right from wrong, and she had failed him.

I don't know where my father heard this story. Perhaps his mother, my ajji, told it to him. Perhaps he made it up. But his point in telling it to me was crystal clear. He felt it was his duty to teach me right from wrong and that if he didn't do so, I would eventually resent his failure and indulgence. When I first heard the story, I was struck by the gall of the boy, hitting his grandmother. Part of me wondered whether she actually knew that he was stealing the bananas. If she didn't know, how was she in any way blameworthy? But none of that part of the story applied to my case. I had pilfered the chocolate, and my father had warned me that I'd be sent to jail if I continued along this path.

When I think of this story now, I can't help but think of the presidency and what it has become. Presidents are like the banana boys of our republic, and the segment of the public that supports them at any given time is like the grandmother. As long as presidents give us what we want, whatever that is—subsidies, individual rights, or national security—we have a tendency to look the other way and ignore whether their acts are lawful. We are grateful for the bananas they give us, and don't care much about their provenance.[1]

Given that so many of us are quick to praise presidents who supply the policies we prefer, is it any wonder that they often get away with unilaterally imposing them? Presidents generally seek to curry favor with their base, supposing that they should dance with those who brought them to the Oval Office. So, when their base is pleased, presidents conclude that they have done the right thing.

But these two familiar reactions are the slow road to a banana republic. If we wish to keep presidents under the law, we have to recommit to the quaint notion that the meaning of a law is fixed until its text is changed. And we have to recommit to neutrality as we judge the legality of the executive's acts. If we don't, we have no fixed compass and no sound basis for criticizing a president for breaching the law. After all, if presidents can legally acquire authority through their transgressive acts, then they are merely exercising an entirely constitutional option when they seek to expand their authority. If you tell presidents that they can acquire authority by violating existing norms, we shouldn't be surprised when they take up that option.

Relatedly, we cannot have an executive constrained by a fixed Constitution when we have a Congress and a judiciary that are free to change the Constitution via their acts and pronouncements. Presidents fully recognize that ours is a living Constitution, and when they see the other two branches amending the Constitution, they cannot be blamed for also trying to bend that unstable, shifting, and mutable framework to their further advantage.

Woodrow Wilson famously praised the idea of an organic Constitution and lauded a president who seized the initiative, who sought to be as "big a man as he can." Should "Congress be overborne by him, it will be no fault of the makers of the Constitution,—it will be from no lack of constitutional powers on its part, but only because the President has the nation behind him, and Congress has not." After referencing the president's power of persuasion, however, Wilson sang a different tune, highlighting what presidents should never do:

> There are illegitimate means by which the President may influence the action of Congress. He may bargain with members, not only with regard to appointments, but also with regard to legislative measures. He may use his local patronage to assist members to get or retain their seats. He may interpose his powerful influence, in one covert way or another, in contests for places in the Senate. He may also overbear Congress by arbitrary acts which ignore the laws or virtually override them. He may even substitute his own orders for acts of Congress which he wants but cannot get. Such things are not only deeply immoral, they are destructive of the fundamental understandings of constitutional government and, therefore, of constitutional government itself. They are sure, moreover, in a country of free public opinion, to bring their own punishment, to destroy both the fame and the power of the man who dares to practise them. No honorable man includes such agencies in a sober exposition of the Constitution or allows himself to think of them when he speaks of the influences of "life" which govern each generation's use and interpretation of that great instrument, our sovereign guide and the object of our deepest reverence. Nothing in a system like ours can be constitutional which is immoral or which touches the good faith of those who have sworn to obey the fundamental law. The reprobation of all good men will always overwhelm such influences with shame and failure.[2]

For a moment, consider the various acts that Wilson decried as "deeply immoral." What is especially curious to the modern ear is his claim that an "honorable man" will not envision such possibilities "when he speaks of the influences of 'life' which govern each generation's use and interpretation of that great instrument, our sovereign guide and the object of our deepest reverence." He is asserting that no honorable living constitutionalists could contemplate that their organic Constitution might eventually authorize, even celebrate, an executive's ability to "ignore laws or virtually override them" or to substitute the executive's orders for the laws of Congress.

In making this claim, Wilson certainly contemplated the prospect that living constitutionalists (or presidents) might one day assert that our nation's lived experience had transformed the president's relationship to Congress and its laws. To say that something is unfathomable is to at least fathom the possibility. Rather than embracing the possibility that the executive's relationship to law might alter over time, Wilson blanched from the implication, resorting to unhelpful preaching. He never begins to explain why some changes to the presidency are welcome, moral, and pose no threat to constitutionalism while others would be the opposite.

This takes me to the second point: Wilson was a remarkably poor Wilsonian, at least when it came to law execution. He had failed to fully internalize the lessons of his own theory. More than a century after he wrote, we have learned that there was nothing uniquely sacrosanct about the presidency's eighteenth-century duty to execute law. As compared to the fading original meanings of the Faithful Execution Clause and Presidential Oath Clause, the "influences of 'life'" have proven too potent. The meanings of the two clauses have not remain untouched. No one reading these clauses today should be fooled into thinking that modern practices satisfy what many people would regard as their ordinary meaning, much less their original meaning.

Indeed, the enduring lesson of living constitutionalism is that there are no checks or duties that the present (or presidents) must honor eternally. There are no sacred constitutional cows. Everything—

individual rights, the scope of congressional power, the role of the judiciary—is up for continual reconsideration and reimagination. In this environment, we cannot expect to maintain an impregnable fortress around the original presidency, or even those parts that have somehow remained intact since the Founding.

You see, contrary to what many suppose, the living presidency is not a bug of modern approaches to constitutional law. The living presidency is rather a central, defining feature of our living Constitution, part of its deep code. So long as we have a living Constitution, we will endure a living presidency that not only enjoys an outsized influence on the Constitution's ongoing informal transformation but also expands executive power.

No one should doubt that fickle opponents of a living presidency will continue to denounce it as "imperial" when they oppose the incumbent's political agenda. But when a favorite sits in the Oval Office, many of these erstwhile critics will insist—with neither a trace of irony nor much concern about future implications—that a controversial presidential action is entirely legal because, after all, prior presidents have done something vaguely similar. The presidency is alternatively imperial or living, as political convenience dictates.

Notes

Acknowledgments

Index

Notes

Introduction

Epigraph: Quoted in Bob Woodward and Carl Bernstein, *The Final Days* (New York: Simon & Schuster, 1976), 61.

1. Arthur M. Schlesinger Jr., *The Imperial Presidency* (Bridgewater, NJ: Replica Books, 1998).
2. James Madison, *Federalist*, no. 48, Avalon Project, Yale Law School Lillian Goldman Law Library, http://avalon.law.yale.edu/18th_century /fed48.asp.
3. US Const., art. II, § 1.
4. "Bush: 'I'm the Decider' on Rumsfeld," *CNN*, April 18, 2006, http://www.cnn.com/2006/POLITICS/04/18/rumsfeld.
5. Joseph A. Schumpeter, *Capitalism, Socialism and Democracy*, 5th ed. (London: Allen & Unwin, 1976), 81–86.
6. *Youngstown Sheet & Tube Co v. Sawyer*, 343 US 579, 610–611 (1952) (Frankfurter, J., concurring).
7. *NLRB v. Noel Canning*, 573 US 513, 570, 593 (2014) (Scalia, J., concurring).
8. Patricia L. Bellia, "The Story of the *Steel Seizure* Case," in Christopher H. Schroeder and Curtis A. Bradley, eds., *Presidential Power Stories* (New York: Foundation Press, 2009), 250.

9. Abraham Lincoln, "The 'Divided House' Speech" (June 17, 1858), in L. E. Chittenden, ed., *Abraham Lincoln's Speeches* (New York: Dodd, Mead, 1896), 71.

CHAPTER 1. KINGLY BEGINNINGS

1. "The Story behind *Time*'s Trump 'King Me' Cover," *Time*, June 7, 2018, http://time.com/5303844/donald-trump-king-cover.
2. President Washington faced such criticism from the press, as well as from Thomas Jefferson and Thomas Paine. See Shannon Duffy, "Press Attacks," Fred W. Smith National Library for the Study of George Washington at Mount Vernon, https://www.mountvernon.org/library /digitalhistory/digital-encyclopedia/article/press-attacks; Jeffrey H. Morrison, *The Political Philosophy of George Washington* (Baltimore: Johns Hopkins University Press, 2009), 83.
3. Saikrishna Bangalore Prakash, *Imperial from the Beginning: The Constitution of the Original Executive* (New Haven, CT: Yale University Press, 2015), ch. 1.
4. Some argue for reading the Constitution in the "bright light" of the Declaration. See, for example, George F. Will, "Foreword," in Randy E. Barnett, *Our Republican Constitution: Securing the Liberty and Sovereignty of We the People* (New York: Broadside Books, 2016), xi.
5. James Madison, *Federalist*, no. 41, Avalon Project, Yale Law School Lillian Goldman Law Library, http://avalon.law.yale.edu/18th_century /fed41.asp.
6. Prakash, *Imperial from the Beginning,* 31–34, 334n53.
7. James Madison, "Tuesday July 17," in Max Farrand, ed., *The Records of the Federal Convention of 1787,* 4 vols. (New Haven, CT: Yale University Press, 1911), 2:35.
8. James Madison, *Federalist*, no. 48, Avalon Project, Yale Law School Lillian Goldman Law Library, http://avalon.law.yale.edu/18th_century /fed48.asp.
9. Prakash, *Imperial from the Beginning,* 34–35.
10. Charles de Secondat, Baron de Montesquieu, *The Spirit of the Laws* (1748; Kitchener, ON: Batoche Books, 2001), 173–174. James Madison acknowledged Montesquieu as the basis for the idea that "[t]he

accumulation of all powers, legislative, executive, and judiciary, in the same hands, whether of one, a few, or many, and whether hereditary, self-appointed, or elective, may justly be pronounced the very definition of tyranny." James Madison, *Federalist,* no. 47, Avalon Project, Yale Law School Lillian Goldman Law Library, http://avalon.law.yale .edu/18th_century/fed47.asp.

11. Prakash, *Imperial from the Beginning,* 16.

12. George Washington to John Jay, August 15, 1786, in W. W. Abbot et al., eds., *The Papers of George Washington: Confederation Series,* 6 vols. (Charlottesville: University of Virginia Press, 1995), 4:213.

13. George Washington to James Madison, March 31, 1787, in Abbot, *Papers of George Washington,* 5:115.

14. James Madison, "Saturday June 2d," in Farrand, *Records,* 1:88.

15. Rufus King, "Friday 1 June," in Farrand, *Records,* 1:71.

16. James Madison, "Tuesday July 17," in Farrand, *Records,* 2:36, quoting James McClurg.

17. Nicholas Gilman to Joseph Gilman, July 31, 1787, in Farrand, *Records,* 3:66.

18. Madison, "Saturday June 2d," in Farrand, *Records,* 1:86–87, quoting John Dickinson.

19. Prakash, *Imperial from the Beginning,* 17.

20. James Madison, "Virginia Plan, May 29," in Farrand, *Records,* 1:21.

21. US Const., art. II, § 1, cl. 8.

22. Paul Leicester Ford, ed., *The Writings of Thomas Jefferson,* vol. 1 (New York: G. P. Putnam's Sons, 1892), 112.

23. James Wilson, "Of Government," in Robert Green McCloskey, ed., *The Works of James Wilson,* 2 vols. (Cambridge: Harvard University Press, 1967), 1:292–293.

24. Thomas Jefferson to James Madison, March 15, 1789, in Julian P. Boyd, ed., *The Papers of Thomas Jefferson,* 43 vols. (Princeton, NJ: Princeton University Press, 1958), 14:661.

25. Madison, "Saturday June 2d," in Farrand, *Records,* 1:83.

26. Pierce Butler to Weedon Butler, May 5, 1788, in Farrand, *Records,* 3:302.

27. Thomas Paine to the Citizens of the United States, Letter II, November 19, 1802, in Moncure Daniel Conway, ed., *The Writings of Thomas Paine,* vol. 3 (New York: G. P. Putnam's Sons, 1895), 388.

28. Jonathan Elliot, ed., *The Debates in the Several State Conventions on the Adoption of the Federal Constitution*, vol. 3 (Philadelphia: J. B. Lippincott, 1836), 58.

29. Luther Martin, "Genuine Information," in Farrand, *Records*, 3:181, 216.

30. Elliot, *Debates*, 485.

31. "Cato IV," November 8, 1787, in John P. Kaminski et al., ed., *The Documentary History of the Ratification of the Constitution*, 28 vols. (Charlottesville: University of Virginia Press, 1983), 14:9.

32. Thomas Jefferson to John Adams, November 13, 1787, in Boyd, *Papers of Thomas Jefferson*, 12:351.

33. John Adams to Roger Sherman, July 22, 1789, *Founders Online*, National Archives, https://founders.archives.gov/documents/Adams/99-02 -02-0696, recounting comments made in 1788 by William V, Prince of Orange.

34. John Adams to Roger Sherman, July 18, 1789, *Founders Online*, https://founders.archives.gov/documents/Adams/99-02-02-0682.

35. Max Farrand, "Compromises of the Constitution," *American Historical Review* 9, no. 3 (1904): 486.

36. Edward J. Larson, *The Return of George Washington: 1783–1789* (New York: William Morrow, 2014), 232.

37. Montesquieu, *Spirit of the Laws*, 84.

38. Eric Nelson, *The Royalist Revolution: Monarchy and the American Founding* (Cambridge: Belknap Press of Harvard University Press, 2014), 232.

39. Frank Prochaska, *The Eagle and the Crown: Americans and the British Monarchy* (New Haven, CT: Yale University Press, 2008), 17.

40. Samuel Johnson, *A Dictionary of the English Language*, 10th ed. (London, 1792), entry for "monarch"; Thomas Sheridan, *A General Dictionary of the English Language*, vol. 2 (London, 1780), entry for "monarch."

41. John Adams to Benjamin Rush, June 9, 1789, in Charlene Bangs Bickford et al., eds., *Documentary History of the First Federal Congress*, vol. 16 (Baltimore: Johns Hopkins University Press, 2004), 727.

42. Articles of Confederation, art. XIII, Avalon Project, Yale Law School Lillian Goldman Law Library, http://avalon.law.yale.edu/18th_century /artconf.asp.

43. US Const., art. I, § 7, cl. 3.

44. US Const., art. II, § 3.
45. "Cassius VI," December 21, 1787, in Kaminski et al., *Documentary History*, 5:500.
46. *Youngstown Sheet & Tube Co. v. Sawyer*, 343 US 579, 587 (1952).
47. Vernon Bogdanor, *The Monarchy and the Constitution* (Oxford, UK: Oxford University Press, 1995), 1.

CHAPTER 2. WHY PRESIDENTS AMEND THE CONSTITUTION

1. James Madison, "Friday June 1st 1787," in Max Farrand, ed., *The Records of the Federal Convention of 1787*, 4 vols. (New Haven, CT: Yale University Press, 1911), 1:66.
2. Jonathan Elliot, ed., *The Debates in the Several State Conventions on the Adoption of the Federal Constitution*, 5 vols. (Philadelphia: J. B Lippincott, 1836), 2:58.
3. Saikrishna Bangalore Prakash, *Imperial from the Beginning: The Constitution of the Original Executive* (New Haven, CT: Yale University Press, 2015), 23–24, 45, 244.
4. William G. Howell, *Thinking About the Presidency: The Primacy of Power* (Princeton, NJ: Princeton University Press, 2013), 56.
5. George Washington to Joseph Jones and James Madison, December 3, 1784, in Andrew Stewart, ed., *The American System* (Philadelphia: Henry Carey Baird, 1872), 369.
6. James Madison, *Federalist*, no. 51, Avalon Project, Yale Law School Lillian Goldman Law Library, http://avalon.law.yale.edu/18th_century /fed51.asp.
7. Lord Bolingbroke, "Remarks on the History of England, letter 1," in *The Works of Lord Bolingbroke with a Life*, vol. 1 (Philadelphia: Cary and Hart, 1841), 296.
8. James Madison, "Saturday June 2," in Farrand, *Records*, 1:81–82.
9. George Washington, "Farewell Address" (September 19, 1796), in Bruce Frohnen, ed., *The American Republic: Primary Sources* (Indianapolis: Liberty Fund, 2002).
10. Prakash, *Imperial from the Beginning*, 19–20.
11. Alexander Hamilton, *Federalist*, no. 72, Avalon Project, Yale Law School Lillian Goldman Law Library, http://avalon.law.yale.edu/18th _century/fed72.asp.

12. James Madison, *Federalist,* no. 51, Avalon Project, Yale Law School Lillian Goldman Law Library, http://avalon.law.yale.edu/18th_century /fed51.asp.

13. Douglass Adair, "Fame and the Founding Fathers," in Trevor Colbourn, ed., *Fame and the Founding Fathers* (New York: W. W. Norton, 1974), 11.

14. John Adams, "Diary of John Adams," in Charles Francis Adams, ed., *The Works of John Adams, Second President of the United States,* vol. 2 (Boston: Charles C. Little and James Brown, 1850), 6.

15. John Jay, *Federalist,* no. 4, Avalon Project, Yale Law School Lillian Goldman Law Library, http://avalon.law.yale.edu/18th_century/fed04 .asp.

16. James Madison, "Helvidius Number IV" (September 14, 1793), in Morton J. Frisch, ed., *The Pacificus-Helvidius Debates of 1793–1794* (Indianapolis: Liberty Fund, 2007), 87.

17. Siena College Research Institute, "US Presidents Study Historical Rankings: 2018 Rankings," https://scri.siena.edu/us-presidents-study -historical-rankings; C-SPAN, "Presidential Historians Survey, 2017: Total Scores / Overall Rankings," https://www.c-span.org/president survey2017/?page=overall.

18. Arthur M. Schlesinger Jr., "Rating the Presidents: Washington to Clinton," *Political Science Quarterly* 112, no. 2 (Summer 1997): 179, quotation on 180.

19. Alan Brinkley, "The 43% President," *New York Times,* July 4, 1993, 22.

20. Siena College Research Institute, "US Presidents Study Historical Rankings: 2018 Rankings."

21. David Herbert Donald, *Lincoln* (New York: Touchstone, 1995), 13.

22. Julian E. Zelizer, "What's Wrong with Presidential Rankings," *CNN,* February 21, 2011, http://edition.cnn.com/2011/OPINION/02/21 /zelizer.presidential.rankings/.

23. John King, "Bush 43: 'History Will Ultimately Judge . . . I'm a Content Man,'" *CNN,* April 25, 2013, https://www.cnn.com/2013/04/24 /politics/bush-interview-king/index.html/.

24. Drew McCoy, "Lincoln and the Founding Fathers: A Reconsideration," *Journal of the Abraham Lincoln Association* 16, no. 1 (Winter 1995): 1–13.

25. US Const., art. II, §§ 1, 3.

26. William Henry Harrison, *General Harrison's Speech at the Dayton Convention, September 10, 1840* (Boston: Whig Republican Association, 1840), 2, 4–7.

27. For instance, the lead drafter of the 2004 Democratic Party Platform stated that "[t]his platform reflects John Kerry." David E. Rosenbaum and David E. Sanger, "The 2004 Campaign: The Democrats; Democratic Platform Focuses on National Security," *New York Times*, July 4, 2004, https://www.nytimes.com/2004/07/04/us/the-2004-campaign-the-democrats-democratic-platform-focuses-on-national-security.html.

28. Woodrow Wilson, *Constitutional Government in the United States* (New York: Columbia University Press, 1908), 66–67, 69, 77–79.

29. Peter Nicholas, "Hillary Clinton Cold, Calculating? Not According to Bill," *Los Angeles Times*, December 11, 2007.

30. Michael S. Dukakis, "Address Accepting the Presidential Nomination at the Democratic National Convention in Atlanta" (July 21, 1988), American Presidency Project, https://www.presidency.ucsb.edu/node/216671.

31. George Bush, "Address Accepting the Presidential Nomination at the Republican National Convention in New Orleans" (August 18, 1988), American Presidency Project, https://www.presidency.ucsb.edu/node/268235.

32. Andrew Rosenthal, "Bush Now Concedes a Need for 'Tax Revenue Increases' to Reduce Deficit in Budget," *New York Times*, June 27, 1990, A1.

33. "Remarks by the President at Univision Town Hall with Jorge Ramos and Maria Elena Salinas" (September 20, 2012), White House of President Barack Obama, https://obamawhitehouse.archives.gov/the-press-office/2012/09/20/remarks-president-univision-town-hall-jorge-ramos-and-maria-elena-salina.

34. Steve Contorno, "Barack Obama: Position on Immigration Action through Executive Orders 'Hasn't Changed,'" Politifact, November 20, 2014, https://www.politifact.com/truth-o-meter/statements/2014/nov/20/barack-obama/barack-obama-position-immigration-action-through-e/; Dara Lind, "Obama Keeps Trying to Explain Immigration Reform Instead of Actually Doing it," Vox, September 7, 2014, https://www.vox.com/2014/9/7/6116367/obama-immigration-strategy-work-republicans-delay-elections/.

35. Jennifer Epstein, "Obama's Pen-and-Phone Strategy," *Politico*, January 14, 2014, https://www.politico.com/story/2014/01/obama-state -of-the-union-2014-strategy-102151/.

36. Michael Genovese and Todd Belt, *The Post-Heroic Presidency: Leveraged Leadership in an Age of Limits*, 2nd ed. (Santa Barbara, CA: Praeger, 2016), 30.

37. Jeremi Suri, *The Impossible Presidency: The Rise and Fall of America's Highest Office* (New York: Basic Books, 2017).

38. Ryan Struyk, "George W. Bush's Favorable Rating Has Pulled a Complete 180," *CNN*, January 22, 2018, https://www.cnn.com/2018/01/22 /politics/george-w-bush-favorable-poll/index.html/.

39. Emergency Economic Stabilization Act of 2008, 122 Stat. 3765.

40. Neal Devins and Saikrishna Prakash, "The Indefensible Duty to Defend," *Columbia Law Review* 112, no. 3 (April 2012): 507, 516–517.

41. Devins and Prakash, "Indefensible Duty to Defend," 519–520.

42. Neal Devins, "A Loss of Control: Privilege Cases Diminish Presidential Power," *ABA Journal* 84, no. 10 (October 1998): 26–27.

Chapter 3. How Presidents Amend the Constitution

1. Saikrishna Bangalore Prakash, *Imperial from the Beginning: The Constitution of the Original Executive* (New Haven, CT: Yale University Press, 2015), 31–33.

2. Alexander Hamilton, *Federalist*, no. 70, Avalon Project, Yale Law School Lillian Goldman Law Library, http://avalon.law.yale.edu/18th _century/fed70.asp.

3. Hamilton, *Federalist*, no. 70.

4. James Madison, "Friday June 1st," in Max Farrand, ed., *The Records of the Federal Convention of 1787*, 4 vols. (New Haven, CT: Yale University Press, 1911), 1:66.

5. James Madison, "Monday June 4," in Farrand, *Records*, 1:96–97. Perhaps the better example would be the clashes among the second triumvirate of Octavian, Mark Antony, and Marcus Lepidus.

6. US Const., art. II, § 1, cl. 8; § 3.

7. Richard E. Neustadt, *Presidential Power: The Politics of Leadership* (New York: John Wiley & Sons, 1960), 9, italics omitted.

8. US Const., art. II, § 1.

9. James Madison, *Federalist*, no. 41, Avalon Project, Yale Law School
Lillian Goldman Law Library, http://avalon.law.yale.edu/18th_centur
/fed41.asp.

10. Charles C. Thach Jr., *The Creation of the Presidency, 1775–1789*
Study in Constitutional History (Baltimore: Johns Hopkins Univer
Press, 1922), 138–139.

11. *United States v. Nixon*, 418 US 683, 708, 711 (1974), on exec
privilege; *Youngstown Sheet & Tube Co. v. Sawyer*, 343 US 579,
682 (1952) (Vinson, C. J., dissenting), on emergency powers;
tive Order no. 10340, *Federal Register* vol. 17, no. 71 (1952)
3141, on seizing private property during the Korean War.

12. Bill of Rights, 1 William and Mary, 2nd sess., ch. 2 (1689);
Burnham MacMillan, *The War Governors in the American R*
(New York: Columbia University Press, 1965), 61–63.

13. James Madison, *Federalist*, no. 48, Avalon Project, Yale I
Lillian Goldman Law Library, http://avalon.law.yale.edu/1
/fed48.asp.

14. For example, "Brutus I, To the Citizens of the State of Ne
tober 18, 1787, in John P. Kaminski and Richard Leffler,
ists and Antifederalists: The Debate over the Ratificati
stitution (Madison, WI: Madison House, 1998), 4, 6–9;
"Centinel II," October 24, 1787, in Kaminski and Le
and Antifederalists, 128–129.

15. Abraham Lincoln, "Divided House" (speech, Spring
1858), in L. E. Chittenden, ed., *Abraham Lincoln*
York: Dodd, Mead, 1896), 72.

16. US Const., art. I, § 2, cl. 5; § 3, cl. 6; art. II, § 4.

17. Thomas Jefferson to Thomas Ritchie, Decembe
Leicester Ford, ed., *The Writings of Thomas Jeff*
York: G. P. Putnam's Sons, 1899), 10:171.

18. US Const., art. III, § 1. For a discussion of w
means, see Saikrishna Prakash and Steven D. S
a Federal Judge," *Yale Law Journal* 116, no.

19. William Baude, "The Judgment Power," *Geo*
no. 6 (2008): 1807, 1826–1827, 1832.

20. This is called *suo moto* ("court on its own
Courting the People: Public Interest Liti
India (New York: Cambridge University F

21. *Lujan v. Defenders of Wildlife*, 504 US 555, 573–575 (1992).

22. Elizabeth J. Perry, *Challenging the Mandate of Heaven: Social Protest and State Power in China* (New York: Routledge, 2002), ix.

23. Robert W. Bennett, *Taming the Electoral College* (Stanford, CA: Stanford University Press, 2006), 14.

24. Neal R. Peirce, *The People's President: The Electoral College in American History and the Direct-Vote Alternative* (New York: Simon & Schuster, 1968), 60, 67, 76.

25. Paul F. Boller Jr., *Presidential Campaigns: From George Washington to George W. Bush* (New York: Oxford University Press, 2004), 9.

26. Andrew Jackson, "Protest," April 15, 1834, in James D. Richardson, ed., *A Compilation of the Messages and Papers of the Presidents 1789–1908,* 11 vols. (Washington, DC: Bureau of National Literature and Art, 1908), 3:90.

27. Daniel Webster, "The Presidential Protest," in *The Works of Daniel Webster,* 18th ed., vol. 4 (Boston: Little, Brown, 1877), 144–145.

28. Though modern vice presidents have been elected the same way as presidents, no one believes that they enjoy the same electoral connection, much less a popular mandate.

29. Andrew Jackson, "Veto Message," July 10, 1832, in Richardson, *Compilation,* 2:576.

30. "The Bank Veto," July 11, 1832, in *Register of Debates in Congress,* vol. 8 (Washington, DC: Gales and Seaton, 1833), 1225.

31. Jon Meacham, *American Lion: Andrew Jackson in the White House* (New York: Random House, 2008), 267.

32. Meacham, *American Lion,* 267.

33. Henry Clay, "Removal of the Public Deposits" (speech, December 26, 1833), in Calvin Colton, ed., *The Works of Henry Clay,* vol. 2 (New York: Barnes and Burr, 1863), 115–117.

34. Robert A. Dahl, "Myth of the Presidential Mandate," *Political Science Quarterly* 105, no. 3 (1990): 355–372.

35. Jimmy Carter, "Inaugural Address" (speech, January 20, 1977), The Miller Center, University of Virginia, https://millercenter.org/the-presidency/presidential-speeches/january-20-1977-inaugural-address.

36. Leigh Ann Caldwell, "Paul Ryan: Trump Achieved 'An Enormous Political Feat,'" *NBC News,* November 9, 2016, https://www.nbcnews.com/politics/paul-ryan/paul-ryan-trump-achieved-enormous-political-feat-n681451.

37. Goldwin Smith, "The Contest for the Presidency," in James Knowles, ed., *The Nineteenth Century: A Monthly Review* 32, no. 187 (London: Sampson Low, Marston & Co., 1892), 345.

38. Theodore J. Lowi, *The Personal President: Power Invested, Promise Unfulfilled* (Ithaca, NY: Cornell University Press, 1985), 97.

39. "Presidential Job Approval," American Presidency Project, https://www.presidency.ucsb.edu/statistics/data/presidential-job-approval.

40. Presidential Job Approval Center, Gallup, https://news.gallup.com/interactives/185273/presidential-job-approval-center.aspx; Charles Franklin, "Nixon, Watergate, and Partisan Opinion," https://medium.com/@PollsAndVotes/nixon-watergate-and-partisan-opinion-524c4314d530.

41. Sidney M. Milkis and Michael Nelson, *The American Presidency: Origins and Development, 1776–2018*, 8th ed. (Los Angeles: CQ Press, 2019), 136.

42. James Grant, *Mr. Speaker! The Life and Times of Thomas B. Reed, the Man Who Broke the Filibuster* (New York: Simon & Schuster, 2011), xi.

43. For a discussion of realignment generally, see David Brady and Joseph Stewart Jr., "Congressional Party Realignment and Transformations of Public Policy in Three Realignment Eras," *American Journal of Political Science* 26, no. 2 (1982): 333–360.

44. Milkis and Nelson, *American Presidency*, 524, 534, 542, 552, 560–564, 575.

45. David Maraniss, "First Lady Launches Counterattack," *Washington Post*, January 28, 1998, https://www.washingtonpost.com/wp-srv/politics/special/clinton/stories/hillary012898.htm.

46. Alex Wigglesworth, "Trump Again Appears to Cast Doubt on Russia Investigation: 'Witch Hunt!'" *Los Angeles Times*, July 27, 2017, https://www.latimes.com/politics/la-pol-updates-trump-tweets-russia-spread-negative-information-fox-news-htmlstory.html.

47. James Madison, *Federalist*, no. 51, Avalon Project, Yale Law School Lillian Goldman Law Library, http://avalon.law.yale.edu/18th_century/fed51.asp.

48. "Senate Spouses," US Senate, https://www.senate.gov/artandhistory/history/common/generic/SenateSpouses.htm.

49. For a discussion of the importance of favors dispensed by the White House, see Kenneth E. Collier, *Between the Branches: The White House*

Office of Legislative Affairs (Pittsburgh: University of Pittsburgh Press, 1997), 18, 70, 99, 106, 142–150.

50. Collier, *Between the Branches,* 103–104.

51. Daryl J. Levinson and Richard H. Pildes, "Separation of Parties, Not Powers," *Harvard Law Review* 119, no. 8 (2006): 2385.

52. Michael Nelson, ed., *The Evolving Presidency: Landmark Documents,* 6th ed. (Los Angeles: CQ Press, 2019), 79–80.

53. Beverly J. Ross and William Josephson, "The Electoral College and the Popular Vote," *Journal of Law and Politics* 12, no. 4 (1996): 712–713.

54. Susan Dunn, *Roosevelt's Purge: How FDR Fought to Change the Democratic Party* (Cambridge: Belknap Press of Harvard University Press, 2010), 214–217.

55. Dunn, *Roosevelt's Purge,* 260.

56. Alex Seitz-Wald, "Arizona GOP Sen. Jeff Flake, Appalled by Trump, Won't Seek Re-Election," *NBC News,* October 24, 2017, https://www .nbcnews.com/politics/congress/arizona-republican-sen-jeff-flake -won-t-seek-reelection-dismayed-n813841; Michael Collins, "Sen. Bob Corker Won't Seek Third Term," *USA Today,* February 27, 2018, https://www.usatoday.com/story/news/politics/2018/02/27/sen-bob -corker-wont-seek-third-term/364818002.

57. Associated Press, "Mark Sanford Loses South Carolina Primary after President Trump Endorses Opponent," *Washington Times,* June 13, 2018, https://www.washingtontimes.com/news/2018/jun/13/mark -sanford-loses-south-carolina-primary-after-pr.

58. George Washington to Count de Moustier, May 25, 1789, in W. W. Abbot et al., eds., *The Papers of George Washington: Presidential Series,* vol. 2 (Charlottesville: University Press of Virginia, 1989), 390.

59. See Prakash, *Imperial from the Beginning,* 187–189.

60. Saikrishna B. Prakash, "Fragmented Features of the Constitution's Unitary Executive," *Willamette Law Review* 45, no. 3 (2009): 703–704.

61. Bruce Ackerman, "Abolish the White House Counsel: And the Office of Legal Counsel, Too, While We're at It," *Slate,* April 22, 2009, https:// slate.com/news-and-politics/2009/04/abolish-the-white-house -counsel-and-the-office-of-legal-counsel.html.

62. Charlie Savage, *Power Wars: Inside Obama's Post 9/11 Presidency* (New York: Little, Brown, 2015), 278–279, 484.

63. William Safire, "Essay: 3 Scandals and Out," *New York Times,* June 24, 1996, https://www.nytimes.com/1996/06/24/opinion/essay-3-scandals-and-out.html.

64. Ackerman, "Abolish the White House Counsel."

65. Savage, *Power Wars,* 661–663.

66. Michael Isikoff, "On Libya, President Obama Evaded Rules on Legal Disputes, Scholars Say," *NBC News,* June 21, 2011, http://www.nbcnews.com/id/43474045/ns/politics-white_house/t/libya-president-obama-evaded-rules-legal-disputes-scholars-say/#.XLYiIZNKiu4.

67. US Const., art. II, § 1, cl. 7.

68. Constitutionality of the Qui Tam Provisions of the False Claims Act, July 18, 1989, *Opinions of the Office of Legal Counsel,* vol. 13 (Washington, DC: Department of Justice, 1996): 207–240, quotation on 232.

69. Matthew J. Ouimet, *The Rise and Fall of the Brezhnev Doctrine in Soviet Foreign Policy* (Chapel Hill: University of North Carolina Press, 2003), 67.

70. Bill Gertz, *The China Threat: How the People's Republic Targets America* (Washington, DC: Regnery Publishing, 2000), 110, attributing the quotation to Lenin.

71. Savage, *Power Wars,* 665, alterations omitted.

72. *Who Framed Roger Rabbit?* Directed by Robert Zemeckis. Burbank, CA: Touchstone Pictures, 1988.

CHAPTER 4. THE LIVING PRESIDENCY
IN A LIVING CONSTITUTION

1. Arthur M. Schlesinger Jr., *The Imperial Presidency* (Bridgewater, NJ: Replica Books, 1998).

2. US Const., art. V.

3. Articles of Confederation, art. XIII.

4. US Const., art. VII.

5. US Const., art. VII.

6. David A. Strauss, *The Living Constitution* (New York: Oxford University Press, 2010), 120–125.

7. Strauss, *Living Constitution,* 52–53, 120–121.

8. US Const., art. I, § 8; US Const., art. I, § 7.
9. Woodrow Wilson, "The New Freedom" (1913), Teaching American History, http://teachingamericanhistory.org/library/document/the-new-freedom/.
10. William J. Brennan Jr., "The Constitution of the United States: Contemporary Ratification," *South Texas Law Review* 27, no. 3 (1986): 433–445, 438, italics added.
11. Brennan, "Constitution," 444.
12. US Const., art. I, § 1.
13. *Gibbons v. Ogden,* 22 US 1, 195 (1824).
14. To be clear, the Constitution did grant Congress sweeping legislative authority over the federal district and the territories. US Const., art. I, § 8, cl. 17; US Const., art. IV, § 3, cl. 2. In these geographical areas, it could regulate abortion, labor conditions, manufacturing, and everything else. In these regions, there were no subject matter constraints on the scope of federal legislative power.
15. Alexander Hamilton, *Federalist,* no. 78, Avalon Project, Yale Law School Lillian Goldman Law Library, http://avalon.law.yale.edu/18th_century/fed78.asp.
16. James Madison, *Federalist,* no. 45, Avalon Project, Yale Law School Lillian Goldman Law Library, http://avalon.law.yale.edu/18th_century/fed45.asp.
17. US Const., art. I, § 10, cl. 1. The case most associated with the defanging of the clause is *Home Building & Loan Ass'n v. Blaisdell,* 290 US 398 (1934).
18. *Barnes v. Glen Theatre, Inc.,* 501 US 560 (1991); *Brandenburg v. Ohio,* 395 US 444 (1969).
19. *Gideon v. Wainwright,* 372 US 335 (1963).
20. Cass R. Sunstein, *Radicals in Robes: Why Extreme Right-Wing Courts Are Wrong for America* (New York: Basic Books, 2005), 243, 247–252.
21. Strauss, *Living Constitution,* 1–2.
22. Strauss, *Living Constitution,* 121.
23. Schlesinger, *Imperial Presidency,* 13.
24. Schlesinger, *Imperial Presidency,* 1.
25. Schlesinger, *Imperial Presidency,* 285.
26. Bruce Ackerman, *The Decline and Fall of the American Republic* (Cambridge: Harvard University Press, 2010), 6.

27. Bruce Ackerman and David Golove, "Is NAFTA Constitutional?," *Harvard Law Review* 108, no. 4 (1995): 799–929.

28. Ackerman and Golove, "Is NAFTA Constitutional?" 861–896.

29. Henry Clay, "On the Removal of the Deposits" (December 26, 1833), in Calvin Colton, ed., *The Speeches of Henry Clay,* 2 vols. (New York: A. S. Barnes & Co., 1857), 1:585.

30. Henry Clay, "On the Sub-Treasury Bill" (September 25, 1837), in Colton, *Speeches,* 2:81.

31. Peter M. Shane, *Madison's Nightmare: How Executive Power Threatens American Democracy* (Chicago: University of Chicago Press, 2009).

32. Shane, *Madison's Nightmare,* 46, 54.

33. Bruce Ackerman, "Legal Acrobatics, Illegal War," *New York Times,* June 20, 2011.

34. Shane, *Madison's Nightmare,* 4, 25; Barbara Peck, "Office Hours: What Has the Obama Presidency Meant for the Growth of Presidential Power?" *Ohio State University Law School Magazine,* Spring 2011, https://moritzlaw.osu.edu/all-rise/2011/05/what-has-the-obama -presidency-meant-for-the-growth-of-presidential-power.

35. Alexander Hamilton, *Federalist,* no. 65, Avalon Project, Yale Law School Lillian Goldman Law Library, http://avalon.law.yale.edu/18th _century/fed65.asp.

36. *Ex parte Merryman,* 17 F. Cas. 144 (C.C.D. Md. 1861) (No. 9487).

37. There are, of course, ambiguities in Congress's laws, and presidents are prone to exploit them when their agendas and the interests of their allies align. In Chapter 8, I discuss the exploitation of statutory ambiguities, real and imagined.

38. William G. Howell and Terry M. Moe, *Relic: How Our Constitution Undermines Effective Government, and Why We Need a More Powerful Presidency* (New York: Basic Books, 2016).

39. Howell and Moe, *Relic,* 144.

40. Woodrow Wilson, *Congressional Government: A Study in American Politics* (Boston: Houghton, Mifflin, 1901), xvi, 282–285.

41. Eric A. Posner and Adrian Vermeule, *The Executive Unbound: After the Madisonian Republic* (New York: Oxford University Press, 2010), 4–5.

42. *Hollingsworth v. Virginia,* 3 US 378 (1798).

43. "13th Amendment to the U.S. Constitution: Abolition of Slavery" (1865), available at https://www.ourdocuments.gov/doc_large_image .php?flash=false&doc=40.

44. "Congressional Pay Amendment," Memorandum Opinion for the Counsel to the President (November 2, 1992), in *Opinions of the Office of Legal Counsel* 16 (Washington, DC: Office of Legal Counsel, 1998), 87.

45. Kim Eisler, "Eisenhower's 'Mistakes,'" *New York Times,* July 28, 1997.

46. Andrew Jackson, Veto Message (July 10, 1832), in James D. Richardson, ed., *A Compilation of the Messages and Papers of the Presidents,* 20 vols. (New York: Bureau of National Literature, 1897), 3:1139, 1144–1154.

47. William J. Clinton, "Statement on Signing the National Defense Authorization Act for Fiscal Year 1996" (February 10, 1996), in *Weekly Compilation of Presidential Documents* 32, no. 7 (Washington, DC: Government Printing Office, 1996), 261.

48. Clinton, "Statement on Signing the National Defense Authorization Act," 261.

49. Thomas Jefferson to Abigail Smith Adams, July 22, 1804, *Founders Online,* National Archives, https://founders.archives.gov/documents /Jefferson/99-01-02-0125.

50. The Supreme Court held that the executive had an exclusive power to recognize foreign nations and that Congress's law impermissibly interfered with that power. *Zivotofsky v. Kerry,* 135 S. Ct. 2076 (2015).

51. Charlie Savage and Sheryl Gay Stolberg, "In Shift, U.S. Says Marriage Act Blocks Gay Rights," *New York Times,* February 23, 2011.

52. *McCulloch v. Maryland,* 17 US 316, 402 (1819).

53. "President Jackson's Proclamation Regarding Nullification" (December 10, 1832), Avalon Project, Yale Law School Lillian Goldman Law Library, http://avalon.law.yale.edu/19th_century/jack01.asp#1.

54. Henry Clay, "On the Removal of the Deposits" (December 26, 1833), in Colton, *Speeches,* 1:607.

55. For a general discussion of Whig criticisms of Jackson, see William S. Stokes, "Whig Conceptions of Executive Power," *Presidential Studies Quarterly* 6, nos. 1/2 (1976): 16–35.

56. Abraham Lincoln, Order to General Scott (April 27, 1861), in John G. Nicolay and John Hay, eds., *Abraham Lincoln: Complete Works, Comprising His Speeches, Letters, State Papers, and Miscellaneous Writings,* vol. 2 (New York: Century, 1894), 39.

57. Transcript of the Proclamation (January 1, 1863), National Archives, https://www.archives.gov/exhibits/featured-documents/emancipation -proclamation/transcript.html.

58. For a general defense of Lincoln's assumption of emergency powers, see Michael Stokes Paulsen, "The Constitution of Necessity," *Notre Dame Law Review* 79, no. 4 (2004): 1257–1297.

59. For a discussion of these early presidents, see Saikrishna Bangalore Prakash, "The Imbecilic Executive," *Virginia Law Review* 99, no. 7 (2013): 1361–1433.

60. Wilson, *Congressional Government*, 311–315.

61. Woodrow Wilson, *Constitutional Government in the United States* (New York: Columbia University Press, 1908), 60.

62. Wilson, *Constitutional Government*, 69.

63. Wilson, *Constitutional Government*, 70.

64. Wilson, *Constitutional Government*, 69.

65. Wilson, *Constitutional Government*, 71–72.

66. Theodore Roosevelt, *Theodore Roosevelt: An Autobiography* (New York: Charles Scribner's Sons, 1920), 357–362.

67. Sir David Frost with Bob Zelnick, *Frost/Nixon: Behind the Scenes of the Nixon Interviews* (New York: HarperCollins, 2007), 94.

68. *Youngstown Sheet & Tube Co. v. Sawyer,* 343 US 579 (1952).

69. *Youngstown Sheet & Tube Co.,* 610–611.

70. *Youngstown Sheet & Tube Co.,* 610.

71. *Inland Waterways Corp. v. Young,* 309 US 517, 524 (1940).

72. *Powell v. McCormack,* 395 US 486, 546–547 (1969).

73. *Missouri v. Holland,* 252 US 416, 433 (1920).

74. *Youngstown Sheet & Tube Co.,* 612–613.

75. Henry Clay, "On the Seminole War" (January 1819), in Colton, *Speeches,* 1:203.

76. *Youngstown Sheet & Tube Co.,* 610.

77. Curtis A. Bradley and Trevor W. Morrison, "Historical Gloss and the Separation of Powers," *Harvard Law Review* 126, no. 2 (2012): 411–485, 430–431.

78. "Constitutionality of the Qui Tam Provisions of the False Claims Act," Memorandum Opinion for the Attorney General (July 18, 1989), *Opinions of the Office of Legal Counsel* 13 (Washington, DC: Office of Legal Counsel, 1996), 232–233.

79. "Constitutionality of the Qui Tam Provisions," 232n17 (quoting *Walz v. Tax Commission,* 397 US 664, 678 [1970]).

80. *National Labor Relations Board v. Noel Canning,* 573 US 513 (2014).

81. *National Labor Relations Board,* 530–533, 546–547.

82. *National Labor Relations Board,* 530, 539, 543.

83. *National Labor Relations Board*, 538.
84. Charlie Savage, *Power Wars: Inside Obama's Post 9-11 Presidency* 299 (New York: Little, Brown, 2015), italics omitted.

CHAPTER 5. FROM CONSTITUTIONAL DEFENDER
TO CONSTITUTIONAL AMENDER

1. Jacques Necker, *An Essay on the True Principles of Executive Power in Great States*, vol. 1 (London: G.G.J and J. Robinson, 1792), 1.
2. The two presidents are George W. Bush and Donald J. Trump. See James Q. Wilson, John J. DiIulio Jr., Meena Bose, and Matthew Levendusky, *American Government: Institutions and Policies*, 16th ed. (Boston: Cengage Learning, 2019), 335.
3. "A Jerseyman: To the Citizens of New Jersey" (November 6, 1787), in Merrill Jensen et al., eds., *The Documentary History of the Ratification of the Constitution*, 27 vols. (Madison: State Historical Society of Wisconsin, 1976–2016), 3:146, 149; italics omitted.
4. "Cassius VI" (December 21, 1787), in Jensen et al., *Documentary History*, 5:500.
5. "George Washington to the Senate, with Jefferson's Note to Washington" (February 28, 1793), *Founders Online*, National Archives, https://founders.archives.gov/documents/Jefferson/01-25-02-0268; italics added.
6. "Jefferson's Opinion on the Constitutionality of a National Bank" (1791), Avalon Project, Yale Law School Lillian Goldman Law Library, http://avalon.law.yale.edu/18th_century/bank-tj.asp.
7. James Madison, Veto Message (March 3, 1817), in James D. Richardson, ed., *A Compilation of the Messages and Papers of the Presidents*, 20 vols. (New York: Bureau of National Literature, 1897), 2:569, 570.
8. James Monroe, Veto Message (May 4, 1822), in Richardson, *Compilation*, 2:711.
9. Andrew Jackson, Veto Message (July 10, 1832), in Richardson, *Compilation*, 3:1139, 1145, 1154.
10. Thomas Jefferson to Abigail Smith Adams, July 22, 1804, *Founders Online*, National Archives, https://founders.archives.gov/documents/Jefferson/99-01-02-0125.

11. George Washington to the House of Representatives of the United States, March 30, 1796, in Richardson, *Compilation*, 1:186, 188.

12. *McCulloch v. Maryland*, 17 US 316 (1819).

13. Andrew Jackson, Veto Message (July 10, 1832), in Richardson, *Compilation*, 3:1139, 1144–1154; Paul Finkelman, "Roger Brooke Taney," in Melvin I. Urofsky, ed., *Biographical Encyclopedia of the Supreme Court: The Lives and Legal Philosophies of the Justices* (Washington, DC: CQ Press, 2006), 533.

14. "South Carolina Ordinance of Nullification" (November 24, 1832), Avalon Project, Yale Law School Lillian Goldman Law Library, http://avalon.law.yale.edu/19th_century/ordnull.asp.

15. Andrew Jackson, Proclamation (December 10, 1832), in Richardson, *Compilation*, 3:1203, 1204, 1218.

16. George Washington, Sixth Annual Address (November 19, 1794), in Richardson, *Compilation*, 1:154, 158.

17. Abraham Lincoln, First Inaugural Address (March 4, 1861), in Richardson, *Compilation*, 7:3206, 3212; italics and internal quotations omitted.

18. *Planned Parenthood of Southeastern Pennsylvania v. Casey*, 505 US 833 (1992); *Citizens United v. Federal Election Commission*, 558 US 310 (2010).

19. 5 USC § 3331.

20. US Const., art. V.

21. 5 USC § 3331. Federal judges also take a separate judicial oath. See 28 USC § 453.

Chapter 6. From First General to Declarer of Wars

1. Zachary Cohen, "Congress Passes $700B Defense Bill, Sends to Trump's Desk," *CNN*, November 16, 2017, https://www.cnn.com/2017/11/16/politics/ndaa-defense-policy-passes-congress/index.html.

2. *Youngstown Sheet & Tube Co. v. Sawyer*, 343 US 579, 641 (1952).

3. Robert H. Jackson "Acquisition of Naval and Air Bases in Exchange for Over-Age Destroyers," in John T. Fowler, ed., *Official Opinions of the Attorneys General of the United States* 39 (Washington, DC: Government Printing Office, 1941), 484.

4. *Youngstown Sheet & Tube Co.*, 582–584; Maeva Marcus, *Truman and the Steel Seizure Case: The Limits of Presidential Power* (Durham, NC: Duke University Press, 1994), 1–2, 58.

5. James Madison, "Helvidius Number IV" (September 14, 1793), in Morton J. Frisch, ed., *The Pacificus-Helvidius Debates of 1793–1794* (Indianapolis: Liberty Fund, 2007), 87.

6. US Const., art. I, § 8, cl. 11.

7. Michael D. Ramsey, *The Constitution's Text in Foreign Affairs* (Cambridge: Harvard University Press, 2007), 229–237; Saikrishna Bangalore Prakash, "Unleashing the Dogs of War: What the Constitution Means by 'Declare War,'" *Cornell Law Review* 93, no. 1 (2007): 45–121.

8. Saikrishna Bangalore Prakash, *Imperial from the Beginning: The Constitution of the Original Presidency* (New Haven, CT: Yale University Press, 2015), 142–170.

9. Act of November 29, 1794, ch. 1, § 1, 1 Stat. 403.

10. *Little v. Barreme*, 6 (2 Cranch) US 170, 177–178 (1804).

11. Alexander Hamilton, *Federalist*, no. 69, Avalon Project, Yale Law School Lillian Goldman Law Library, http://avalon.law.yale.edu/18th _century/fed69.asp.

12. US Const. art. I, § 8, cl. 12.

13. Rosara Joseph, *The War Prerogative: History, Reform, and Constitutional Design* (Oxford, UK: Oxford University Press, 2013), 96–99; Eric Nelson, *The Royalist Revolution: Monarchy and the American Founding* (Cambridge: Harvard University Press, 2014), 221.

14. Michael D. Ramsey, "Textualism and War Powers," *University of Chicago Law Review* 69, no. 4 (2002), 1543–1938.

15. Sir Robert Walpole, "Second Parliament of George II: Fourth Session (9 of 9, begins 12/5/1738)," in *The History and Proceedings of the House of Commons*, vol. 10: *1737–1739* (London: Chandler, 1742), http://www.british-history.ac.uk/report.asp?compid=37805.

16. John Adams to Samuel Adams, "February 14, 1779," in Francis Wharton, ed., *The Revolutionary Diplomatic Correspondence of the United States*, vol. 3 (Washington, DC: Government Printing Office, 1889), 48.

17. Saikrishna Bangalore Prakash, "Exhuming the Seemingly Moribund Declaration of War," *George Washington Law Review* 77, no. 1 (2008): 89–140, 118–119.

18. Prakash, "Exhuming," 111.

19. Articles of Confederation, art. IX, Avalon Project, Yale Law School Lillian Goldman Law Library, http://avalon.law.yale.edu/18th_century/artconf.asp#art9.

20. Saikrishna Bangalore Prakash, "The Separation and Overlap of War and Military Powers," *Texas Law Review* 87, no. 2 (2008): 299–386, 369.

21. Prakash, "Separation and Overlap," 353.

22. Prakash, "Separation and Overlap," 352–353.

23. Prakash, "Separation and Overlap," 369, 371.

24. Articles of Confederation, art. IX.

25. James Madison, *Federalist,* no. 41, Avalon Project, Yale Law School Lillian Goldman Law Library, http://avalon.law.yale.edu/18th_century/fed41.asp; John Jay, in John P. Kaminski et al., eds., "New York Convention Debates," *The Documentary History of the Ratification of the Constitution: Ratification of the Constitution by the States: New York,* vol. 22 (Madison: State Historical Society of Wisconsin, 2008), 1824.

26. US Const., art. I, § 8, cl. 14; Articles of Confederation, art. IX.

27. US Const., art. 1, § 8, cl. 12–13.

28. US Const., art. II, § 2, cl. 1.

29. US Const., art. I, § 7, cl. 3.

30. US Const., art. II, § 2.

31. Alexander Hamilton, *Federalist,* no. 69, Avalon Project, Yale Law School Lillian Goldman Law Library, http://avalon.law.yale.edu/18th_century/fed69.asp.

32. Prakash, "Separation and Overlap," 312–315, 321–324.

33. James Wilson, Pennsylvania Ratifying Convention (December 11, 1787), in Phillip B. Kurland and Ralph Lerner, eds., *The Founders' Constitution,* vol. 1 (Chicago: University of Chicago Press, 1987), 231.

34. Rufus King and Nathaniel Gorham, Response to Elbridge Gerry's Objections (October 31, 1787), in John P. Kaminski and Gaspare J. Saladino, eds., *The Documentary History of the Ratification of the Constitution: Ratification of the Constitution by the States; Massachusetts,* vol. 4 (Madison: State Historical Society of Wisconsin, 1997), 190.

35. Thomas Jefferson to James Madison, September 6, 1789, in *The Papers of Thomas Jefferson,* Princeton University, https://jeffersonpapers.princeton.edu/selected-documents/thomas-jefferson-james-madison.

36. Alexander Hamilton, "Pacificus Number 1" (Philadelphia, June 29, 1793), in Frisch, *Pacificus-Helvidius Debates*, 16.

37. Thomas Jefferson to James Madison, March 24, 1793, *Founders Online*, https://founders.archives.gov/documents/Jefferson/01-25-02-0408.

38. George Washington to William Moultrie, August 28, 1793, *Founders Online*, https://founders.archives.gov/documents/Washington/05-13 -02-0381.

39. George Washington, "Farewell Address" (September 19, 1796), in Bruce Frohnen, ed., *The American Republic: Primary Sources* (Indianapolis: Liberty Fund, 2002), 76.

40. US Marine Corp., "The Marines' Hymn" (1929), available at https://www.marineband.marines.mil/About/Library-and-Archives /The-Marines-Hymn/.

41. Prakash, "Unleashing the Dogs of War," 69–70.

42. Prakash, "Separation and Overlap," 332–333.

43. Prakash, "Separation and Overlap," 327–330.

44. Prakash, "Separation and Overlap," 348–350.

45. Prakash, "Separation and Overlap," 341–345.

46. Prakash, "Separation and Overlap," 343.

47. Prakash, "Separation and Overlap," 343.

48. For a history of the naval war with France, see Alexander DeConde, *The Quasi-War: The Politics and Diplomacy of the Undeclared War with France, 1797–1801* (New York: Scribner's, 1966).

49. George Washington, Veto Message of George Washington, April 5, 1792, Avalon Project, Yale Law School Lillian Goldman Law Library, https://avalon.law.yale.edu/18th_century/gwveto1.asp.

50. Prakash, *Imperial from the Beginning*, 165–166.

51. George Washington, Veto Message of George Washington: February 28, 1797, Avalon Project, Yale Law School Lillian Goldman Law Library, https://avalon.law.yale.edu/18th_century/gwveto2.asp.

52. Prakash, "Unleashing the Dogs of War," 99–100.

53. Act of July 9, 1798, ch. 68, § 1, 1 Stat. 578.

54. An Act for the protection of the Commerce and Seamen of the United States, against the Tripolitan Cruisers, ch. 4, 2 Stat. 129 (1802).

55. An Act for declaring War between the United Kingdom of Great Britain and Ireland and the dependencies thereof, and the United States and their territories, ch. 102, 2 Stat. 755 (1812); An Act for the protection of the commerce of the United States against the Algerine cruisers, ch. 90, § 2, 3 Stat. 230 (1815).

56. David S. Heidler, "The Politics of National Aggression: Congress and the First Seminole War," *Journal of the Early Republic* 13, no. 4 (1993): 501–530, 502–508.

57. Heidler, "Politics of National Aggression," 508.

58. Heidler, "Politics of National Aggression," 502.

59. William Marcy to Zachary Taylor, January 13, 1846, in *Messages of the President of the United States on the Subject of the Mexican War* (Washington, DC: Wendell and Van Benthuysen, 1848), 90: "Sir: I am directed by the President to instruct you to advance and occupy, with the troops under your command, positions on or near the east bank of the Rio del Norte, as soon as it can be conveniently done with reference to the season and the routes by which your movements must be made."

60. An Act Providing for the Prosecution of the Existing War between the United States and the Republic of Mexico, ch. 16, 9 Stat. 9 (1846).

61. Amy S. Greenberg, *A Wicked War: Polk, Clay, Lincoln, and the 1846 Invasion of Mexico* (New York: Alfred A. Knopf, 2012), 103–109.

62. Abraham Lincoln, "Abraham Lincoln Protests the War" (December 22, 1847), *Digital History*, http://www.digitalhistory.uh.edu/disp_textbook.cfm?smtid=3&psid=3672.

63. James G. Randall, *Constitutional Problems under Lincoln* (Urbana: University of Illinois Press, 1951), 36–37n15.

64. Abraham Lincoln, "July 4th Message to Congress" (July 4, 1861), Miller Center, University of Virginia, https://millercenter.org/the-presidency/presidential-speeches/july-4-1861-july-4th-message-congress.

65. Act of August 6, 1861, ch. 63, § 3, 12 Stat. 326; Act of March 3, 1863, ch. 81, § 1, 12 Stat. 755.

66. Randall, *Constitutional Problems under Lincoln*, 166–167; Russell F. Weigley, *A Great Civil War: A Military and Political History, 1861–1865* (Bloomington: Indiana University Press, 2000), 216–217.

67. Francis D. Wormuth and Edwin B. Firmage, *To Chain the Dog of War: The War Power of Congress in History and Law*, 2nd ed. (Urbana: University of Illinois Press, 1989), 144–151.

68. Stanley Sandler, *The Korean War: No Victors, No Vanquished* (London: University College London Press, 1999), 47–74.

69. United Nations, 82 (1950), Resolution of 25 June 1950, http://unscr.com/en/resolutions/doc/82.

70. United Nations, 84 (1950), Resolution of 7 July 1950, http://unscr.com /en/resolutions/doc/84.

71. Larry Blomstedt, *Truman, Congress, and Korea: The Politics of America's First Undeclared War* (Lexington: University Press of Kentucky, 2016), 23.

72. Richard F. Grimmett, *Instances of Use of United States Armed Forces Abroad, 1798–2006* (Washington: Congressional Research Service, 2007), 15.

73. Blomstedt, *Truman, Congress, and Korea*, 32.

74. Blomstedt, *Truman, Congress, and Korea*, 33.

75. Blomstedt, *Truman, Congress, and Korea*, 33.

76. Blomstedt, *Truman, Congress, and Korea*, 31.

77. *Congressional Record*, 81st Cong., 2d sess., June 28, 1950, 9323, available at https://www.govinfo.gov/content/pkg/GPO-CRECB-1950 -pt7/pdf/GPO-CRECB-1950-pt7-11-1.pdf.

78. *Congressional Record*, 81st Cong., 2d sess., June 28, 1950, 9323.

79. Blomstedt, *Truman, Congress, and Korea*, 34.

80. Blomstedt, *Truman, Congress, and Korea*, 36.

81. Blomstedt, *Truman, Congress, and Korea*, 27.

82. Blomstedt, *Truman, Congress, and Korea*, 36.

83. US Department of State, "Authority of the President to Repel the Attack in Korea" (July 3, 1950), in *Department of State Bulletin* 23, no. 574 (July 3, 1950): 173–177, quotation on 177.

84. US Department of State, "Authority of the President to Repel the Attack in Korea," 177; Act of March 3, 1811, ch. 47, 2 Stat. 666.

85. US Department of State, "Armed Actions Taken by the United States without a Declaration of War, 1789–1967," Research Project 806A, Historical Studies Division, Bureau of Public Affairs (1967), 1, 2–3.

86. Wormuth and Firmage, *To Chain the Dog of War*, 135–151.

87. Arthur Schlesinger Jr., *The Imperial Presidency* (Boston: Houghton Mifflin, 1973), 51.

88. Caroline Krass, US Department of Justice, "Authority to Use Military Force in Libya" (April 1, 2011), 1, 10, https://www.justice.gov/sites /default/files/olc/opinions/2011/04/31/authority-military-use-in-libya _0.pdf.

89. US Department of Justice, "Authority to Use Military Force in Libya," 10.

90. US Department of Justice, "Authority to Use Military Force in Libya," 10.

91. US Department of Justice, "Authority to Use Military Force in Libya," 12–13.

92. Walter Dellinger, "Proposed Deployment of United States Armed Forces into Bosnia" (November 30, 1995), in *Opinions of the Office of Legal Counsel,* vol. 19 (Washington, DC, 2002), 327, 332.

93. John C. Yoo, "The President's Constitutional Authority to Conduct Military Operations against Terrorists and Nations Supporting Them" (September 25, 2001), in Nathan Forrester, ed., *Opinions of the Office of Legal Counsel,* vol. 25 (Washington, DC: Office of Legal Counsel, 2012), 188.

94. John M. Harmon, "Presidential Power to Use the Armed Forces Abroad without Statutory Authorization," in Margaret Colgate Love, ed., *Opinions of the Office of Legal Counsel,* vol. 4A (Washington, DC, 1985), 187–188 (citing the Korean War as precedent for use of force overseas); Steven A. Engel, US Department of Justice, "April 2018 Airstrikes against Syrian Chemical-Weapons Facilities" (May 31, 2018), 6, https://www.justice.gov/sites/default/files/opinions/attachments/2018/05/31/2018-05-31-syrian-airstrikes_1.pdf.

95. Paul M. Edwards, *Korean War Almanac* (New York: Facts on File, 2006), 543.

96. Bruce Cumings, *The Korean War: A History* (New York: Modern Library, 2010), 35.

97. Cumings, *Korean War,* 35.

98. *Youngstown Sheet & Tube Co.,* 343 US at 641.

99. Dwight Eisenhower, "The President's News Conference of March 10, 1954," in *Public Papers of the Presidents of the United States, Dwight D. Eisenhower: January 1 to December 31, 1954* (Washington, DC: Government Printing Office, 1960), 306.

100. Schlesinger, *Imperial Presidency,* 177–178.

101. Schlesinger, *Imperial Presidency,* 177–178.

102. Joint Resolution to Promote the Maintenance of International Peace and Security in Southeast Asia, Pub. L. No. 88-408, 78 Stat. 384 (1964).

103. Francis X. Clines, "The Sting of Tear Gas and Regret," *New York Times,* August 21, 1996, https://www.nytimes.com/1996/08/21/us/the-sting-of-tear-gas-and-regret.html.

104. Randolph D. Moss, "Authorization for Continuing Hostilities in Kosovo" (December 19, 2000), in *Opinions of the Office of Legal Counsel,* vol. 24 (Washington, DC: Office of Legal Counsel, 2006), 347–349.

105. Jide Nzelibe, "A Positive Theory of the War-Powers Constitution," *Iowa Law Review* 91, no. 3 (2006): 993–1062.

106. Saikrishna Bangalore Prakash, "Military Force and Violence, but Neither War nor Hostilities," *Drake Law Review* 64, no. 4 (2016): 995–1026, 1016–1018 (discussing the various theories and citing criticism of the inconsistent explanations and justifications).

107. Joint Resolution to Authorize the Limited Use of the United States Armed Forces Against the Islamic State of Iraq and the Levant, https://obamawhitehouse.archives.gov/sites/default/files/docs/aumf_02112015.pdf.

108. Walter Dellinger, "Placing of United States Armed Forces under United Nations Operational or Tactical Control" (May 8, 1996), in *Opinions of the Office of Legal Counsel,* vol. 20 (Washington, DC: Office of Legal Counsel, 2002), 182, 185.

109. US Department of Justice, "Standards of Conduct for Interrogation under 18 USC §§ 2340-2340A" (August 1, 2002), 39, https://www.justice.gov/olc/file/886061/download.

110. Adam Liptak, "The Reach of War: Penal Law; Legal Scholars Criticize Memos on Torture," *New York Times,* June 25, 2004, https://www.nytimes.com/2004/06/25/world/the-reach-of-war-penal-law-legal-scholars-criticize-memos-on-torture.html.

111. Charlie Savage, "Barack Obama Q&A," *Boston Globe,* December 20, 2007, http://archive.boston.com/news/politics/2008/specials/Candidate QA/ObamaQA/.

112. Pub. L. No. 113-66, div. A, title X, subtitle D, § 1035, 127 Stat. 672, 851 (December 26, 2013); Pub. L. No. 113-76, div. C, title VIII, § 8111, 128 Stat. 5, 131 (January 17, 2014); Eric Schmitt and Charlie Savage, "Bowe Bergdahl, American Soldier, Freed by Taliban in Prisoner Trade," *New York Times,* May 31, 2014, https://www.nytimes.com/2014/06/01/us/bowe-bergdahl-american-soldier-is-freed-by-taliban.html.

113. Felicia Schwartz, "Congressional Report Says Administration Misled Congress on Bergdahl Swap," *Wall Street Journal,* December 10, 2015, https://www.wsj.com/articles/congressional-report-says-administration-misled-congress-on-bergdahl-swap-1449763881.

114. "Wednesday, July 10, 1776," in Worthington Chauncey Ford, ed., *Journals of the Continental Congress 1774–1789*, vol. 5 (Washington, DC: Government Printing Office, 1906), 539; "Friday, January 5, 1781," in Gaillard Hunt, ed., *Journals of the Continental Congress 1774–1789*, vol. 19 (Washington, DC: Government Printing Office, 1912), 27–28.

115. Act of March 3, 1799, ch. 45, 1 Stat. 743.

116. Joint Resolution Concerning the War Powers of Congress and the President, Avalon Project, Yale Law School Lillian Goldman Law Library, http://avalon.law.yale.edu/20th_century/warpower.asp.

117. John C. Yoo, "Kosovo, War Powers, and the Multilateral Future," *University of Pennsylvania Law Review* 147, no. 5 (2000): 1673–1731, 1677–1679.

118. Libya and War Powers, S. Hrg. 112–89, Senate Committee on Foreign Relations, June 28, 2011 (Washington: Government Printing Office, 2011), 7–9.

119. Moss, "Authorization for Continuing Hostilities in Kosovo," 346–347.

120. David B. Rivkin Jr., and Lee A. Casey, "Constitutional Warp," *Wall Street Journal*, January 31, 2007, https://www.wsj.com/articles/SB117021777306393414.

121. Blomstedt, *Truman, Congress, and Korea*, 53.

Chapter 7. From Chief Diplomat to Sole Master of Foreign Affairs

1. Saikrishna Bangalore Prakash, *Imperial from the Beginning: The Constitution of the Original Executive* (New Haven, CT: Yale University Press, 2015), 119–120.

2. Theophilius Parsons, "The Essex Result" (1778), in Charles S. Hyneman and Donald S. Lutz, eds., *American Political Writing during the Founding Era 1760–1805*, vol. 1 (Indianapolis: Liberty Fund, 1983), 494.

3. Saikrishna B. Prakash and Michael D. Ramsey, "The Executive Power over Foreign Affairs," *Yale Law Journal* 111, no. 2 (2001): 231–356, 274.

4. John Jay to George Washington, January 7, 1787, in Henry P. Johnston, ed., *The Correspondence and Public Papers of John Jay*, vol. 4: *1794–1826* (New York: G.P. Putnam's Sons, 1893), 227.

5. N.Y. Const. of 1777, art. XXVIII.

6. George Washington to Sidi Mohammed, December 1, 1789; and George Washington to Louis XVI, October 9, 1789; both in Dorothy Twohig, ed., *The Papers of George Washington: Presidential Series*, vol. 4 (Charlottesville: University Press of Virginia, 1987), 354, 152.

7. Abraham Sofaer, *War, Foreign Affairs, and Constitutional Power* (Cambridge, MA: Ballinger, 1976), 65.

8. Prakash and Ramsey, "Executive Power over Foreign Affairs," 298–300.

9. Jefferson's Opinion on Powers of the Senate Respecting Diplomatic Appointments (April 24, 1790), in Julian P. Boyd, ed., *The Papers of Thomas Jefferson*, vol. 16 (Princeton, NJ: Princeton University Press, 1961), 379.

10. Alexander Hamilton, "Pacificus No. 1," in Morton J. Frisch, ed., *The Pacificus-Helvidius Debates of 1793–1794* (Indianapolis: Liberty Fund 2006), 12–13.

11. Hamilton, "Pacificus No. 1," 13.

12. George Washington to Sidi Mohammed, in Twohig, *Papers of George Washington*, 354.

13. Prakash and Ramsey, "Executive Power over Foreign Affairs," 309.

14. Prakash, *Imperial from the Beginning*, 172–175.

15. "Proclamation of Neutrality, April 22, 1793," in Frisch, *Pacificus-Helvidius Debates*, 1; Anthony J. Bellia Jr. and Bradford R. Clark, "The Federal Common Law of Nations," *Columbia Law Review* 109, no. 1 (2009): 1–93, 49–52.

16. 4 *Annals of Cong.* 11 (1793).

17. Neutrality Act, ch. 50, 1 Stat. 381 (1794).

18. *US v. Curtiss-Wright Export Corp.*, 299 US 304, 319 (1936).

19. Harold Hongju Koh, *The National Security Constitution: Sharing Power after the Iran-Contra Affair* (New Haven, CT: Yale University Press, 1990), 94.

20. *Zivotofsky v. Kerry*, 135 S. Ct. 2076, 2079 (2015).

21. US Const., art. I, § 3.

22. US Const., art. VI.

23. Michael D. Ramsey, "The Treaty and Its Rivals," in Gregory H. Fox, Paul R. Dubinsky, and Brad R. Roth, eds., *Supreme Law of the Land? Debating the Contemporary Effects of Treaties within the United*

States Legal System (New York: Cambridge University Press, 2017), 290.

24. Ramsey, "The Treaty and Its Rivals," 290.

25. Alexander Hamilton, *Federalist,* no. 75, Avalon Project, Yale Law School Lillian Goldman Law Library, http://avalon.law.yale.edu/18th_century/fed75.asp.

26. James Wilson in Merrill Jensen, ed., *Documentary History on the Ratification of the Constitution,* vol. 2 (Madison: State Historical Society of Wisconsin, 1976), 563.

27. US Const., art. I. § 7.

28. US Const., art. V.

29. "Message from the President in Answer to the Resolution of the House," March 30, 1796, in *Annals of Congress,* vol. 5 (Washington, DC: Gales and Seaton, 1849), 760–762.

30. Earl M. Maltz, "The Constitution and the Annexation of Texas," *Constitutional Commentary* 23, no. 3 (2006): 381–423, 387–390.

31. Joint Resolution for Annexing Texas to the United States, 5 Stat. 797 (1845).

32. Joint Resolution for the Admission of the State of Texas into the Union, 9 Stat. 108 (1845).

33. Joint Resolution to Provide for Annexing the Hawaiian Islands to the United States, 30 Stat. 750 (1898).

34. *Guide to Congress,* 7th ed. (Washington, DC: CQ Press, 2013), 234.

35. Four other treaties from the nineteenth century enjoyed majority support in the Senate but were not rerouted to the House for its approval. See *Guide to Congress,* 234, listing proposed treaties with Hawaii, Mexico, Nicaragua, and Great Britain.

36. US Const., amend. XVII. To be clear, most states were complying with the principle of popular elections prior to the passage of the amendment.

37. Bruce Ackerman and David Golove, "Is NAFTA Constitutional?" *Harvard Law Review* 108, no. 4 (1995): 799–929, 825–828.

38. Ackerman and Golove, "Is NAFTA Constitutional?" 802–803.

39. Ackerman and Golove, "Is NAFTA Constitutional?" 893–895.

40. Ackerman and Golove, "Is NAFTA Constitutional?" 803.

41. Oona A. Hathaway, "Treaties' End: The Past, Present, and Future of International Lawmaking in the United States," *Yale Law Journal* 117, no. 7 (2008): 1236–1372, 1308–1309.

42. Edward S. Corwin, *The Constitution and World Organization* (Princeton, NJ: Princeton University Press, 1944), 32.
43. Stephen P. Mulligan, *International Law and Agreements: Their Effect upon U.S. Law* (Washington, DC: Congressional Research Service, 2018), 7–8.
44. David Bodansky and Peter Spiro, "Executive Agreements+," *Vanderbilt Journal of Transnational Law* 49, no. 4 (2016): 885–929, esp. 921–922.
45. *Whitman v. American Trucking Ass'n,* 531 US 457, 468 (2001).
46. US Const., art. I, § 10.
47. Bradford R. Clark, "Domesticating Sole Executive Agreements," *Virginia Law Review* 93, no. 7 (2007): 1573–1661, esp. 1581–1583.
48. Michael D. Ramsey, "Executive Agreements and the (Non)Treaty Power," *North Carolina Law Review* 77, no. 1 (1998): 133–240, esp. 174–183.
49. Michael P. Van Alstine, "Executive Aggrandizement in Foreign Affairs Lawmaking," *UCLA Law Review* 54, no. 2 (2006): 309–371, esp. 319.
50. David J. Barron and Martin S. Lederman, "The Commander in Chief at the Lowest Ebb–A Constitutional History," *Harvard Law Review* 121, no. 3 (2008): 941–1111, esp. 1043–1045.
51. Ramsey, "Executive Agreements," 235–236.
52. Curtis A. Bradley and Jack L. Goldsmith, "Presidential Control over International Law," *Harvard Law Review* 131, no. 5 (2018), 1217–1220.
53. Duncan B. Hollis and Joshua J. Newcomer, "'Political' Commitments and the Constitution," *Virginia Journal of International Law* 49, no. 3 (2009): 507–584, esp. 510–511, 516, 565.
54. "Joint Comprehensive Plan of Action" (July 14, 2015), *International Legal Materials* 55 (2016): 108–109.
55. Under Secretary for Political Affairs Wendy R. Sherman, "Briefing to the Press on the Iran Nuclear Deal," US Department of State, https://2009-2017.state.gov/p/us/rm/2015/245007.htm.
56. Julia Frifield, Assistant Secretary of Legislative Affairs, US Department of State to Mike Pompeo, November 19, 2015, https://perma.cc/C32V-LKYK.
57. See Secretary of State Rex W. Tillerson, "Joint Statement to the Media," US Department of State, https://www.state.gov/secretary/20172018tillerson/remarks/2017/12/276255.htm; Secretary of State Mike Pompeo, "After the Deal: A New Iran Strategy," US Department of State,

https://www.state.gov/secretary/remarks/2018/05/282301.htm; Secretary of State John Kerry, "Remarks on the One-Year Anniversary of the JCPOA," US Department of State, https://2009-2017.state.gov/secretary/remarks/2016/07/259972.htm.

58. President Donald Trump, "Remarks by President Trump on the Joint Comprehensive Plan of Action," White House, https://www.whitehouse.gov/briefings-statements/remarks-president-trump-joint-comprehensive-plan-action/.

59. John Kerry (@JohnKerry), "My thoughts on President Trump's Iran statement," Twitter, May 8, 2018, 12:15 p.m.

60. Barack Obama, "There are few issues more important to the security of the United States than the potential spread of nuclear weapons, or the potential for even more destructive war in the Middle East," Facebook, May 8, 2018, https://www.facebook.com/barackobama/posts/10155854913976749.

61. Kay Armin Serjoie, "'The Americans Cannot Be Trusted': How Iran Is Reacting to Trump's Decision to Quit Nuclear Deal," *Time,* May 9, 2018.

62. Nader Mardani and Mohammad Mehdi Hooshmand, "JCPOA: A Dialectical Paradigm of Treaty and Other Instruments," *Journal of Politics and Law* 9, no. 3 (2016): 70–84, esp. 82.

63. Ulysses S. Grant, Seventh Annual Message, December 7, 1875, https://www.presidency.ucsb.edu/documents/seventh-annual-message-3.

64. See, for example, Executive Order No. 13337, 69 *Federal Register* 25299 (2004).

65. *Sisseton–Wahpeton Oyate v. US Dept. of State,* 659 F. Supp. 2d 1071, 1081 (D.S.D. 2009).

66. Jackson S. Kern, "Abrogate the Acquiescence: Why Congress Should Take on the President over the Keystone XL Pipeline," *Seattle Journal of Environmental Law* 3, no. 1 (2013): 123–153, 150–151.

67. Curtis A. Bradley and Trevor W. Morrison, "Historical Gloss and the Separation of Powers," *Harvard Law Review* 126, no. 2 (2012): 411–485, esp. 418.

68. Charlie Savage, *Power Wars: Inside Obama's Post-9/11 Presidency* (New York: Little, Brown, 2015), 679.

69. Virginia A. Seitz, "Unconstitutional Restrictions on Activities of the Office of Science and Technology Policy in Section 1340(A) of the Department of Defense and Full-Year Continuing Appropriations Act,

2011," US Department of Justice, https://www.justice.gov/file/18346
/download.

70. Savage, *Power Wars,* 679–680.

71. For example, Omnibus Appropriations Act of 2009, Pub. L. No. 111-8,
§ 7054, 123 Stat 524 (2009).

72. David Barron, "Constitutionality of Section 7054 of the Fiscal Year
2009 Foreign Appropriations Act," US Department of Justice,
https://www.justice.gov/sites/default/files/olc/opinions/2009/06/31
/section7054_0.pdf.

73. *Zivotofsky v. Kerry,* 135 S. Ct. 2076, 2087 (2015).

74. *Dames & Moore v. Regan,* 453 US 654, 679, quoting *Youngstown
Sheet & Tube Co. v. Sawyer,* 343 US 579, 637 (1952) (Jackson, J.,
concurring).

CHAPTER 8. FROM DUTIFUL SERVANT OF THE LAWS TO SECONDARY LAWMAKER

1. Aaron Wildavsky, "The Two Presidencies," *Trans-Action* 4, no. 2
(1966): 7–14.

2. US Const., art. II, § 3.

3. *Youngstown Sheet & Tube Co. v. Sawyer,* 343 US 579, 587 (1952).

4. Jacques Necker, *An Essay on the True Principles of Executive Power
in Great States,* vol. 1 (London: G. G. J. and J. Robinson, 1792), 4.

5. *Mistretta v. United States,* 488 US 361, 427 (1989) (Scalia, J.,
dissenting).

6. Roger Sherman in Max Farrand, ed., *The Records of the Federal
Convention of 1787,* vol. 1 (New Haven, CT: Yale University Press,
1966), 65.

7. The Federal Farmer, "Letter XIV," in John P. Kaminski, ed., *The Documentary History of the Ratification of the Constitution,* vol. 20 (Madison: Wisconsin Historical Society Press, 2004), 1035–1042, 1042.

8. Alexander Hamilton, *Federalist,* no. 73, Avalon Project, Yale Law
School Lillian Goldman Law Library, http://avalon.law.yale.edu/18th
_century/fed73.asp. The presidential veto "establishes a salutary check
upon the legislative body, calculated to guard the community against
the effects of faction, precipitancy, or of any impulse unfriendly to the
public good, which may happen to influence a majority of that body."

9. "Cato IV," in Herbert J. Storing, ed., *The Complete Anti-Federalist,* vol. 2 (Chicago: University of Chicago Press, 1981), 113–116.

10. US Const., art. II, § 3.

11. Saikrishna Bangalore Prakash, *Imperial from the Beginning: The Constitution of the Original Executive* (New Haven, CT: Yale University Press, 2015), 92–94.

12. "An Act Declaring the Rights and Liberties of the Subject and Settling the Succession of the Crown," 1 William & Mary 2nd. sess., ch. 2.

13. William Symmes Jr., to Peter Osgood Jr., Andover, MA, November 15, 1787, in Kaminski, *Documentary History,* 4: 236–245, 242.

14. US House of Representatives, "Institution: Presidential Vetoes," https:// history.house.gov/Institution/Presidential-Vetoes/Presidential-Vetoes/.

15. Michael J. Gerhardt, "Constitutional Construction and Departmentalism: A Case Study of the Demise of the Whig Presidency," *University of Pennsylvania Journal of Constitutional Law* 12, no. 2 (2010): 425–459, esp. 438–439.

16. David P. Currie, *The Constitution in Congress: Democrats & Whigs, 1829–1861* (Chicago: University of Chicago Press, 2005), 169.

17. George Washington, "Veto Message," in James D. Richardson, ed., *A Compilation of the Messages and Papers of the Presidents,* vol. 1 (New York: Bureau of National Literature Inc., 1897), 203.

18. Ryan S. Walters, *The Last Jeffersonian: Grover Cleveland and the Path to Restoring the Republic* (Bloomington, IL: WestBow Press, 2012), xix.

19. US House of Representatives, "Presidential Vetoes," https://history .house.gov/Institution/Presidential-Vetoes/Presidential-Vetoes/.

20. US House of Representatives, "Presidential Vetoes."

21. James Madison, *Federalist,* no. 48, Avalon Project, Yale Law School Lillian Goldman Law Library, http://avalon.law.yale.edu/18th_century /fed48.asp.

22. *United States v. Shreveport Grain & Elevator Co.,* 287 US 77, 85 (1932).

23. 48 USC §§ 821, 1423(a).

24. *Yakus v. United States,* 321 US 414, 458 (1944); *American Power & Light Co. v. SEC,* 329 US 90, 100 (1946); *National Broadcasting Co. v. United States,* 319 US 190, 216 (1943).

25. See, for example, 15 USC §§ 77-z3, 78mm(a)(1), delegating sweeping authority to the Securities and Exchange Commission. For a more general discussion, see David J. Barron and Todd D. Rakoff, "In

Defense of Big Waiver," *Columbia Law Review* 113, no. 2 (2013): 265–345.

26. *Chevron USA Inc. v. National Resources Defense Council*, 467 US 837 (1984).

27. Elena Kagan, "Presidential Administration," *Harvard Law Review* 114, no. 8 (2001): 2245–2385, 2301–2303.

28. *United States v. Midwest Oil Co.*, 236 US 459, 483 (1915).

29. Mark Mazur, assistant secretary for tax policy, Department of the Treasury, to Fred Upton, chairman, House Committee on Energy and Commerce, July 9, 2013, https://perma.cc/3LJ9-3WTC.

30. 12 USC § 5211(a)(1).

31. David M. Herszenhorn and David E. Sanger, "Bush Approves $17.4 Billion Auto Bailout," *New York Times,* December 19, 2008.

32. "Transcript: President Bush on Auto-Industry Bailout," *Fox News,* December 19, 2008, https://www.foxnews.com/politics/transcript -president-bush-on-auto-industry-bailout.

33. For a discussion of the Obama administration's actions, statements, and claims, see *US House of Representatives v. Burwell*, 185 F. Supp. 3d 165, 175–176 (D.D.C. 2016).

34. Jennifer Haberkorn, "House GOP Wins Obamacare Lawsuit," *Politico,* May 12, 2016, https://www.politico.com/story/2016/05/house-gop -wins-obamacare-lawsuit-223121.

35. *US House of Representatives,* 175.

36. Pub. L. No. 113-76, div. C, title VIII, § 8111, 128 Stat. 5, 131 (January 17, 2014); Government Accountability Office, "Department of Defense—Compliance with Statutory Notification Requirement," August 21, 2014, https://www.gao.gov/products/B-326013#mt=e-report.

37. "Administration Views Provided to the Government Accountability Office," available at https://lawfare.s3-us-west-2.amazonaws.com /staging/s3fs-public/uploads/2014/08/GAO-Response-question-3 -FINAL.pdf.

38. Consolidated Appropriation Act of 2012, Public Law 112-74, 125 Stat. 786, 1195–1196.

39. Arshad Mohammed and Patricia Zengerle, "U.S. Sidesteps Decision Whether to Cut Off Aid to Egypt," Reuters, July 25, 2013, https://www .reuters.com/article/uk-egypt-protests-usa-aid-idUKBRE96O1CL 20130726.

40. For a defense of the claim that the Constitution requires judicial review of the constitutionality of congressional laws, see Saikrishna B. Prakash and John C. Yoo, "The Origins of Judicial Review," *University of Chicago Law Review* 70, no. 3 (2003): 887–982, 890–893.

41. An Act in addition to the act, entitled "An act for the punishment of certain crimes against the United States," ch. 74, § 2, Stat. 596 (1798).

42. Prakash, *Imperial from the Beginning,* 308–309.

43. Prakash, *Imperial from the Beginning,* 105–106.

44. Deputy Attorney General James M. Cole, August 29, 2013, "Memorandum for All United States Attorneys: Guidance Regarding Marijuana Enforcement," available at https://www.justice.gov/iso/opa/resources/3052013829132756857467.pdf.

45. Secretary of Homeland Security Janet Napolitano, June 15, 2012, "Exercising Prosecutorial Discretion with Respect to Individuals Who Came to the United States as Children," https://www.dhs.gov/xlibrary/assets/s1-exercising-prosecutorial-discretion-individuals-who-came-to-us-as-children.pdf.

46. *Bordenkircher v. Hayes,* 434 US 357, 364 (1978).

47. Woodrow Wilson, *Constitutional Government in the United States* (New York: Columbia University Press, 1908), 66–67.

48. Wilson, *Constitutional Government,* 71.

Chapter 9. How to Recage the Executive Lion

1. Daniel Webster, *Mr. Webster's Speech on the President's Protest: Delivered in the Senate of the United States, May 7, 1834* (Washington, DC: Gales and Seaton, 1834), 23.

2. Webster, *Speech on the President's Protest,* 23.

3. Aditya Bamzai, "Taft, Frankfurter, and the First Presidential For-Cause Removal," *University of Richmond Law Review* 52, no. 4 (2018): 691–748, 694.

4. Gerald R. Ford, "Imperiled, Not Imperial," *Time,* November 10, 1980, 30. I have argued that as compared to the Founding, the modern presidency is more powerful in some respects and weaker in others. Saikrishna Bangalore Prakash, "Imperial and Imperiled: The Curious State of the Executive," *William and Mary Law Review* 50, no. 3

(2008): 1021. As noted at the outset, I have spent little space in this book discussing where the presidency has grown weaker.

5. "Declaration of Independence: A Transcription," *America's Founding Documents,* National Archives, https://www.archives.gov/founding -docs/declaration-transcript.

6. James Wilson, "Comparison of the Constitution of the United States, with That of Great Britain," in Robert G. McCloskey, ed., *The Works of James Wilson,* 2 vols. (Cambridge: Harvard University Press, 1967), 1:319.

7. Wilson, "Comparison," 1:319.

8. 31 USC § 502(a); 19 USC § 2171(b)(1).

9. Kathy Goldschmidt, *State of the Congress: Staff Perspectives on Institutional Capacity in the House and Senate* (Washington, DC: Congressional Management Foundation, 2017), 17, http://www.congress foundation.org/storage/documents/CMF_Pubs/cmf-state-of-the -congress.pdf.

10. Goldschmidt, *State of the Congress,* 24.

11. Goldschmidt, *State of the Congress,* 24.

12. Goldschmidt, *State of the Congress,* 17.

13. Baron de Montesquieu, "Book XI: Of the Laws Which Establish Political Liberty, with Regard to the Constitution," in *The Complete Works of M. De Montesquieu,* vol. 1 (London: T. Evans and W. Davis, 1777), https://oll.libertyfund.org/titles/montesquieu-complete-works -vol-1-the-spirit-of-laws.

14. For a discussion of such statutes, see "A Guide to Emergency Powers and Their Use," Brennan Center for Justice, December 8, 2018, https://www.brennancenter.org/analysis/emergency-powers.

15. Elizabeth Goitein, "Trump's Hidden Powers," Brennan Center for Justice blogpost, December 5, 2018, https://www.brennancenter.org/blog /trump-hidden-powers.

16. George Washington, "Message to the House Regarding Documents Relative to the Jay Treaty" (March 30, 1796), Avalon Project, Yale Law School Lillian Goldman Law Library, http://avalon.law.yale.edu/18th _century/gw003.asp.

17. Washington, "Message to the House."

18. Washington, "Message to the House."

19. Randy Beck, "Qui Tam Litigation against Government Officials: Constitutional Implications of a Neglected History," *Notre Dame Law*

Review 93, no. 3 (2018): 1235–1316, 1235–1236; Evan Caminker, "The Constitutionality of Qui Tam Actions," *Yale Law Journal* 99, no. 2 (1989): 341–388, 341–342.

20. Washington, "Message to the House"; *The Debates and Proceedings in the Congress of the United States, Fourth Congress, First Session* (Washington, DC: Gales and Seaton, 1855), 771–784.

21. *The ABM Treaty and the Constitution: Joint Hearings before the Committee on Foreign Relations and the Committee on the Judiciary, United States Senate, One Hundredth Congress, First Session* (Washington, DC: Government Printing Office, 1987), 81–105; S. Res. 167 (1987); John Yoo, "Politics as Law?: The Anti-Ballistic Missile Treaty, the Separation of Powers, and Treaty Interpretation," *California Law Review* 89 (2001): 851–915, 860.

22. Philip R. Trimble and Alexander W. Koff, "All Fall Down: The Treaty Power in the Clinton Administration," *Berkeley Journal of International Law* 16, no. 1 (1998): 55–70, 62–64.

23. Jane A. Hudiburg and Christopher M. Davis, *Resolutions to Censure the President: Procedure and History* (Washington, DC: Congressional Research Service, 2019), 5, 6, 8.

24. *Youngstown Sheet & Tube Co. v. Sawyer,* 343 US 579, 654 (1952).

Conclusion

1. Confession: At times, I might have appeared as an apologist for our banana boys. See Saikrishna B. Prakash and Michael D. Ramsey, *The Goldilocks Executive,* 90 Tex L. Rev. 973 (2012). That article celebrates the fact that the presidency is not yet fully liberated from law. That claim and approach were in keeping with my preference for always finding the silver lining. I should add that at the time I had not fully grappled with what our presidency has become and may yet become.

2. Woodrow Wilson, *Constitutional Government in the United States* (New York: Columbia University Press, 1908), 70–71.

Acknowledgments

Thanks to my able, cheerful, and industrious research assistants: Joseph Barakat, Erin Brown, Joseph Calder, Scott Falin, David Goldman, Victoria Granda, Will Hall, Hanaa Khan, Josh Lefebvre, Katie Montoya, Arjun Ogale, Avery Rasmussen, Christian Talley, Jordan Walsh, and T. J. Whittle.

For helpful comments, criticism, and discussion, thanks to Mike Ramsey, John Harrison, Paul Stephan, participants at the faculty workshops at the University of North Carolina School of Law and the University of San Diego School of Law, and to my wonderful colleagues at the Miller Center and the University of Virginia School of Law. Thanks also to Lee J. Strang and the University of Toledo College of Law for inviting me to give the Stranahan Lecture, where I tested some claims and themes. Similar thanks are due to Michael S. Paulsen, the University of St. Thomas Law School, and the *University of St. Thomas Law Journal* for inviting me to a conference on presidential powers. Parts of this book draw upon ideas presented in the resulting article: "The Past, Present, and Future of Presidential Power," *University of St. Thomas Law Journal* 14, no. 3 (2018): 627–649. Gratitude also to two anonymous readers who offered copious and incisive criticisms; to my dean, Risa Goluboff, for her support; and to University of Virginia's superb law librarians.

Finally, thanks to the great and good men and women at Harvard University Press. Thomas LeBien supplied sage advice and valuable suggestions early in the process. James Brandt ably took over, providing excellent guidance and a seamless transition. Mihaela-Andreea Pacurar shepherded me through the long process. Julie Carlson, Anne McGuire, and Louise Robbins made some needed and terrific edits and rather welcome suggestions.

Index